The

CALIFORNIA
DAYS *of*
RALPH WALDO
EMERSON

The
CALIFORNIA
DAYS *of*
RALPH WALDO
EMERSON

BRIAN C. WILSON

University of Massachusetts Press
Amherst and Boston

Copyright © 2022 by University of Massachusetts Press
All rights reserved
Printed in the United States of America

ISBN 978-1-62534-643-8 (paper); 644-5 (hardcover)

Designed by Sally Nichols
Set in Minion Pro and The Pretender
Printed and bound by Books International, Inc.

Cover design by Derek Thornton, Notch Design
Cover photo by Carleton E. Watkins, *Yosemite Valley, California,* ca. 1865.
Courtesy Prints and Photographs Division,
Library of Congress, LC-DIG-ppmsca-09983.

Library of Congress Cataloging-in-Publication Data

Names: Wilson, Brian C., 1960– author.
Title: The California days of Ralph Waldo Emerson : a travelogue / Brian C.
Wilson.
Description: Amherst : University of Massachusetts Press, [2022] | Includes
bibliographical references and index.
Identifiers: LCCN 2021054327 (print) | LCCN 2021054328 (ebook) | ISBN
9781625346438 (paperback) | ISBN 9781625346445 (hardcover) | ISBN
9781613769218 (ebook) | ISBN 9781613769225 (ebook)
Subjects: LCSH: California—Description and travel. | Emerson, Ralph Waldo,
1803–1882—Travel—California. | Emerson, Ralph Waldo, 1803–1882—Last
years. | Authors, American—19th century—Biography.
Classification: LCC F866 .W755 2022 (print) | LCC F866 (ebook) | DDC
814/.3 [B]—dc23/eng/20211123
LC record available at https://lccn.loc.gov/2021054327
LC ebook record available at https://lccn.loc.gov/2021054328

British Library Cataloguing-in-Publication Data
A catalog record for this book is available from the British Library.

TO MY MOTHER,
MARION N. WILSON

CONTENTS

PREFACE

The attraction and superiority of California are in its days. It has better days, and more of them than any other country.

—Ralph Waldo Emerson, *Journals* (April 1871)

In the spring of 1871, Ralph Waldo Emerson (1803–82), the dean of American Transcendentalism and one of America's most celebrated lecturers and essayists, boarded a train in Concord, Massachusetts, bound for a month-and-a-half-long tour of California. It took some cajoling, but Emerson was convinced to travel to the West by his friend, the Boston railroad magnate John Murray Forbes. Fearing that the philosopher had overworked himself while recently teaching a course at Harvard, Forbes volunteered to underwrite all the expenses, including a private Pullman Palace Car, for a luxury trip across the continent. By all accounts, the journey became one of the highlights of Emerson's life. Among his traveling companions were Forbes and his family; his daughter Edith Emerson Forbes and son-in-law, William Forbes; Garth Wilkinson James (brother of Henry and William James); and a young Boston lawyer named James Bradley Thayer.

Along the way, Emerson met such luminaries as George Pullman in Chicago, Mormon church president Brigham Young in Salt Lake City, the Unitarian minister Horatio Stebbins and the photographer Carleton Watkins in San Francisco, the educator Jeanne Carr in Oakland, and, in Yosemite, the conservationist Galen Clark and the naturalist John Muir, who counted Emerson's visit as one of the turning points in his life. Emerson also learned that, despite his declining mental powers, his brand of Transcendentalism was still very much in demand out west, and he found himself unexpectedly lionized in the Bay Area, especially by the Unitarian congregation of the late Thomas Starr King, Emerson's ardent California disciple.

The California Days of Ralph Waldo Emerson retells this epic journey by means of a travelogue in which I contextualize the journey within Emerson's life and thought, as well as within the history of California and the West. Emerson's trip followed the line of the Yankee diaspora across the continent, and at every step he encountered its representatives, as noted above, each of whose stories illuminates the impress of New England culture on the West. In California, too, the Emerson party encountered Native American, Chinese, and Hispanic cultures that challenged their Yankee prejudices, as did the perceived rawness of the rampantly commercial society developing there, which troubled Emerson greatly. Equally significant, of course, was the encounter with the natural landscape of the West, from the snows of the Rockies to the vastness of the Pacific to the sublimities of Yosemite, all of which the book refracts through the Transcendentalist sensibilities of Emerson and his companions.

Finally, *The California Days of Ralph Waldo Emerson* is also about the personal story of Emerson himself: only 67 at the time of the trip but already showing unmistakable signs of the aphasia that would soon rob him of his words, Emerson nevertheless exuded good cheer and bore the hardships of the trip with remarkable fortitude and good-humored stoicism. Most of Emerson's biographers have treated his last decade as a remorseless decline, but his California trip clearly shows that Emerson was still capable of wonder, surprise, and a capacity for friendship that puts the lie to the presumed unrelieved darkness of his last years.

A note here is in order to acknowledge the sources without which this book would not have been possible. The inclusion of James Bradley Thayer in the Emerson party was fortuitous for posterity, because Emerson himself wrote very little about the journey west. All that remains from his hand are a few letters and an itinerary jotted into one of his notebooks. At one point during the trip, while they were riding through Yosemite, Emerson admonished Thayer to follow Dr. Johnson's rule: "Always take notes on the spot. A note is worth a cartload of recollections." Sadly, Emerson did not take his own advice, and sadly, too, although Emerson apparently wrote three letters a week back home, only a few of these missives survive. At that time, unless expressly forbidden by the correspondent, letters were frequently public documents to be passed around to family and friends. It is likely that many of Emerson's California letters would have been very popular and thus, passed around more than most, were eventually lost.

Thayer, however, was a conscientious correspondent, writing almost daily to his wife Sophia, who saved all of his letters. Moreover, inspired by Emerson's death in 1882, Thayer used the letters for a talk to his club, which he then turned into a short book that he had published two years later as *A Western Journey with Mr. Emerson*. Travelogues about the American West and California were immensely popular throughout the nineteenth century, ranging from the dryly promotional, such as Charles Nordhoff's *California: For Health, Pleasure and Residence* (1872), to the sensational, such as Richard F. Burton's *The City of the Saints* (1861), to the broadly comic, such as Mark Twain's uproarious *Roughing It* (1872). Thayer probably surmised that with the public's continued interest in Ralph Waldo Emerson, a western travelogue featuring the Concord Sage would be a welcome addition to the genre. Thayer was also aware that during the thirteen years that had elapsed since the journey, California and the West had undergone great changes, such that his observations would have some interesting documentary value. Despite these selling points, however, and an elegant prose style, Thayer had to pay for the publication of *A Western Journey* out of his own pocket, and the publisher, Little, Brown and Co., had trouble selling out the initial print run of one thousand after two years, at which time it surrendered the copyright back to Thayer. The book thus enjoyed scant success, garnering only a few newspaper reviews and some appreciative letters from family and friends, but no wider or lasting fame.

Although proud of *A Western Journey with Mr. Emerson*, Thayer was all too sensible of its limitations. In his preface, he deprecated his book as "almost too slight a performance; the pudding is small, and the plums are few." He asked his readers that "these savings from oblivion . . . be regarded as a sort of *wreccum maris* [i.e., flotsam and jetsam],—to use our pleasant law-Latin,—something not nearly so good as one could wish, but better than nothing." Perhaps remembering Emerson's admonition, Thayer regretted that he hadn't been even more diligent in recording the trip, "but it would not have seemed quite friendly, in such a company, to play the part of a mere Boswell; nor should I have been willing to tamper with my own quiet enjoyment of the situation by doing that." "It will be remembered, also," he added, "that some things which really were preserved [in letters] must naturally be omitted here, as being of too personal a nature for publication."

This last observation was an understatement. Given Thayer's Victorian sense of privacy, many names in *A Western Journey with Mr. Emerson* were censored and replaced with Mr. — or Miss — and the like. Even the composition of the fellowship itself was not obvious from Thayer's description of it in his book. Moreover, in his effort to foreground Emerson and record his orbiter dicta, Thayer omits or hurries over many interesting incidents of the trip. Happily, though, other sources exist. Thayer's original letters are on deposit in the Harvard Law Library, and despite his atrocious handwriting and tendency to cram two pages onto one by overwriting the page at right angles (a common practice to save paper and postage), many of the gaps of his published narrative can be filled in. This, and the existence of another cache of letters by Will and Edith Forbes in the archives of the Massachusetts Historical Society, some letters from Ellen Tucker Emerson at the Concord Free Public Library, not to mention published reminiscences of several people met along the way and tourist guides from the period, gives much added detail. What's more, given our distance from the trip not by thirteen years but by a century and a half, we have the benefit of modern scholarship on the West, which I use to reflect critically on many of the incidents narrated by Thayer. For example, in the presence of certain peoples (e.g., African Americans, Mormons, Native Americans, Chinese, Irish) and certain personalities (e.g., Brigham Young, John Muir), Emerson and his party responded in ways typical of the prejudices of elite eastern tourists of the time, especially Yankee tourists. Thus, while I faithfully record their perceptions in *The California Days of Ralph Waldo Emerson*, I also supply a wider perspective so as to shed light on some of their blind spots, as well as to flesh out the travelogue for a contemporary audience unfamiliar with nineteenth-century western history. Those wishing to know more about the ample secondary literature that I used to guide my interpretations can consult the notes at the end of the book.

All in all, Emerson's 1871 journey west is a fascinating and entertaining *story*, and this is the main reason that I felt it bore retelling. Of course, personal motivations played a part too, primarily having to do with nostalgia. Born and raised in California, but having spent the last 25 years in the Midwest, I craved an opportunity to get back to the state, if only in my imagination. The Emerson trip was the perfect vehicle, and I have enjoyed every minute of this project. Little did I know when I began this book, however, that by the time I completed it in 2020—just shy of the trip's 150th anniversary—California would be entering into a new phase of its history marked by environmental disasters, political turmoil, and pandemic disease. But just as Emerson's life was characterized by a certain dogged resilience in the face of challenges, so too I hope Californians can still find within themselves the resilience necessary to work together to make the state the demi-paradise it was meant to be.

BRIAN C. WILSON

Kalamazoo, Michigan

September 2020

ACKNOWLEDGMENTS

Writing a book like this, one incurs many happy debts, and I would like to acknowledge some of them. First, the archivists and librarians who cheerfully made available the documentary materials on which this book is based: Jane Kelly and Ed Moloy, Historical and Special Collections, Harvard Law School Library; Anna Clutterbuck-Cook and Dan Hinchen, Massachusetts Historical Society; Anke Voss and Jessie Hopper, William Munroe Special Collections, Concord Free Public Library; Margaret E. Bancroft and Leslie A. Morris, Ralph Waldo Emerson Memorial Association; Mike Wurtz, Holt-Atherton Special Collections and Archives, University of the Pacific Library; and Carol Acquaviva, Anne T. Kent California Room, Marin County Public Library. Thanks too to Beatrice F. Manz of the Forbes Family Archive Committee for permission to quote from the Edith Emerson Forbes and William Hathaway Forbes Papers housed at the Massachusetts Historical Society. Second, I thank all those who read the manuscript in whole or in part: Tom Bailey, Lisle Dalton, John Geisler, Tyler Green, Rob Lehman, Megan Leverage, Tim Light, Richard Merkel, Jon Stone, Mike Wurtz, and Deborah Yeager. I also thank my ever-encouraging editor at the University of Massachusetts Press, Matt Becker, the two anonymous reviewers for their helpful suggestions, and Rachael DeShano and Nancy Raynor for their editorial expertise in the production of this book. Finally, a special appreciation to my wife, Cybelle Shattuck, for all her support, and to "the kids," Sadie and Minnie.

The

CALIFORNIA
DAYS *of*
RALPH WALDO
EMERSON

INTRODUCTION

I find it a great & fatal difference whether I court the Muse, or the Muse courts me: That is the ugly disparity between age & youth.

—Ralph Waldo Emerson, *Journals* (July 1866)

Ralph Waldo Emerson was tired and depressed. It was April 10, 1871, and in a letter to the English thinker Thomas Carlyle, Emerson wrote: "I hope the ruin of no young man's soul will here or hereafter be charged to me as having wasted his time or confounded his reason." The motivation for this plea was that Emerson was about two-thirds of the way through a lecture series at his beloved Harvard but finding the task all but overwhelming. The theme of the series, the Natural History of the Intellect, was meant to be nothing less than a grand synthesis of everything he had learned about the human mind over the years, a culminating work that he hoped would be his testament to the future. However, at the very moment he needed it most, Emerson's own intellect was failing him—and he knew it. While old age was "not disgraceful," Emerson had once observed, it was nevertheless "immensely disadvantageous."

Even as Emerson's powers were on the decline, his reputation as "America's Philosopher" was still on the rise. At this point in his life he enjoyed a level of popularity—in some cases adulation—that must have been surprising considering the bitter controversy that greeted the beginning of his career back in the 1830s. Emerson, a graduate of Harvard (class of 1821), had been a Unitarian clergyman, but in the wake of the death of his beloved first wife, Ellen Tucker, and his growing doubts about the dogmatism of even so liberal a faith as Unitarianism, he abandoned his Boston ministry, eventually relocating to the nearby village of Concord to pursue a vocation as an independent thinker, essayist, and lecturer. Here, in the company of his second wife, Lydia ("Lidian") Jackson, he spent the rest of his life, raising three children, Ellen, Edith, and Edward (their youngest, Waldo, died of scarlet fever at five years old).

By the time of his move to Concord in 1834, Emerson had been decisively influenced by idealist currents from Germany and England, especially the works of Samuel Taylor Coleridge and Carlyle. Emerson now conceived of God as pure spirit, pervading everything in the universe down to the "blowing clover and the falling rain." Since the essence of spirit ultimately transcended the material world, however, and could only be known intuitively, this theological position came to be called Transcendentalism.

What was perhaps most distinctive about Emerson's brand of Transcendentalism was, first, his insistence on the right of each individual to use his or her intuition freely to achieve the truth of spirit and, second, the indispensable role of nature in this process. He expressed these ideas anonymously in his first book, *Nature* (1836), which both excited and puzzled his contemporaries. Emerson's best-known work even today, *Nature* functions as a kind of gnomic guidebook, leading the soul from an understanding of the natural world at the merely material level to an ecstatic realization of the spirit behind nature. When Emerson himself achieved this level of realization, he famously declared that he had become "a transparent eye-ball" through which "the currents of Universal Being circulate"—that he had become "part or particle of God." Importantly, Emerson believed that such peak experiences never came secondhand, through book learning or the teaching of others, nor through churches, clergy, or the Bible. They came only when one had established "an original relation to the universe" by means of unmediated contemplation of the natural world. In this process, institutions were largely superfluous.

Quickly identified as the author of *Nature*, Emerson's newfound notoriety made him a daring choice to deliver the annual Phi Beta Kappa lecture at Harvard in 1837. Entitled "The American Scholar," this address continued Emerson's emphasis on spiritual freedom by calling on Americans to create art and literature worthy of their homeland and independent of the past, especially "the courtly muses of Europe." Keeping with the themes of *Nature*, such art and literature would be possible only when "the ancient precept, 'Know thyself,' and the modern precept, 'Study nature,' [became] at last one maxim." The address was generally well received, and perhaps the graduating class of the Harvard Divinity School thought they would get a similarly anodyne speech when they asked Emerson to address them the following year. What they got, however, was the "Divinity School Address," a highly poetical but nevertheless spectacularly blunt rejection of scripture, miracles, and the whole of historical Christianity. Emerson even had the temerity to attack what he saw as the "noxious exaggeration about the *person* of Jesus" perpetuated by the churches, which according to him were "not built on his principles, but on his tropes." It was not clear what kind of response Emerson was expecting from his "Divinity School Address," but the backlash came quickly and was brutal. One prominent Unitarian divine, Andrews Norton, condemned the lecture as nothing less than "the latest form of infidelity." Emerson wisely stayed out of the fray, which raged back and forth between defenders and detractors for several weeks before dying down. It made Emerson famous, but much to his chagrin, he was now persona non grata at Harvard.

Nevertheless, time, the healer of all wounds and the softener of all heresies, eventually worked wonders. Through the 1840s and 1850s, Emerson continued to publish popular essays and poetry in books and magazines, including in the Transcendentalist journal called *The Dial*, which he edited for a time with Margaret Fuller. Some of his essays, such as "Self-Reliance" (1841) and "The Over-Soul" (1841), and his poems, such as "Woodnotes" (1840) and "Hamatreya" (1847), became firm fixtures in the American literary canon. His books, *Representative Men* (1850) and *English Traits* (1856), were international bestsellers. Moreover, through his indefatigable appearances on the Lyceum lecture circuit and his public stances on the antislavery movement, women's rights, and other issues, the usually retiring Emerson became celebrated as an immensely popular public figure both at home and abroad. By the 1860s, one historian has described him as "the Patriarch of American letter, . . . a wonder of the Western world as well known as Niagara Falls or Lowell mills."

Thus, in 1866, the year after the end of the Civil War, Emerson finally found himself welcomed back to his Cambridge alma mater. Harvard awarded him an honorary LLD degree at commencement, the alumni elected him to the Board of Overseers, and he was again asked to give the annual Phi Beta Kappa address after an absence of exactly thirty years. His rehabilitation, Emerson must have felt, was almost complete—all that was lacking now was for him to be invited to teach. This would have to wait until 1869, when the visionary Charles W. Eliot was elected Harvard's president. Eliot wished to shake up the staid institution and liberalize the curriculum by creating a system of electives, thereby giving undergraduates a modicum of choice in their programs of study. This innovation, Eliot said, had been inspired by Emerson's essay "Self-Reliance." President Eliot also decided to create a lecture series in which distinguished thinkers from outside the institution would be invited to create informal courses for upperclassmen called the University Lectures. A delighted Emerson was selected as one of the inaugural lecturers. He jumped at the chance to offer a course titled the Natural History of the Intellect. Ever since 1848, he had been hoping to expand this topic into the book that would be his magnum opus.

The task of preparing the Harvard course, however, proved even more daunting than Emerson could have predicted. Even though he had a year to prepare, the course called for sixteen lectures, which would be delivered over six weeks (all for a mere $8.75 per lecture). Not only did the sixty-seven-year-old Emerson find that he didn't quite have the intellectual horsepower to fill out the spaces between the discrete ideas and themes he had elaborated in his notebooks but that he was also a master of procrastination, occupying himself with a myriad of other tasks, both professional and domestic. Thus, by the time the April 1870 start date rolled around, Emerson still had not managed to create a coherent course, which is not surprising given that he had never been much of a systematic thinker. Nonetheless, he forged ahead. Thirty students attended the first of his lectures, but only four persevered to the end, and these students were frustrated by the haphazard nature of Emerson's "anecdotes of the intellect." Feeling defeated and tired, Emerson canceled the last two lectures. Soon after, he wrote to Carlyle that he was relieved it was over and bemoaned his dismal performance. And yet, almost in the same breath, he confidently predicted that a revised version of the course would be a success next year. This was not to be, though. Emerson was apparently even more befuddled at the lecture podium during the 1871 iteration of the class, frequently losing his place in his notes or his train of thought completely. By the end of lecture fourteen of the second Natural History of the Intellect series, much to his despair and frustration, he again knew he could not go on.

Significantly, Emerson was not the only one who noticed that he was floundering. His family and friends worried as well. One was his longtime friend John Murray Forbes, the immensely successful Boston business tycoon and railroad magnate, who came to his rescue with a tantalizing offer: to cancel the rest of the lectures and accompany him and his family on an all-expense-paid trip to California via the newly completed transcontinental railroad. In his reply, Emerson, loath to accept favors from friends, was coy at first, but in the end he managed to argue himself into going:

R. W. EMERSON TO J. M. FORBES.
Concord, Sunday Evening, 26 March 1871.

My dear Friend, —Your brave offer, which startled me yesterday, has kept my thoughts pretty steadily at work all to-day. And I am hardly ready to-night to decide. I have been postponing some serious tasks till my Cambridge work (which is a more serious strain than you would imagine) is ended, and to postpone these again, I fear seems to threaten the breaking of my contracts. . . . On the other side is the brilliant opportunity you offer me to see the wonderful country, and under every advantage, and with friends so dear and prized, and with yourself the leader. And I have the whisper that the adventure may add so much strength to body and mind as to compensate the shortened time on my return. Add that my wife and Ellen and Edward are unanimous in urging the journey. The result is that at this moment I lean to your munificent proposal, and shall prepare to go with you; but I shall reserve, for a day or two yet, a right to reconsider the decision of this moment. Meantime I value dearly the great heart that makes the proposition.

R. W. Emerson

Despite what Emerson said in his letter to Forbes, his wife Lidian was apparently not quite so enthusiastic about the journey, evidently favoring a shorter trip to Florida over a long trip to California. However, she knew that some kind of a vacation was necessary, and son Edward and elder daughter, Ellen, had no such reservations. Moreover, Emerson already knew that his youngest daughter, Edith, and her husband, William Hathaway Forbes, John Murray's son, would also be making the trip. With such a wealth of support, it was quickly decided by all: Emerson would abandon his labors at Harvard and go west. In a letter to Carlyle about the journey, Emerson seemed grumpily resigned to Forbes's plan "to carry me off to California, the Yosemite, the Mammoth trees, and the Pacific." And yet, in the face of a devastating intellectual defeat, it was clear that the invitation to California came as a huge relief to Emerson.

THE ATTRACTIONS OF CALIFORNIA

Besides his desire to escape an onerous task, many other things pulled Emerson toward California. He had long had an abiding interest in the West in general, and one scholar even claims that *Nature* was inspired as much by Emerson's interest in the exploration of the West as by any experience he had traveling in Europe. He avidly read the works by explorers such as John S. Frémont, Bayard Taylor, and Francis Parkman, whose *The Oregon Trail* (1849) was a classic of its type. Emerson wholeheartedly accepted the idea that it was America's "manifest destiny" to control the continent from east to west. This was necessary, he believed, for the creation of a democratic society that would overcome the gross imperfections of Europe and Asia. The irony of how this was to be accomplished, however, was not lost on Emerson. As he wrote in his journal of 1849, the year of the gold rush, the "good World-soul understands us well," and thus, "how simple the means" to populate the West: "Suddenly the Californian soil is spangled with a little gold-dust here and there in a mill-race in a mountain cleft; an Indian picks up a little, a farmer, and a hunter, and a soldier, each a little; the news flies here and there, to New York, to Maine, to London, and an army of a hundred thousand picked volunteers, the ablest and keenest and boldest that could be collected, instantly organize and embark for this desart [*sic*], bringing tools, instruments, books, and framed houses, with them. Such a well-appointed colony as never was planted before arrive with the speed of sail and steam on these remote shores, bringing with them the necessity that the government shall instantly proceed to make the road which they themselves are all intimately engaged to assist." Emerson's estimation of this messy and frequently violent process was quite clear eyed, describing it as "a rush and a scramble of needy adventurers, . . . a general jail-delivery of all the rowdies of the rivers" motivated by "the very commonplace wish to find a short way to wealth." Nevertheless, "Nature watches over all, and turns this malfeasance to good": "California gets peopled and subdued, civilized in this immoral way, and on this fiction a real prosperity is rooted and grown. 'T is a decoy-duck; 'T is tubs thrown to amuse the whale; but real ducks, and whales that yield oil, are caught. And out of Sabine rapes, and out of robbers' forays, real Romes and their heroisms come in fullness of time." Indeed, for Emerson this process of society building was inevitable, because the "whole creation is made of hooks and eyes, of bitumen, of sticking-plaster; and whether your community is made in Jerusalem or in California, of saints or of wreckers, it coheres in a perfect ball. Men as naturally make a state, or a church, as caterpillars a web." Emerson found the particulars of this "natural" process fascinating, and shortly after receiving Forbes's offer, he made a special trip to the Boston Athenaeum to borrow two books to give him the most up-to-date information on the state: Charles Loring Brace's *The New West: or, California in 1867–1868* (1869) and John Shertzer Hittell's *The Resources of California* (1863). Both books, with their wealth of statistics, confirmed for Emerson that now, twenty years after the epochal event at Sutter's Mill that set off the gold rush, was a good time for him to go west to see for himself whether his faith in the meliorating, community-building ways of the "World-soul" was justified.

There was another motivation for Emerson to take this trip besides witnessing the handiwork of the "sublime and friendly Destiny by which the human race is guided." His son Edward, who had made the overland trip to California in 1862, brought back tantalizing stories of the Far West. Anxious to enlist in the Union Army, Edward had been persuaded by his father that he needed to improve his health and toughen himself up if ever he were to be a soldier. In response, Edward proposed going to California, to which Emerson agreed, in part because Edward's friend Cabot Russell would be his companion on the journey, but also because a family friend, Abel Adams, generously bankrolled the adventure. Edward and Cabot set out from Concord on May 12, a few days after the funeral of Henry David Thoreau. By railroad, they reached the then railhead at Omaha, Nebraska, a week later, where they joined a wagon train of gold seekers and immigrants. For two months Edward rode across the plains on the train, which, always mindful of Indian attacks, hopped from Fort Kearney to Fort Laramie to Fort Bridges and then south to Salt Lake City. Mail service was slow, and Emerson fretted about his son: "If we don't hear tomorrow we shall have to make war on the Mormons," he anxiously joked. Edward was perfectly safe, however, although Cabot Russell turned back at this point. Bearing a letter of introduction to Brigham Young from a former governor of the territory, Alfred Cumming, Edward stayed in that city for several days. He then pushed on across the Great Basin by horseback and stagecoach to Carson City, Nevada, after which it took four days of jouncing roads to cross the Sierra Nevada into California, with a stop in Sacramento and then San Francisco, where he tarried for only a week, guest of the Reverend Thomas Starr King. Apparently war fever had gotten the best of him after the Confederate advance on Washington, for despite his host's best efforts to get him to stay to see "the jaw-teeth of the Sierra in the Yosemite gorge, the Fremont gold vein, and the Titan trees," Edward soon caught a boat to Panama, quickly crossed the Isthmus, and embarked to New York, where he arrived on September 25, planning to enlist.

In a letter to Ralph Waldo Emerson recounting Edward's visit, King rationalized Edward's precipitate departure, writing that "he needs not go to see the Yosemite, if there is something tougher in him than the texture of its pinnacles." Unfortunately, Edward was not quite as tough as that, and the overland experience did little to improve his robustness. On arrival back East, Edward was so ill that he had to take refuge in his uncle William's Staten Island home for a day or two before making the short journey to Concord. Reluctant to give up his chance at glory in battle, especially when his companion Cabot Russell had already joined up, Edward nevertheless realized that he was not fit for a soldier's life. What's more, John Murray Forbes confided to Edward that the enlistment of his own son William terrified him. As the only living son of Ralph Waldo Emerson, Forbes argued, Edward did not have the right to put his father through the same kind of daily anguish. Edward therefore reconsidered and enrolled at Harvard instead. His California adventure, however, proved to be a high point in his life, and his experience there was undoubtedly why he wholeheartedly recommended the trip to his father.

Of course, making the trip to California would be much easier in 1871 than it had been for the original forty-niners or even for Edward, because the transcontinental railroad now connected the coasts. This, too, Emerson believed was a gift of the "World-soul": "The timeliness of this invention of the locomotive must be conceded. . . . We could not else have held the vast North America together which we now engage to do." Indeed, during Emerson's lifetime, not only the invention of the locomotive but also the massive expansion of railroad routes must have seemed something of a miracle. "An unlooked for consequence of the railroad," he wrote in "The Young American" (1844), "is the increased acquaintance it has given the American people with the boundless resources of their own soil. . . . [I]n this country it has given a new celerity to time, or anticipated by fifty years the planting of tracts of land, the choice of water privileges, the working of mines, and other natural advantages. Railroad iron is a magician's rod, in its power to evoke the sleeping energies of land and water." The first American steam engine was run on just four miles of track constructed to cart granite to the site of the Bunker Hill Monument in Boston in 1827. Since then, track mileage had grown to 9,021 miles in 1850, and to 35,085 miles by 1865. With the completion of the transcontinental railroad at Promontory, Utah, four years later, California was now easily accessible by rail.

The arrival of the transcontinental railroad transformed California, socially, politically, and commercially. The physical connection to the rest of the Union brought not only waves of new migrants but also growing numbers of well-heeled tourists as well. Small numbers of pioneer sightseers had been coming to California since the 1850s, but one had to be a hardy adventurer to make the trip and enjoy it: except for San Francisco, little tourist infrastructure yet existed in the state. Nevertheless, early literary tourists such as Bayard Taylor, Horace Greeley, and Charles Nordhoff had all written glowing reports of California's natural splendors, and in anticipation of the completion of the transcontinental railroad, entrepreneurs had already begun to plot out internal routes of travel and build hotels and other facilities to accommodate the anticipated rush of visitors. They were not disappointed. Over the next twenty years, tourism would grow to become a major industry in California. Although Emerson could not have known this, his decision to travel to the state in 1871 was perfect timing: enough of an infrastructure had been developed by this time to tour the sights of California in relative comfort, yet the flow of tourists had not reached the flood stage. That would happen soon enough, but for the time being, crowds would not be a problem for the California tourist, and sights could still be approached with the aura of newness.

Finally, seeing the role that transplanted Yankees were playing in California undoubtedly also influenced Emerson's decision to visit.

Ethnocentric to a fault, Emerson not only believed in the Manifest Destiny of the United States to colonize the continent but also that New Englanders—the latest and highest manifestation of the "Anglo-Saxon race"—would lead the movement. Thus while he had some interest in the Indigenous, Hispanic, and Asian cultures of California, it is safe to say that he was most concerned with those aspects of California that had become assimilated to the United States through what one anonymous 1848 immigrant called "that all-pervading solvent and amalgam, the universal Yankee nation." And indeed, although New Englanders never formed more than 10 percent of the population of California during the Mexican period, they were present there early on. Some even became highly influential by marrying into prominent Californio families, as described in *Two Years before the Mast* (1840) by Bostonian (and Emerson's former pupil) Richard Henry Dana. What's more, Yankee settlers such as Massachusetts native Thomas O. Larkin, merchant, newspaper correspondent, and American consul in Monterey, not only encouraged more New Englanders to come West but was also instrumental in fomenting rebellion against Mexico and then promoting American annexation and statehood, which would come in 1850.

Gold, of course, the irresistible instrument of the Emersonian "World-soul," hastened the process considerably, and Yankees played a role in this too. The credit for the discovery goes to Maine-born Samuel Brannan, who came to California at the behest of Brigham Young, the leader of that most Yankee of new religious movements, the Church of Jesus Christ of Latter-day Saints. Brannan became a member of the church in 1842 and was sent with a Mormon expedition to see if California was a good place for the church to plant itself. When Brannan's Mormon colony, New Hope, quickly failed, he first fell back on his experience as a journalist, founding California's first newspaper, the *California Star*, and then turned merchant at Sutter's Mill on the American River near Sacramento. It was here that work on the millrace revealed the presence of gold, which Brannan quickly advertised to world, setting off the "rush of '49." Many answered the siren call, including many more New Englanders, some of whom came to the gold diggings in meticulously organized colonies formed like joint-stock companies, such as the Boston & California Joint Mining & Trading Company. As the name implied, the company was designed not only for mining but also for merchandizing—although few got rich off the former, many found their fortunes in the latter. Again, the Yankee exodus to California was never huge during this period, especially when compared with the number of Yankees who flooded the Midwest. By 1870, the federal census counted some 37,210 New Englanders in California, which was only about 6 percent of the population there. Nevertheless, institution builders par excellence, New Englanders, as Emerson had predicted, would long play an outsized role in the commercial and political development of the state.

Yankee culture had also taken root on the West Coast by the 1870s. Boston newspapers and magazines, such as the *Boston Herald* and the *Atlantic Monthly*, were freely available (if a bit out of date), and books from New England's publishing center, Hartford, Connecticut, made up much of the stock in almost every book and stationary store in the state. In light of this, it is no surprise to find that Emerson's works were well known in California and probably had been since the gold rush, carried there by immigrating Yankees as prized cultural talismans from their native New England. The travel writer, Bayard Taylor, for example, once found himself in 1859 in a remote mining town called, appropriately enough, Timbuctoo, but even here he found in the office of a local mining engineer "a choice collection of standard works," including a set of Emerson, "whom one would not expect to find in the midst of such barren material toil." Emerson's works were also ubiquitous in the growing number of private subscription libraries in the state, and selections from his essays were routinely included in newspapers as fillers.

And yet, reading their favorite authors was not enough for California's Yankees: they also demanded that they come west to see what God had wrought. In 1869, California's most celebrated literary magazine, the *Overland Monthly*, called on a whole host of Yankee literary luminaries—Whittier, Bryant, Lowell, Longfellow, Holmes, and Emerson—to come to California, because only they could appreciate and describe its "new civilization." Thus, when a writer for the *Oakland Daily News* caught wind of Emerson's journey in 1871, he thought it was especially fitting that the "Sage of Concord" would be "the literary pioneer and forerunner of [all] the philosophers, poets and scientists who will take a trip to California," for he alone would "see, not 'the nakedness of the land,' but the rich and gorgeous scenery with which Nature has decked it." Whether or not he knew it, Emerson would find in California an enthusiastic population of Yankee stalwarts who were more than eager to welcome him as New England's representative man.

THE CALIFORNIA FELLOWSHIP

By the date of departure, April 11, 1871, the Forbeses' traveling party to California—"New England's best," according to Emerson—had grown to eleven, with one more to be added along the way. In addition to Emerson, these included John Murray Forbes (1813–98) and his wife, Sarah Swain Hathaway Forbes (1813–1900); two of their daughters, Alice Hathaway Forbes (1838–1917) and Sarah Hathaway Forbes (1853–1917), and their son, William Hathaway Forbes (1840–97), who was married to Emerson's younger daughter, Edith (1841–1929). Family friends were invited also: Garth Wilkinson James (1845–83), Sarah Parkman Shaw Russell (1811–88), and Annie Keene Anthony (1839–1922). Rounding out the group was Boston lawyer and Harvard law professor James Bradley Thayer (1831–1902).

The Emersons had long been close to the Forbes family. Emerson first met John and Sarah Forbes on March 25, 1857, after giving a lecture at the Lyceum in Milton, Massachusetts. As a young man, Forbes had grown wealthy as a merchant in Canton, China, where he worked for years, with only a few trips back to the States. It was on one of these infrequent trips, in 1834, that he married Sarah Hathaway of New Bedford. Upon his return to the United States for good in 1846, Forbes organized a group of Boston capitalists to invest in the newly burgeoning business of railroads, eventually becoming the president of the Chicago, Burlington, and Quincy (CB&Q) Railroad. Through shrewd management of his railroad enterprises, Forbes had amassed a fortune that would last for generations. He and Sarah settled into a life of luxury in Milton, where they raised their six children, including Alice (33 at the time of the California trip), William (31), and Sarah (the baby of the family, only 18 in 1871).

Emerson had at first been wary of associating with Boston capitalists and their materialism, but in Forbes he found a man whose Republican politics and cultural preferences, not to mention his practical good sense, coincided with his own. The two became extremely close friends. Forbes, Emerson later wrote, was "an American to be proud of," a man of great talents and charm who nevertheless little "suspects, with his sympathy for man and his respect for lettered and scientific people, that he is not likely, in any company, to meet a man superior to himself." In addition to his baronial mansion in Milton, Forbes wholly owned the coastal island, Naushon, making him, according to Emerson, "the only squire in Massachusetts." In 1858, John and Sarah Forbes invited the Emerson clan for the first of many visits to the island, where they were lodged in luxury at the Forbeses' opulent and fully staffed summer cottage. Seven miles long with wooded hills, open meadows, freshwater ponds, and miles of beach, Naushon Island was enchanting. One could spend days fishing, hunting, riding, boating, or doing nothing at all but walking or meditating in the sunshine. Emerson's children especially loved their visits there, and even the reluctant Lidian was induced to come on occasion. For Emerson, it was nothing less than "Prospero's Island."

It was probably on Naushon during the summer of the Emersons' first visit that William Hathaway Forbes met and fell in love with Edith Emerson, although the details of their courtship are sketchy. Because none of their early letters survives, the best we can say is that their relationship developed in those short times when the families came together on vacations or holidays, either on the island or in Milton. The course of true love did not run smoothly, however. In 1860, Will was expelled from Harvard for a fraternity prank gone wrong and despaired that he would "never have any hope of Edith Emerson now." Banished to a clerk's position in the Boston office of the CB&Q Railroad, Will hoped to mend his reputation by enlisting with the Union Army at the outbreak of the Civil War. He served gallantly and would rise to the rank of lieutenant colonel in the 2nd Massachusetts Cavalry. A daring and reckless officer, Will had a horse shot out from under him and was captured in an 1864 skirmish with Mosby's Raiders outside Washington, D.C. He spent months in a Confederate prison, which made Edith literally sick with worry, which even a stint at Dr. Schieferdecker's, a popular New York water-cure establishment, did not help. Finally paroled and given leave to return home to Milton, Will wasted little time in proposing to Edith, and their engagement was publically announced on March 6, 1865 (two days after Lincoln's Second Inaugural, as Emerson noted in his journal). If Edith *had* to be married, Emerson was pleased by the choice of groom: "I am rejoiced," he wrote to John Murray Forbes, "to give my little country girl into the hands of this brave protector," although, perhaps tongue-in-cheek, he had his doubts about who was getting the better end of the bargain: "I hope she may know how to deserve her felicity. . . . She does not please in advance as much as she merits, but can sometimes surprise old friends who tho't they knew her well, with deeper and better thoughts."

The marriage between Will and Edith would have to wait, however. Dropping Edith off in Concord after announcing their engagement to his parents in Washington D.C., Will returned to his duties at the Virginia front on March 31, 1865. Now under the command of General George Armstrong Custer, Will continued to participate in cavalry attacks on Confederate forces until he was ordered by General Phil Sheridan to report to Appomattox. There, by happenstance, he witnessed the surrender of Robert E. Lee to Ulysses S. Grant on April 9, 1865. Now, with the war over and Will safely returned to his family in Milton, the Emerson women threw themselves into preparations for the wedding, which took place in the Emersons' front parlor on October 3, with the local Unitarian minister presiding in the presence of what seemed to be half the population of Concord. The bride and groom then set off to honeymoon on the coast before setting up housekeeping in Milton. Before the wedding, Emerson and his eldest daughter, Ellen, had referred to nuptials as "the Day of Judgement and the End of the World," but the pathos behind their joke was real: "There are several agreeable circumstances about that child's going away," Emerson wrote, "but there is a sad one and that is she is gone. Yes she was an idle minx, but she has gone and that troubles me."

And yet, there were many advantages to the marriage. Over the next few years, the Emerson and Forbes families grew closer than ever, continuing to vacation together on Naushon Island almost every year. Moreover, John Murray Forbes secured Edward Emerson a job in Iowa working for the CB&Q Railroad, and when this didn't work out due to ill health, Will Forbes, whom Edward idolized, took him under his wing. Together they ran a commercial vineyard growing Concord grapes until Edward eventually decided to go back to Harvard and become a doctor. Perhaps even more consequential was that Will Forbes took over Emerson's finances, investing his and Lidian's money wisely and, in at least one occasion, saving the couple from being outrageously cheated by an unscrupulous cousin. So successful was Will in stewarding their money that in his last years, Emerson was relieved of the burden of having to earn a living by continuous lecturing. Indeed, by 1871, his bank account was stable enough that when he was presented with the opportunity of taking a long vacation to California, financial considerations were of no account.

The rest of the California fellowship was made up of close friends of the Emerson and Forbes families. The twenty-six-year-old Garth Wilkinson James was the third son of Henry James Sr. and younger brother of William and Henry James Jr. Named for the British Swedenborgian J. J. Garth Wilkinson, but known as "Wilkie" to his friends and family, he, like his brothers, had spent a childhood being shuttled back and forth to Europe by the mercurial Henry Sr., who was ever dissatisfied with the quality of his children's education. The "adipose and affectionate Wilkie," as his father once referred to him, was easygoing and had little of the drive that characterized his older brothers, once confessing that all he wished to do with his life was go into the dry-goods business. His father had other plans for him, however, and in 1860, at Ralph Waldo Emerson's recommendation (they had known each since 1842), Wilkie was sent with his younger brother Robert to Franklin Sanborn's Concord Academy. Here he became good friends with the Emerson children, Ellen, Edward, and Edith. To all, Wilkie was a great favorite. Julian Hawthorne, also a student at the academy at the time, later described Wilkie as "incomparable": "Besides being the best dressed boy in the school, and in manners and talk, the most engaging, his good humor was inexhaustible. He was of middle height, broad-shouldered and symmetrical, with a good head, well set, and a smiling countenance. . . . He was sixteen years old when he came to us, but appeared older by two or three years, being self-possessed and having the bearing of a man of the world. In the company of the ladies he was entirely at his ease, and devoted; they all loved him." Ellen Emerson, who often stayed with the James family, once described William as "the happiest, queerest boy in the world" and Henry Jr. as "the most lovely, gentle and good," whereas Wilkie was "equally queer and equally good but very different." Perhaps the difference was that unlike the two older James brothers, Wilkie was affable, undemanding, and blessedly unneurotic.

Wilkie's halcyon days ended abruptly in 1862. Under the influence of Franklin B. Sanborn, master of the Concord Academy, ardent abolitionist and personal friend of John Brown, Wilkie had enlisted in the Union Army. Only 17, he nevertheless made a good soldier, serving in battle first with the 44th Massachusetts Infantry and then with the 54th Massachusetts, an all-Black regiment commanded by Robert Gould Shaw. Present at the attack on Fort Wagner on July 18, 1863, when Shaw was killed at the head of his troops, Wilkie himself was grievously wounded in the side and back by a shell burst and then a canister ball that lodged in his foot. The hospital was a nightmare that Wilkie barely survived. That he did survive was mere chance: a family friend, William C. Russell, happened to be searching for his own son in the hospital, none other than Edward's companion Cabot Russell, who, it was later learned, had died in the attack with Colonel Shaw. Instead, the senior Russell stumbled onto Wilkie, whom he arranged to be returned to his family in Boston. Healing was painfully slow, and he never fully recovered from either of his wounds. Nevertheless, Wilkie returned to his regiment and soldiered on until the end of the war, mustering out four months after the South surrendered. After the war, finding no employment in Boston, Wilkie traveled to Florida in 1866 to try his hand at cotton farming, using as capital money lent to him by his father and John Murray Forbes. Despite local hostility and harassment by the Ku Klux Klan due to his support of Black labor, not to mention a bout of malaria, bad weather, and insect pests, Wilkie persevered on the plantation until 1871, when he finally sold what he could and returned to Boston. It was at this point that Forbes invited him to accompany his party to California. If anyone needed a frolic, it was Wilkie James.

Less is known about the next two Boston members of the traveling party, Annie Anthony and Sarah Russell. The thirty-two-year-old Annie Keene Anthony was a cousin of John Murray Forbes. Her father was John Gould Anthony (1804–77), a noted naturalist in charge of the conchology department of Harvard's Museum of Comparative Zoology, where he was a colleague of Louis Agassiz and a friend of William James. We don't know exactly why Annie was invited on this trip to California, although we do know that she was in the middle of a turbulent on-again, off-again engagement to George Garrison, the ne'er-do-well son of the abolitionist William Lloyd Garrison. Perhaps the journey offered her a break from a trying romantic situation in Boston. In any case, she was known to be a "genial and sunny" person with "a talent for making friends," so her addition to the company, like Wilkie's, was a happy one.

As for Sarah Parkman Shaw Russell, or simply Mrs. Russell as everyone called her, she was described by Bronson Alcott as a frequent attendee at Margaret Fuller's "Conversations" in Boston and a Fourierist, who, along with her husband, George Robert Russell (1800–1866), was a die-hard supporter and financial backer of George Ripley's utopian

Brook Farm. It was perhaps through the 1841 Brook Farm experiment that she first met Emerson and his family. We know that Mrs. Russell had been a friend of the Forbes family even longer, as both George Russell and John Murray Forbes had started their business careers with the same Boston-based Far East import firm, Perkins & Co. Their friendship eventually resulted in the 1863 marriage of the Russells' son Henry Sturgis, to Mary Hathaway Forbes, after which the two families took a long vacation together in Paris. Witty, energetic, and unflappable, the good sense of sixty-year-old Mrs. Russell made her a favorite with her traveling companions, and perhaps John Murray Forbes included her precisely because he knew he could count on her buoyancy. Forbes also liked her because she was famously informal. As one of her admirers once said of Mrs. Russell, "her manner was direct and frank and cheerful, and with her perfect candor and vigorous good-sense, it scattered the trivial and smirking artificialities of social intercourse as a clear wind from the north-west cools and refreshes the sultry languors of August."

EMERSON'S AMANUENSIS

The last of the Boston travelers was James Bradley Thayer, forty years old at the time of the trip. Thayer had been born in Haverhill, midway between Concord and Boston. During his childhood, his family was always in a precarious position, as his father, Abijah, never quite found his calling, whether as an editor of small-town newspapers, a silkworm farmer, or a commodities broker. Nevertheless, Thayer enjoyed a good primary and secondary education in the schools of Northampton, Massachusetts, where he converted to the Baptist faith and contemplated becoming a missionary to the western territories. This vocation was short-lived, however, and he soon encountered Unitarianism, in which faith he would become extremely active for the rest of his life. In 1848, Thayer entered Harvard College, where he distinguished himself as a brilliant student, graduating in 1852 as class orator. During his college years, he taught at the Milton Academy to make ends meet, and it was probably there that he met the Forbes family for the first time. Two years later, after debating a career in either law or divinity, he entered Harvard Law School, graduating in 1856 and afterward practicing law in Boston, where he became especially noted for his expertise in corporate law.

FIGURE 1. *James Bradley Thayer,* ca. 1870s. —Courtesy of the Harvard Law School Library, Historical and Special Collections.

It is not known when or where Thayer first met Ralph Waldo Emerson, although he did hear Emerson speak several times during the 1850s. We know, for example, that Thayer was in the audience at Harvard in 1851 when Emerson delivered his incendiary speech "The Fugitive Slave Law," which, Thayer remembered, "elicited hisses, shouts, and catcalls." "Through all this," according to Thayer, "there never was a finer spectacle of dignity and composure than he presented." Friendship with Emerson was solidified in 1861 when Thayer married Sophia Ripley (1833–1914). "Sophy" was the daughter of Brook Farm founders George and Sophia Ripley and granddaughter of the Reverend Ezra Ripley, who was the beloved minister of the Concord Unitarian Church, denizen of the Old Manse, and Ralph Waldo Emerson's step-grandfather. From then on, the Thayer and Emerson families were very close, with Thayer serving as Emerson's personal lawyer and confidant for the rest of the older man's life.

Again, the circumstances for Thayer agreeing to join the fellowship on the eve of the trip to California are not known, but it is easy to suspect that Thayer saw this both as a golden opportunity to visit the West and as a unique opportunity, through the liminality of travel, to get to know better a man whose life and thought he deeply admired. For Emerson's part, he was lucky to have Thayer along, for not only did Thayer prove a hardy traveler, boon companion, and ever-ready conversation partner, but he would also come to serve as the faithful, if ad hoc, chronicler of the western adventures to come.

Chapter 1
FROM EAST TO FAR WEST
(APRIL 11 TO APRIL 17, 1871)

Who shall think he has come late into nature, or has missed anything
excellent in the past, who seeth the admirable stars of possibility, and
the yet untouched continent of hope glittering with all its mountains in
the vast West?

—Ralph Waldo Emerson, "The Method of Nature" (1841)

On Tuesday, April 11, 1871, Ralph Waldo Emerson set off from his home,
affectionately called "Bush," and headed for the Concord Depot to catch
the train to Boston. A familiar figure in town for decades, everyone
knew Emerson by sight and may have remarked on how he had aged of
late. He had always been sloped shouldered, but now he was to an even
greater degree. And while always tall and thin, he was now thinner than
ever and not as tall as he had once been—according to Oliver Wendell
Holmes Sr., Emerson always claimed to be six feet, "but his son thinks he
could hardly have straightened himself to that height in his later years."
Emerson's fine brown hair, thick in his youth, was now thinning, but his
gait was still strong and his face had changed little over the years: thin
with a high forehead, his most distinctive features were still his nose—
hawklike or "accipitrine" in the Latinate jargon of the day—and his eyes,
which were the "strongest and brightest blue"—"sea-captains'" eyes as
one of his daughters described them. His voice remained strong, too,
and he could still modulate it from its natural baritone to a deep bass for
emphasis if he wished to. Emerson had long been accustomed to arduous
overland journeys given his years on the Lyceum circuit, so he traveled
light. Along with a trunk packed for the trip by Ellen, he carried only
a bright purple satchel or carpetbag, stuffed with books and papers to
amuse himself on the long trip to California.

Already waiting for Emerson at the Boston & Worcester Depot were Mrs. Russell, James Bradley Thayer, Wilkie James, and Will and Edith Forbes (the rest of Forbes family and Annie Anthony would join them in Burlington, Iowa). Also at the depot was a farewell committee consisting of Ellen and Edward Emerson; Sophia Ripley Thayer and her sister Mary Ripley Simmons; Mrs. Russell's daughter Emily; and Henry James Sr. Edith recorded in her diary that Ellen had come that morning to their home in Milton to arrange for Edith and Will's children—Ralph, Edith ("Violet"), and William Cameron ("Cam")—to be sent to her and Lidian for babysitting. Ellen expressed some trepidation at having to look after "the young Vandals in Concord," but despite her worries, Edith gave her "cheering assurances that those children would be wiser and better next June" on the party's return. At last, Thayer bid a heartfelt farewell to Sophy, who insisted on seeing him off despite a persistent cold. The group then boarded the cars of the Boston and Albany Railroad, which departed for the west at precisely three o'clock.

Now comfortably ensconced in a drawing-room car, the little group sped across central Massachusetts, stopping only briefly at Springfield, where they transferred from the drawing-room car to a Wagner sleeping car. Despite the comfortable berths, Thayer found sleep difficult as the "night was a jolty one," and too much strong tea the day before wouldn't let him sleep past 6:00 a.m. As they were passing through Syracuse, Thayer dressed and climbed out of his berth and strolled up to the drawing-room car. Here, he whiled away the hours until breakfast chatting with "an entertaining youth" from Kendallville, Indiana, who "talked with a degree of simplicity and enthusiasm about his horses and his races and with so much sympathy and appreciation with his four legged friends, being withal by nature a really good fellow, that it was fun to hear him."

Thayer returned to the Wagner sleeping car around nine o'clock and found Emerson and the rest of the party all dressed and chatting away as though they had never gone to bed. Thayer especially noted that "a fresher and more cheerful object than Mrs. Russell one would be hard to find." At Rochester, the party "breakfasted with a bout of sumptuous leisure" at Congress Hall and then boarded the "Arlington," a Pullman Palace Car that would take them to Chicago via Niagara Falls and Ontario, Canada. Thayer was quite bowled over by the luxury of it all:

"It is the most comfortable thing I have ever saw. . . . Everything is quiet and in good taste around the car with a certain richness and elegance even, quite unlike the tawdry ornaments one sees in cars." What's more, the car was nearly empty, so the party "had four sections and eight seats (with seats that would hold sixteen persons) among the six." This gave them plenty of room to stretch out and settle in.

By that afternoon they had crossed over into Canada by means of the Niagara Falls Suspension Bridge, built by John Roebling and completed in 1855. With a clear view of the great falls, which had long functioned as a favorite metaphor for the sheer power of nature, Emerson must have cast his mind back to when he first saw them in the summer of 1850. Returning on a steamboat from a talk in Detroit, Emerson happened to run into John Murray Forbes, who persuaded him to take the time to see the falls. "We took a carriage and drove around the circuit," Forbes later wrote. "When we came to Table Rock on the British side, our driver took us down on the outer part of the rock in the carriage. We passed on by rail, and the next day's papers brought us the telegraphic news that Table Rock had fallen over; perhaps we were among the last persons on it!" This was not the last time calamity almost found Emerson at Niagara Falls: in 1863, Emerson nearly died when the American Hotel went up in flames in the middle of the night. Despite the thick smoke that filled his hotel room, he managed to salvage a few of his belongings and manuscripts and make his way downstairs and out into the street, where, with the other displaced guests, he stood mesmerized by the now raging inferno. As a pioneer of the Lyceum lecture circuit, Emerson had long become quite accustomed to the odd inconvenient adventure along the way, and later he made light of the fire, saying that it allowed him to get acquainted with many interesting people he otherwise would not have had the opportunity to meet.

For someone who once wrote "travelling is a fool's paradise," Emerson nevertheless seemed to relish being on the road, and the Lyceum circuit provided the perfect excuse. After leaving the Unitarian ministry in 1832, the Lyceum became indispensable for Emerson's career, allowing him simultaneously to make a living and to build his reputation as one of the leading public intellectuals of his day. Books and articles were efficient in reaching elites, but for connecting with a mass audience in the nineteenth century, there was nothing like the

FIGURE 2. *The Only Route Via Niagara Falls and Suspension Bridge,* ca. 1876.
—Courtesy of the Prints & Photographs Division, Library of Congress, Washington,
D.C., LC-DIG-pga-03608.

lecture. Named after Aristotle's school of philosophy in ancient Athens, the Lyceum was the brainchild of Josiah Holbrook (1788–1854), a schoolteacher from Derby, Connecticut; inspired by similar Mechanics' Institutes in Britain, he wished to make advanced education available to the working classes in America through a network of locally based lecture series. Holbrook published a plan for fee-based "associations for mutual instruction in the sciences, and in useful knowledge generally," and set about traveling the towns of New England to encourage the creation of Lyceum branches. Concord's Lyceum, established in 1829, introduced Emerson to the system and would long serve as an important sounding board to fine-tune his lectures before taking them to a wider public. Emerson quickly found that the growing network of Lyceum associations, along with the speakers bureaus that grew up to service them, were exceedingly convenient as they relieved him of handling advertising, booking halls, and arranging lodgings. Emerson and the Lyceum were made for each other, a perfect example of the kind of synchronicities slyly arranged by the "World Soul."

The Lyceum became an immensely popular institution with Yankees wherever they were. Thus, as New Englanders spread into Upper Canada and the Midwest, the Lyceum soon followed and, eventually, so, too, did Emerson, that "Plato" from the "Yankee Athens," Concord, Massachusetts. By train, steamboat, stagecoach, on horse or on foot, Emerson traveled far and wide in the Yankee diaspora, lecturing primarily, but also sightseeing when time permitted. In 1850, when he made his first extended trip into the Midwest, traveling as far as St. Louis, he took time to visit Mammoth Caves near Bowling Green, Kentucky, which he found impressive, especially after his guide lit off a Roman candle, which illuminated the vastness like no lantern could. Although Lyceum travel could be hard and wearying, especially when connections were missed or the weather was foul, Emerson continued on this circuit year after year, reaching as far west as Iowa, Wisconsin, and Minnesota. People flocked to hear the "celebrated metaphysician," and although not everyone understood what he said, they came to see him anyway as the symbol of the highest cultural aspirations of America. So popular were his appearances that often while lecturing for a Lyceum in one town, Emerson would be confronted by a committee from another, importuning him to extend his itinerary to include an impromptu lecture in that locale. He rarely said no. Because Ellen Emerson was so used to her father being asked to lecture wherever he went, she sensibly insisted on including several of his manuscripts in his trunk for California, just in case he met with a Lyceum or other interested group along the way.

Flying across Ontario, the traveling party spent most of the day chatting or reading. "Everything went smoothly and charmingly during the day," Thayer later wrote, "everything easy and pleasant." He was especially impressed by the 2:00 p.m. dinner service aboard the Palace Car: "The car's bill of fare is passed about—very much like [the Boston restaurant] Parkers . . . and you order your dinner and when it is ready . . . a table is inserted between each pair of seats facing each other, a white table cloth spread, the table set and you dine as if quietly at home,— and all the time you are pelting along over the country like mad." The company paired off for dinner, with Will and Edith sitting together, and Mrs. Russell sitting across from Wilkie James. Thayer was delighted to "to have Emerson for my messmate" at both dinner and tea. After both repasts, Thayer and Wilkie moved to the smoking car for cigars and more conversation. Despite all that he had suffered in the last decade, it is remarkable how upbeat Wilkie remained: "What a most agreeable and sensible little fellow,—how easy and rolly polly he is," Thayer wrote to Sophy back in Boston. "I take as much comfort in his pleasant company as in my cigar."

Back in the Pullman Palace Car, Emerson and Thayer began what would become a favorite sport throughout the trip: debating the reputations of the poets and writers of the day. In *Nature*, Emerson had written that two things that were guaranteed to heighten one's perception of the world were looking out train windows at the countryside and reading and discussing poetry, albeit the former afforded only a "low degree of the sublime" when compared with the latter—but who knows what heights of perception could be achieved if the two were combined? Of course, Emerson had an ulterior motive in always talking about poetry on this trip: it allowed him to think out loud about what should be included in *Parnassus*, the anthology of his favorite poems that he was editing with Edith and Will for publication by Houghton, Osgood of Boston.

Sitting side by side on one of the three divans in the carriage, Emerson regaled Thayer with his opinions on Dante, Goethe, Wordsworth, Longfellow, and William Morris, one of the progenitors of the British Arts and Crafts Movement. Emerson was adamant that Goethe's *Faust*—the first part, that is (he hadn't read the second part)—"was a *destructive* and not an affirmative poem and he didn't like that sort of thing." Thayer pushed back, citing Bayard Taylor's defense of *Faust* as a paean to man's fallibility and ability to learn from mistakes, a reading that would be clear, Thayer pointedly concluded, if one were to read *both* parts one and two. Emerson retreated with a smile and deftly shifted the subject to a discussion of two intuitive faculties of the mind, "fancy" and "imagination," which Coleridge had distinguished as merely associative in the former but transcendental in the latter. Thayer concurred by referring to a similar distinction made by Wordsworth in the new preface to the 1815 edition of his *Lyrical Ballads* (a copy of which just happened to be at hand). Here Wordsworth claimed that a comparison made by the imagination could be identified as such because "a sense of the truth of the likeness, from the moment that it is perceived, grows and continues to grow upon the mind." Emerson agreed: "Yes, imagination is the solemn act of the soul in believing that things have a spiritual significance and it uses words simply as a vehicle for conveying that." Longfellow and William Morris were brought up next, with both garnering Emerson's qualified approval, although he felt that Morris wrote *too* much.

Perhaps needless to say, not all the conversations along the way were so high toned and occasionally devolved into good-natured gossip about family, friends, and acquaintances. At some point, for example, Mrs. Forbes mentioned that Elizabeth Hoar "seemed a very timid person." Although Emerson dearly loved Elizabeth as part of his family, as she had been betrothed to his brother Charles at his death, he nevertheless could not resist lampooning her, saying that only she could come out with a line like, "Well, if the fire *should* burn me." Thayer would often record such barbs in his letters to Sophy, although, because letters were typically read out loud to family and friends, he added caveats such as, "Do not, by the way, read what I say of Mr. Emerson's very freely,—not for instance to [Mrs. Russell's daughter] Mary Russell. I do not care to be reckoned a Boswell. I write to *you*. I care too much for Mr. Emerson and value his suggestions so much and know too much that you do, that I would fain not forget some things that he lets fall," even if they didn't bear repeating to others. Finally, when even the gossip ran out, the tired group turned in around 10:00 p.m., just as the train was crossing the Detroit River into Michigan. It was to be another restless night for Thayer, who woke up every hour, dismayed "at the furious tearing pace west we seemed to be making across Michigan." Sleep came finally, though, and when he next awoke at eight, he could see through his sleeping berth's window the dawn light on Lake Michigan.

GEORGE PULLMAN

Arriving in Chicago around nine that morning, the Emerson party checked into the Sherman House on Clark Street. Opened a decade before, the Sherman House was one of the most elegant hotels in the city: six stories tall, clad in "Athens marble," it boasted a two-story colonnaded portico and a massive central hall, off which could be found opulent dining, drawing, and meeting rooms. Since the train west would not board until nine the next morning, the group had the day before them to idle away as they saw fit. After breakfast, Emerson sat down at one of the writing desks and completed his letter to Carlyle, which he had begun back in Concord on the eve of the trip: "Arrived here and can bring this little sheet to the post-office here," he wrote. "My daughter Edith Forbes, and her husband William H. Forbes, and three other friends, accompany me, and we shall overtake Mr. Forbes senior to-morrow at Burlington, Iowa." He also read a letter just arrived from Ellen, who wrote that Lidian missed him already ("Oh! to think he was here last night, and now he's gone!"). Lidian was somewhat consoled, however, by the delivery of a new oil portrait of "Mr. Emerson," despite the fact that the artist gave him a "look of severe victimization." Thayer, meanwhile, after completing his own letter to Sophy ("write soon and every morning," he commanded), strolled the city streets, at one point taking the 1,605-foot Washington Street traffic tunnel under the Chicago River to visit a couple of lawyers of his acquaintance who lived on Chicago's north side. Thayer, of course, could not have known it, but much of what he saw that day, including the Sherman House, would cease to exist just six months later, swept away by the Great Chicago Fire of October 1871.

Late the next morning at the train station, Emerson and his party were met by none other than George Pullman (1831–97) himself. John Murray Forbes, who long knew Pullman through their railroad connections, had booked a Palace Car named the "Huron" as a special treat for his guests, and Pullman had decided to deliver the car in person and see to its provisioning. Thayer described Pullman as "a man of forty odd, with a longish beard and close cut grayish hair and short; he seemed quiet and modest—a little heavy perhaps and slow; but he had a quiet way of saying a thing that indicated more than his manner." Originally from Upstate New York, Pullman was the son of the quintessential Yankee inventor, James Pullman, who designed a machine for moving houses, barns, and other buildings on wheels. In the 1850s, son George took this invention to Chicago, where the marshy terrain on the shores of Lake Michigan necessitated the raising of whole blocks of buildings to a more elevated grade. So proficient at this was Pullman that it was said he "raised an entire city block of brick stores on Lake Street to the new street level without breaking a single pane of glass."

Growing rich from this enterprise and increasing his wealth after a stint as a miner and merchant in Colorado during the Pike's Peak gold rush, Pullman next turned his attention to building a more comfortable sleeping car. During his frequent travels by rail, Pullman had been singularly unimpressed by the sleeping cars then in service. By incorporating a number of ingenious features into his new design, including berths that folded away near the ceiling, thus freeing up space on the floor of the carriage during the day, Pullman's cars quickly outpaced the competition in terms of both comfort and luxury, and in 1868, he secured the sleeping car contract with the soon-to-be-completed transcontinental railroad. The Pullman Palace Car, which differed from the earlier Pullman sleeping car by the addition of kitchen and food storage facilities, was introduced by Pullman the year before and became standard on "through" lines between Chicago and the East, especially New York and Boston. The first through trip from New York to San Francisco in Pullman Palace Cars was made in May 1870 as a special excursion of the Boston Board of Trade, which included Forbes's brother Robert B. Forbes. Pullman was a stickler for quality, and one way he maintained quality was that he didn't sell his cars outright but leased them to the railroads with a strict set of conditions. Each car was staffed exclusively by Pullman employees trained to exacting standards that were rigorously enforced by a cadre of company spies known as "spotters." What's more, every time a Pullman returned to its hub, its linens, carpets, and other furniture were removed, and the car was scrubbed from top to bottom, ensuring maximum cleanliness each time a car went out. It was a winning system, and by the time Emerson and his party came through, the Pullman Company was worth millions, and Pullman himself was celebrated as one of America's most innovative industrialists.

Standing together on the platform, the two Yankees, Emerson and Pullman, were a study in contrasts: the tall, thin, stooped-shouldered, clean-shaven Emerson next to the short, portly Pullman with his neatly trimmed gray beard. They both had in common, however, an abiding interest in social reform, although they came at it from diametrically opposite directions because Emerson was an ex-Unitarian Transcendentalist and Pullman a devout Universalist (the $80,000 Pullman Memorial Universalist Church in his hometown of Albion, New York, was the result of his largesse). Emersonian self-reliance sought to reform individuals to catalyze larger social movements, whereas the Universalist Pullman believed that although all mankind would be saved—hence Universalism—the old Calvinist dogma still held: depravity lurked at the bottom of the human soul and needed to be managed from the top

down by an elect few. It was this kind of thinking that would lead Pullman in the 1880s to invest millions in an ambitious planned community
south of Chicago. Pullman City would have everything necessary for
the happiness of Pullman's employees: houses, stores, schools, churches,
auditoriums, parks, a hospital, a hotel, a library, and a theater, many of
which were designed in the Gothic Revival style of famed Chicago archi-
tect Solon S. Beman and all electrified by the same great Corliss engine
from the 1876 Centennial Exhibition celebrated by the author Henry
Adams in his famous chapter, "The Dynamo and the Virgin," in *The
Education of Henry Adams* (1900). Pullman believed that by providing
everything his workers needed and excluding what they did not (such
as saloons), they would be content and easily controlled, and the potential for strikes, violence, and other labor unrest would be avoided. At
the dedication of the Pullman Library, the Presbyterian minister David
Swing specifically compared Pullman City to the earlier social experiment of Brook Farm, claiming that whereas the latter was doomed to
failure because it was based on "abstract philosophy," the former would
survive and thrive because it was built on "common sense of the highest
and best order." Indeed, "industry will always surpass philosophy as the
basis of welfare." Emerson, who was famously doubtful of the wisdom
of Brook Farm when he was asked to join, undoubtedly would have been
dubious of this enterprise as well. And he would have been right: when
the economic depression of 1893 hit, Pullman City, for all George Pullman's "common sense" idealism, was the site of labor unrest and violence as intense as anything in Chicago's history.

Of course, Emerson didn't waste time talking about the efficacy of
planned communities with Pullman. His concern was of a much more
immediate and practical nature: Was the Palace Car safe? Thayer reports
that Pullman assured him that the car was strong and could "bear rolling over and over," although "there was one place . . . on the way out
where if we were to go off he thought the car would not hold together,
and that was just as we would go down the Sierra Nevada, rounding
Cape Horn as they call it, where it is 1,400 feet straight down on one side
of the track; if we should go off there, he wouldn't warrant it." Pullman
would warrant, however, that he had done his best to stock the Huron
with all the good things that Forbes had requested, and then some.
Thayer remarked on the "apples and baskets of wine and other luxuries"

being loaded into a small stateroom in the back of the car. Bennett, their conductor for the trip, admitted that things would be a bit crowded for a while, but they would "'eat our way out' pretty soon." Thayer hoped so, for the small stateroom was destined to be the carriage's smoking room once it was empty; until then, all smoking had to be done on the chilly open platform at the end of the car. There were compensations to this arrangement, however: since the Huron would always be the last car of the train, the views of the countryside as they traveled would be unobstructed and thus the best on the train. Even after the stateroom became available later in the trip, Thayer and the other smokers in the party would continue to use the open platform.

Once the car was loaded, the party said their good-byes to Mr. Pullman and boarded. Within minutes, the train was chugging through the Chicago

1538. DRAWING ROOM CAR "HURON."

FIGURE 3. *Interior of the Pullman Palace Car "Huron,"* ca. 1870. —Courtesy of the Society of California Pioneers, San Francisco, CA.

suburbs out to the Illinois countryside. As he settled in, Thayer waxed enthusiastic about how "well economized" the design of the car was, and he marveled at opulence of the Pullman Palace Car in his letter to Sophia: "It is wholly unlike the adorning of our ordinary cars; the ornamenting consists chiefly in a little gilt line sunk in the wood, making little set figures such as suggest the Etruscan pottery and are . . . elegantly neat in their effect; a Brussels carpet of beautiful pattern, little mirrors between the windows which slide up and give you a lamp for the evening with a curved reflector behind it that will light the little table if you choose to have it before you; the dark woodwork, black walnut, inlaid occasionally with the curled root and with mahogany, the low handsome wide seats and all about it is attractive and satisfactory." Far from extravagant and simply pandering to Americans' increasing desire for luxuries, Pullman had defended the elaborate furnishings of his Palace Cars as a civilizing influence, just as much a part of his moralizing project as the parks and libraries of Pullman City: "I have always held," he opined, "that people are very greatly influenced by their physical surroundings. Take the roughest man, a man whose lines have always brought him into the coarsest and poorest surroundings, and bring him into a room elegantly carpeted and furnished and the effect upon his bearing is immediate. The more artistic and refined the mere external surroundings, in other words, the better and more refined the man." Proof of this assertion was the oft-cited opinion that "respectable" women felt safer in the domestic surroundings of a Palace Car than elsewhere on trains, but undoubtedly the fact that only well-to-do white people could secure seats in Pullman cars also had something to do with it.

Forbes was paying $85 a day for the Huron, which included a full complement of staff: a conductor, two porters, and a cook. Drilled to military precision and rigidly hierarchical, the staff performed their duties with maximum efficiency and little fanfare, and it was at least because of their unobtrusive presence that travel on a Pullman Palace Car was so highly praised. Significantly, however, the only member of the staff to be referred to by name by Thayer throughout the journey was Bennett, the conductor, perhaps owing to his having been the much-praised conductor on the Boston Board of Trade trip to California the previous year. But most likely was that Bennett was white and the others were Black. George Pullman had insisted on this arrangement since the beginning because he believed that after years of slavery, not only were Blacks a cheap labor source but they were also more accustomed to rendering service than whites and thus more likely to be obliging to passengers and less demanding of management. Despite the explicit racism of this policy, many African American men embraced this role and flocked to Pullman recruiters when they came to town, especially in the Deep South. The hours were long, sleep was unpredictable, much time was spent away from home, and no matter how hard one worked, a porter could never become a conductor as this position was reserved for whites. Yet the pay was steady, tips could be good, and over time the job as a Pullman porter developed a special status within the Black community. Thus, many Pullman porters and cooks put up with the indignities of the job and the invisibility of their efforts because they knew that this was the best they could do given the racist climate of late nineteenth-century America.

CROSSING THE MISSISSIPPI AND MISSOURI RIVERS

At half-past two, dinner was served from the tiny kitchen and larder, which were located after the first two staterooms as one entered the carriage from the front end. Joining the Emerson party for dinner were Augustus Parsons and his wife, Hannah (the niece and final caretaker of Emerson's beloved, brilliant—if cantankerous—aunt, Mary Moody Emerson [1774–1863]). The Parsons were traveling to Kansas by way of Galesburg, Illinois, and once Emerson and Edith learned they were aboard, they instantly invited them to enjoy Mr. Forbes's bounty. And bountiful it was: as Thayer enumerated the menu, it included "soup, your choice of roast beef, roast lamb or chicken; mashed potatoes, asparagus, peas, tomatoes, canned corn, bread and butter, ice water and English ale; raspberry pie, cottage pudding, cake, nuts and raisins and coffee; oranges and bananas!" Afterward, Thayer and Wilkie headed to the back platform "and smoked looking out at the broad fields, many just growing green, and at the great stretch of sky all blue and softened by the warm air" of the Illinois spring. "What an extraordinary and ludicrously easy, delightful piece of travelling this is," Thayer wrote to his wife while balancing his blotter and inkstand on his lap: "I think you can hardly have an idea what fun this is." The train reached Galesburg a little after 5:00 p.m. Here the Parsons detrained to catch their connection, and the Huron was transferred to a locomotive of the Chicago, Burlington & Quincy line bound for the far West.

As the train sped across the countryside, passing by scenes of settled towns, prosperous farms, and acre after acre of blossoming apple and cherry trees, Emerson opened his purple satchel stuffed with books and papers to occupy him on the trip. He pulled out a German dictionary and was about to go to work deciphering Goethe's *Sprüche in Prosa* (1870), a New Year's gift from George Bancroft, when he turned to Thayer to observe that traveling on the train was an excellent time to study German. This led to the kind of conversation of free association that Emerson was prone to in his old age, perhaps because it exercised his fading memory without taxing it too much. Reciting a line from Goethe about the Roman Grammarian Aelius Donatus led him to reminisce a bit about his acquaintance, the English writer Walter Landor, who had quoted to him poetry by Julius Caesar that had been preserved in Donatus's works as Emerson related in his *English Traits*. Here the conversation lapsed for a moment and Emerson went back to his reading, only to return to Thayer to ask if he had read the eighteenth-century mystic Emanuel Swedenborg, who had been one of Emerson's "representative men." In response, Thayer dutifully quoted Emerson's characterization of Swedenborg: "He goes up and down the world of men, a modern Rhadamanthus in gold-headed cane and peruke, and with nonchalance and the air of a referee, distributes souls." "Yes," Emerson replied, Swedenborg "was like Linnaeus, or those who devised the nomenclature of chemistry,—a sort of classifier of souls." They chuckled about this, but Emerson was quick to recommend Swedenborg's *Arcana* as a book worth reading, as was *The Conjugial Love*, although "'conjugial' was such a silly word." The conversation now shifted to the state of the Unitarian clergy, which prompted Emerson to ruminate about his own difficulties in the ministry, the controversy over communion that led to his resignation, and how he nevertheless identified himself thereafter as a Christian, apparently unwilling to repudiate the label, even though "some one had lately come to him whose conscience troubled him about retaining the name of Christian." Emerson said he himself had no problem with it: "When he was called a Platonist, or a Christian, or a Republican, he welcomed it. It did not bind him to what he did not like. What is the use of going about and setting up a flag of negation?" By now, the sun had begun to set and Bennett, the conductor, was going about lighting the car's lamps. Soon they would cross the Mississippi River to stop overnight in Burlington, Iowa.

Burlington was the connecting hub between the CB&Q Railroad and another Forbes-controlled line, the Burlington and Missouri River (B&MR) Railroad. The party was met at the station by the superintendent of the latter line, Charles Elliott Perkins (1840–1907), who happened to be

John Murray Forbes's nephew. Forbes himself was also on hand to greet the new arrivals. The original plan was for the party to spend the night on the Huron, but Perkins had arranged for Thayer to spend the night with another railroad man, John Worthington Ames, a good friend of Thayer's since their Harvard days (Ames's son would eventually marry one of Thayer's daughters). Coincidentally, Ames's wife, Margaret ("Maggie") Plumley Ames, was an old flame of Wilkie's, both having attended Sanborn's Concord School together. Wilkie therefore tagged along, admitting that his "'heart quite palpitated' at the prospect of seeing her" again. Thayer himself had not met her, but once he did, he, too, became a member of the "swelling chorus of her admirers," babbling later to Sophy that "her hair is so pretty and her manners and her face and everything." After tea with the Ameses, Thayer and Wilkie went off to the Perkins's Federal-style home, called the Apple Trees, where they found the Forbes family already gathered, along with Annie Anthony and the rest of the traveling party. Emerson was already well acquainted with the Perkins family, having been their guest at the Apple Trees while on a Lyceum tour of Iowa back in 1867 (the Perkinses had likewise put up Edward on his 1862 trip to California).

Also present at the Apple Trees was a young man named George Ward Holdrege (1847–1926), who, apparently on the spur of the moment, had been invited to join the Emerson party on their trip to California. Holdrege was an employee of the B&MR, a position secured for him by John Murray Forbes. In the wake of Holdrege's father Henry's 1869 bankruptcy, the younger Holdrege was forced to drop out of Harvard, and Forbes, a family friend, stepped in to help. Scion of an old Quaker family with deep roots in New Bedford, George Holdrege was well known not only to the Forbes family but also to Emerson as well, having met him several times through his schoolmaster, William P. Atkinson, to whose Boston home Emerson was a frequent visitor. Holdrege had also been a classmate of Edward Emerson at Harvard. Of medium height, muscular, wiry, and athletic (he rowed crew for Harvard's varsity team), Holdrege was always described as physically striking: "he had a long thin face with a very high forehead topped with black curly hair" and "piercing brown eyes [that] peered out from under heavy, bushy eyebrows." He was also very dark complected, the "blackest white man who ever lived," in the words of one acquaintance, which accounts for why his childhood nickname, gleefully reported in his biography, is a racist epithet now unmentionable. Holdrege was obviously a favorite of John Murray Forbes, who was always keen to encourage lively young men who showed business potential; the trip to California would allow a good opportunity to get to know Holdrege better. Once the introductions had been made all around and the schedule for the following day outlined by the senior Forbes, the party broke up for the night. Thayer repaired to the Ames house, while Emerson and the rest of the group returned to the Huron to make ready for an early start.

The next morning, Thayer woke before dawn and made his way to the Apple Trees for coffee and to finish a letter to his "dear little woman," asking her to give his "love to the kids, the little brats," especially his son William, whose birthday was that day (April 15). At about eight thirty, the train—a special with the Huron attached—left the Burlington Station. The train stopped at noon in Ottumwa, where the party was joined on the cars by more Boston relatives for a quick lunch, and then off again across Iowa. Thayer was amused to note that they "passed through the towns of 'Russell,' and 'Emerson,' and 'Brooks' and 'Hawthorne' and 'Thayer,'" yet another reminder of the pervasive Yankee influence in the state. The weather that day had been variable, "but pleasant for the most part," and there was "a beautiful sunset." George Holdrege meanwhile was entertaining the party with the story of how he had once hitched a ride on a wagon with a man whose job it was to catch rattlesnakes. Somewhat alarmed by this, George had innocently asked, "Have you been cutting off their heads and saving their rattles?" to which the man replied, "No, I haven't had time. I've just been throwing them in the back of the wagon there." At that moment both men heard the distinctive "whir of a rattler about to strike," and each threw themselves out of the moving wagon, causing the horses to bolt. It took an hour to catch up to the wagon, but at this point Holdrege had resolved to walk.

The train reached Council Bluffs after dark, and as there was no bridge yet over the Missouri River, the Huron would have to be taken over by ferry the next day. The party thus spent the night "camping out" on a sidetrack. Perhaps because rattlesnakes invaded their dreams or because the ventilation system of the car only operated effectively when the car was moving, most in the party slept poorly and awoke "not so fresh," as Thayer put it. But the prospect of breakfast at seven cheered them all up, and the excitement of crossing the Missouri—the farthest West most of the party had ever been—quickly energized them for the day ahead.

Before breakfast, Emerson and Thayer, both of whom were early risers, took a turn around Council Bluffs, a town that began life in 1846 as a way station for Mormon immigrants bound for Utah. It would later become the eastern terminus for the B&MR Railroad. This being a Sunday, the town of some twelve thousand inhabitants was very quiet, although the day was already quite bright. As they walked, Emerson fell into miscellaneous reminiscences again, talking of his friendships with the English writers Arthur Hugh Clough and James Anthony Froude, both of whom he had met during his visit to England in 1848. This somehow led him then to the problematic versification of Shakespeare's *Henry VIII*, which Emerson wrote about in *Representative Men*. A little further on, he spoke movingly about Mary Rotch, a New Bedford Quaker whom he had known ever since he been a supply minister to the Unitarian Church there in 1833. Rotch's brand of Quakerism had had a definite impact on Emerson and may have contributed to his eventual abandonment of the ministry. "She was a thoughtful person, who saw everybody's limitations in matters of religion," Emerson said, "a very noble person, who held to that sense of what she should do, to which the consent of the whole world could not give authority, nor its opposition diminish it. One would say to her, 'Well, Aunt Mary' (everybody called her 'Aunt Mary'), 'what is this "light" that you speak of?' 'It is not a thing,' she would reply, 'to be talked about.'" Thayer, who knew Mary Rotch's grandniece well, had undoubtedly heard such stories before and had no doubt that, when it came to her influence on Emerson, it was from Rotch that "some of the sweetness and charm of our friend [Emerson] came from." Soon they returned to the Huron, famished for the morning meal.

At ten o'clock, as the Sunday bells of Council Bluffs were ringing its citizens to church, Thayer, Mrs. Russell, and Alice Forbes set out in a carriage to explore the bluffs for which the town was named. Thayer commended the "superb view" of the "miles of meadows or 'bottom' as they call it here," "stretching away towards the town of Omaha, that lay scattered loosely over the beautiful easterly slopes of another great bluff" on the far side of the Missouri River. They then drove on to the crumbling bank of the river, which they "found running furiously,— deep, raging, tawny and full of mud," and "cutting fast into the fine prairie earth, so that it was dangerous to go near the edge." Here they could clearly see the great iron piers being sunk into the river to provide the foundation for a railroad bridge that would finally link the B&MR to the Union Pacific.

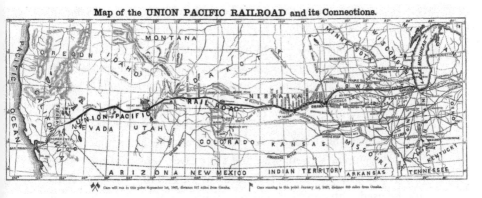

FIGURE 4. *Map of Union Pacific Railroad and Its Connections,* ca. 1867. —Courtesy of the Cornell University Library Maps and Geospatial Information Collection, Ithaca, NY.

Later that morning, the entire party took a small steamboat across the river to Omaha. Here they found that the Huron, which had been ferried over earlier to the Union Pacific Station, had sustained some damage and would have to be repaired. The Union Pacific superintendent said it would take an hour or two. Hiring carriages, the group took the opportunity to tour Omaha, which was about twice the size of Council Bluffs. Ending their drive at a nearby hotel for lunch, the party had scarcely been seated when a messenger from the station interrupted them. Breathlessly, he told them that the repair work had been long completed and they were now holding up the train! They dashed back, and at around 12:30, with all finally aboard, the locomotive and its cars with the Huron in tow slowly chugged off onto the plains of Nebraska.

INTO THE FAR WEST

Leaving Omaha, Emerson finally entered the "vast West" that he had long imagined but had not yet seen. As indicated by his pre-trip perusal of Brace's and Hittell's books on California, Emerson was not willing to enter the West without some concrete intelligence on what he would find. Out beyond the Missouri on the great plains of Nebraska, it was time to break out the guidebook, which most likely was George A. Crofutt's attractive *Great Trans-Continental Tourist's Guide* (1871). Easily available at every station and "sold on the cars," the guide offered a philosophy of travel that Emerson himself undoubtedly approved of: "Now as you are about to leave the busy hum and ceaseless bustle of the city for the broad sweeping plains, the barren patches of desert, and the grand old mountains—for all these varied features of the earth's surface will be encountered before we reach the Pacific coast—lay aside *all* city prejudices and ways for all time . . . and for *once* be *natural* while among nature's loveliest and grandest creations." In addition to the purple prose, the *Guide*, lavishly illustrated with engravings and maps, exhaustively described the distances, elevations, and other particulars of just about every town, station, watering stop, river, and landmark along the way. Thus, despite the unfamiliarity of the country, Crofutt's *Guide* could be used with confidence to keep track of mileage by checking off the features as they passed. This was especially useful for anticipating the infrequent stops for fuel and water that allowed passengers to stretch their legs outdoors, if only for a few minutes.

One such place was the small railroad hamlet of Sidney, Nebraska, which, according to Thayer, consisted of a dozen horses, innumerable one-eared pigs, and a woman in front of small house ringing a bell, hoping to entice some of the passengers to a quick meal. She was not successful: "The woman stopped ringing and stood in the door with arms folded for awhile and then withdrew and did double duty I dare say on her own breakfast." The day was overcast and gray, and the surrounding country was "absolutely without trees, with a soil like a reddish gravel covered by starved intermittent dried up grass and weeds,—flat for the most part but with low elevations a little way off which look as they recede of the color of ashes." Emerson more succinctly described the landscape as "this poor, flat, worn-out common." So far, Thayer reported, the company had seen three antelopes but no buffalos yet (gone were the days when the train would slow so passengers could take potshots at the massive herds milling by the tracks). Nor had they seen any Indians, most likely Pawnees, who, they'd been told, had but a few weeks ago raided horses from a station they'd passed in the night—and this despite the presence of a troop of cavalry stationed nearby. It was typical of the racism of the day that Thayer would, without a thought, include the Native Americans among the wild creatures of the prairie. Unfortunately, nothing on this trip would shake him out of this prejudice, a fact that would come to have dire consequences for Native Americans later in Thayer's career, as will be seen in chapter 8.

Life was pleasant for the passengers of the Huron. Unlike the eastern roads, which ran as fast as forty miles per hour, the Union Pacific ran at a relatively moderate twenty-two, which meant a lot less swaying and jostling for the passengers. The Huron was also heated by an ingenious system of hot-water pipes running under the floor, which diffused an even heat throughout the car, making it warm even in the early mornings. The party quickly fell into a routine, or as Thayer put it, "our life in the cars is funny but easy and comfortable enough." The three Forbes women and Annie Anthony occupied the two staterooms at the front of the carriage. Edith and Mrs. Russell were assigned to the two berths at the left of the first section of the car, while across from them, Emerson slept in the lower berth with Will Forbes above him. In the second section, Wilkie James and George Holdrege slept in berths stacked one above the other. Thayer and the conductor Bennett occupied stacked berths on the opposite side. Thayer had insisted on this arrangement because he was an early riser and the conductor of necessity had to be up before everyone, and thus "when we two are up, the section can be cleaned out and one can sit down like a Christian." Emerson was usually the third person up and would meet Thayer at the washstand "in his shirt sleeves looking wise and funny." Thayer was amazed that Emerson "even manages to shave *in his berth* while the cars are going." Since breakfast couldn't be served until everyone had risen and dressed and the berths and all the bed linens had been stowed away, the party "grew accustomed to a long morning and a late breakfast." Cooking in the tiny kitchen, moreover, was "a slow business" as "dishes have to be prepared separately, and then set to wait till others are done in succession."

During most of the day, everyone either read, wrote letters, stared out the windows at the passing scenery, dozed, or sat quietly talking. Occasionally, Emerson would dip into his purple carpetbag and pull out the proof sheets for *Parnassus*. The poetry volume was but one of the two "serious tasks" Emerson had cited to John Murray Forbes as obstacles to his going to California. And while *Parnassus* was a labor of love, the other task was vexatious in the extreme. In 1870, Emerson had learned of the impending publication of a volume of his uncollected talks and lectures, which had been cobbled together by the English publisher James Camden Hotten. Emerson was outraged by the effrontery, but under the copyright laws of the day he had no legal recourse, although he demanded the moral right of revising the material before it went to press. Hotten made this concession but with the proviso that it had to be done within twelve months. This was galling enough, but the really upsetting aspect of the whole business was that Hotten was not only a notorious literary pirate, publishing unauthorized editions of such American authors as Mark Twain and Bret Harte, but also a pornographer whose catalog included such edifying titles as *Pretty Little Games for Young Ladies & Gentlemen*, *The Romance of Chastisement*, and *Lady Bumtickler's Revels*. Even if Emerson at this point had had the intellectual energy to do the revisions, it was such a distasteful task that he suspected he would never do it, adding substantially to his worries. Better to work on *Parnassus* and forget all about Hotten's ill-begotten volume.

As on an ocean voyage, the most eagerly anticipated activities of the day were the meals, which, after breakfast, consisted of dinner (lunch), tea, and supper. Each temporary table in the car could accommodate only four places, hence the group made an effort to rotate messmates, so that everyone would have a chance to get to know everyone else. Thayer especially coveted those times when he ate with Emerson, as he could never get enough of his conversation, which he endeavored to record as faithfully as he could in his letters to Sophia. At one meal Emerson talked about his Boston friends, Abel Adams and Francis Lowell; his fifty-year class reunion at Harvard; and a classmate named Charles Wentworth Upham, who was noted for his two-volume history of the Salem witchcraft trials. When asked by Thayer if he had read Upham's books, Emerson replied, laughing, "No, he never read any of my books; I don't know why I should read his." Perhaps inspired by his work on the *Parnassus* proofs, Emerson also quoted lines from Tennyson's "The Eagle," and in response, someone else at the table recited Keats's sonnet "On First Looking into Chapman's Homer," which apparently Emerson had forgotten. One of the lines of this poem assigns the discovery of the Pacific Ocean to Cortez, which all knew must be wrong—they would have to look it up first thing on arrival in San Francisco.

At another meal, Emerson told Mrs. Russell the sad story of a vineyardist whom his son Edward had met in California and who had fallen off a bridge and been eaten by an alligator. Perhaps not knowing how seriously the story should be taken, Emerson added, "Nowadays, one must finish off a story well. Perhaps this might not be exact." "But yet observe," Mrs. Russell readily retorted, "the man had a vineyard, and the alligator didn't eat that!" Emerson was taken aback, never knowing when Mrs. Russell was joking, "but he recovered, laughed, and with a nod, slowly and dubiously remarked: 'Yes, that deserves to be considered. But it is, perhaps, not conclusive!'" This provoked general merriment and laughter all around the table. Sadly, the punch line of joke, Edward Emerson's friend, was actually the remarkable Hungarian nobleman Agoston Haraszthy (1812–69), known as the "Father of California Viticulture." Haraszthy was instrumental in introducing European vines to California, and by the early 1860s, his Buena Vista Estate outside Sonoma was widely seen as "the largest vineyard in the world." He overextended himself, however, and descended into bankruptcy in 1867, retreating to Nicaragua in an effort to recoup his fortune. There, on July 6, 1869, while inspecting the construction of a sawmill, Haraszthy slipped from a log bridge and drowned in a rain-swollen river. The fact that his body was never found led to the rumor that Haraszthy had been eaten by an alligator, a story too good not to be true, and thus this detail hardened into legend—precisely as Emerson suspected. Sadly, too, the alligator might as well have eaten the vineyard, since Buena Vista was one of the first wiped out by the phylloxera blight that would eventually devastate wine production in both the United States and Europe in the late 1870s.

Early in the afternoon of April 17, the train pulled into the station at Cheyenne, Wyoming, where it was forced to idle longer than normal because of snow on the tracks further ahead. Out in the fresh air, Thayer was struck by his first views of the snowy grandeur of what the *Guide* called "the back-bone of the American Continent," the Rocky Mountains. "Nowhere else," sermonized the *Guide*, was the "hand of Him who rules the universe . . . more marked." Emerson would have agreed. As he observed in one of his early essays, the exposed granite that "towers into the highest mountains" is simply the grandest visible indication of that which forms the foundation of the entire world and as such is a perfect natural metaphor for the pervasive moral order that undergirds the universe. In the early nineteenth century, explorers were enchanted to find a mountain in the heart of the Rockies stamped with what they interpreted to be a giant cross, making the mountains seem for them a little less of a godforsaken wilderness. Emerson's friend Longfellow had even written a poem, "The Cross of Snow," memorializing the supposed

epiphany. For Emerson, though, such a cross would have seemed to
be gilding the lily, for the simplicity of the naked granite was symbol
enough for him. Notably, the Longfellow poem would not be among
those included in *Parnassus*.

Thayer took the opportunity of the unexpected delay in Cheyenne
to walk to the post office where a little boy accosted him, offering two
prairie dogs in a box for $5 (he declined). Returning to the depot, Thayer
helped Emerson and Alice Forbes kill time by weighing them on the
freight scale. Emerson was surprised when Alice went first and weighed
more than the 140 pounds that Emerson himself normally weighed. He
promised Alice that since he couldn't maintain his usual habits on this
trip, he would soon surpass her, and when Thayer weighed him next
and told him that he actually weighed 140½, he said, "Yes, yes; a hundred and forty and a half! That *half* I prize; it's an indication of better
things!" Some forty-four years before, when Emerson was convalescing
from tuberculosis in St. Augustine, Florida, and found that he was up to
141½, he also cherished that half pound as a sign of his recovery. Perhaps
this trip, too, was already having its intended therapeutic effect.

Soon the train was released and climbed to Sherman, Wyoming, which
at 8,242 feet was the highest point on the trip; from thence it ran down
across the Laramie Plains, where Thayer marked the complete absence of
a "tree or a shrub excepting a low aromatic dusty bush called wild sage,"
which "gives a very powerful odor as you handle it, but seems to be good
for nothing." The party also spied herds of antelopes and packs of prairie dogs, but again there were no buffalo in sight. Since "Mr. Emerson
considers it 'essential to see *one* buffalo,'" a constant vigil was kept for
just such an opportunity, but to no avail. There was a short stop again at
Laramie City, where the car was entertained by a very small boy expertly
riding "a velocipede," after which the train continued up through an
increasing blizzard to the Continental Divide at Creston. By this time it
was dark, and the party had dined and were asleep in their berths.

Chapter 2

SALT LAKE CITY

(APRIL 18 TO APRIL 20, 1871)

Good out of evil. One must thank the genius of Brigham Young for the creation of Salt Lake City—an inestimable hospitality to the Overland Emigrants, and an efficient example to all men in the vast desert, teaching how to subdue and turn it to a habitable garden.

—Ralph Waldo Emerson, *Journals* (October 1863)

When Emerson and the other denizens of the Huron awoke on the morning of April 18, the snowstorm had stopped and the day was excessively bright as the landscape was blanketed in sparkling snow. A happy consequence of this was that the "troublesome, unwholesome dust" of the alkali country they had now entered was abated somewhat, although Thayer still sniffed "a suggestion of saleratus or potash in the air," which aggravated Mr. Forbes's sinuses terribly. Once they passed Church Butte, some nine hundred miles west of Omaha, they stopped briefly at Bridger Station, Wyoming, where Thayer was excited to note the presence of the first Chinese he had yet seen on the journey. They appeared "nice looking fellows dressed in blue blouses and boots and trowsers like the rest of us in this country," but with conical straw hats and carrying "all their goods strung on two sides of a pole that rested at the middle on their shoulder," just as he had seen in the popular geographies. At around noon, the town of Evanston, Wyoming, was reached, where the party received their mail. The train then began its headlong decent, twenty-six hundred feet into Salt Lake Valley.

Although it was dinnertime, the party ignored Bennett's protestations and stood in a crowd on the open back platform, transfixed by "the inexpressible beauty of great towering peaks, covered with snow, that rose high about us." As the train gathered speed, the canyons—Echo,

Weber, Devil's Gate—became deeper and more narrow, and then, "when every variety [of natural feature] seemed to have been exhausted," they were all "suddenly silenced and stunned by a succession of high, magnificent isolated buttresses of red rock, curiously rounded and, as it were, carved." Canyon after canyon flew by, revealing such curious formations as Hanging Rock, Pulpit Rock, and the Devil's Slide. Then, close by the town of Ogden, Utah, the train finally "slid swiftly out" of the canyon lands onto "the vast, fat plains of the Salt Lake region, where cherries and peaches were in blossom, and men were ploughing." Here, the first glimpses of the Great Salt Lake could be seen to the west. At Ogden Station, the Huron was detached from the Union Pacific train and joined to a Utah Central locomotive for the short thirty-six-mile trip south to Salt Lake City. It was golden twilight by this time—suppertime now—but the snow-capped mountains to the immediate east caught and reflected the last rays of the setting sun, keeping the group rapt on the back platform, undoubtedly ignoring yet again the frustrated conductor's call to table.

SALT LAKE CITY

Nestled near a spur of the Wasatch Mountains, Salt Lake City was just emerging from the frontier stage in 1871. Although as a Mormon settlement it was far better planned than most, it still retained much of the scruffiness that marked the majority of outposts in the Far West. Shortly after arriving in the valley in 1847 and declaring, "This is the place," Brigham Young (1801–77) set his lieutenants to staking out the future city based on a design for the "City of Zion" bequeathed to him by the Mormon prophet and founder, Joseph Smith Jr. This meant designating a central block as Temple Square and using this as the base and meridian point for a grid of spacious streets and public squares (as it turned out, given the exigencies of geography, Temple Square would always be slightly off center, and the far eastern part of the city remained less developed because it sat on a naturally occurring "bench" higher than the rest of the city). A main street south of Temple Square was designated as a commercial zone, while land was set aside contiguous to the city for those farmers who did not wish to commute to their lands. Home lots were a generous one and one-quarter acres, and given Young's stipulation that these could not be subdivided and sold, and that water in town was relatively abundant owing to an ingenious series of irrigation ditches capturing runoff from the nearby mountains, most yards were given over to extensive vegetable gardens and orchards, which must have much pleased Emerson, the gardener manqué.

Crofutt's *Guide* praised the attributes of Salt Lake City in its best boosterish fashion: the "principal material used in building the city was stone and 'adobes' (sun-dried brick), hence it presents the appearance of a European town," and "the numerous shade trees and gardens, give the city an indescribable air of coolness, comfort and repose." Others were not so impressed. The travel writer Charles Nordhoff, for example, wrote: "There is an air of strain and hardship about every thing": "After twenty-five years of hard work, unceasing industry, their houses are small and mean; their gardens are badly kept; the whole place has the cheap, shabby, and temporary look of a new settlement. The Tabernacle is a huge, vast building; it will accommodate thirteen thousand people with seats, but the plaster is rough; the pews—models of comfort in their shape—are unpainted; the magnificent organ, which it took five years and a half to build, has a case very well shaped, but of shabby stained pine; and in the whole city, the high wall around Brigham Young's houses is the only permanent and respectable structure I saw—the only evidence of luxury, for it is a substantial wall." Nevertheless, whether one chose to notice its advantages or its defects, there was always something alluring and exotic about Salt Lake City that attracted tourists from the beginning, precisely because it was a Mormon settlement. For example, in *The City of the Saints* (1861), the English adventurer Richard Burton described Mormons as the Muslims of America and Salt Lake City as their Mecca, and he portrayed their temples, strict patriarchy, and polygamy in terms worthy of the Old Testament or the Qur'an. Burton's was one of the earliest (and perhaps least condemnatory) of many subsequent books and articles that viewed Mormonism through an Orientalizing lens, which piqued the curiosity of many Americans. Indeed, now that the "Trans-Continental Railroad has brought within easy reach [this] land as full of fascination as ever the scenes of the Arabian Nights," as one traveler put it, a stop at Salt Lake City had become de rigeur on any Far West tour.

The train carrying the Emerson party arrived at the Salt Lake station around seven in the evening, just as they were finishing their supper. The Huron was soon decoupled from the rest of the train and pushed onto a

FIGURE 5. *Salt Lake City and Wahsatch Mountains,* engraving by Meeder & Chubb after photograph by A. Wills from Henry T. Williams, *The Pacific Tourist,* 1876. —Author's collection.

sidetrack. Here the party intended to spend the night in order to tour the city first thing in the morning. Not content to sit in the carriage all night, however, someone in the party noticed a handbill being circulated advertising a performance of a melodrama called *The Wildcat: or Marriage by Moonlight.* Thayer, Will and Alice Forbes, Annie Anthony, Holdrege, Wilkie, and—much to the surprise of Thayer—Emerson himself decided to take in the show, which was to begin at eight at the Salt Lake Theatre. Setting out in an open carriage, Thayer found it "queer as we drove up in the evening to cross the brooks that run gurgling down along all the sidewalks and saw in the dark the enormous elephant backed roof of the 'Tabernacle' (like the top of a hat) surrounded by a wall considerably higher than our heads, and grasped (correctly) as to the house and surroundings of 'President Young' as they call him." A few minutes later, they pulled up at the ornate portico of the theater near Temple Square.

Ever since the days of Joseph Smith Jr., Mormons had had a great love of plays, music, and dancing. It brought great pleasure therefore, when, soon after the termination of the so-called Mormon War against

the federal government in 1858, Brigham Young announced to the people of Salt Lake City that "he was going to build a big 'fun hall,' or theatre, where the people could go and forget their troubles occasionally,
in a good, hearty laugh." After the Tabernacle, the Salt Lake Theatre,
which opened in 1862, was one of the more substantial buildings in the
city, having a capacity of some fifteen hundred. It was constructed of
brick covered in white plaster, and its architecture was of a boxy Greek
Revival design, with two-story pilasters at its corners and large Doric
columns marking the main lobby entrance. In its early years, the theater
depended largely on an acting troupe of local Mormons (one of Young's
daughters, Alice Clawson, was a leading player), but with the coming
of the railroad, more professional troupes from the East made it a regular stop on their circuits of the West. With the coming of the railroad,
the theater had become a magnet for tourists because Brigham Young
himself often attended, sitting in the front row in a large rocking chair
reserved for him. His many wives and children could also frequently be
observed seated in a private area on the main floor in the dress circle or
in their raised box to the right of the stage.

Taking their seats around 7:30, Emerson and his group had plenty of
time to people-watch. Unfortunately, neither President Young nor any
of his family was in attendance. Indeed, as this was the last night of *The
Wild Cat*, the audience in general was quite sparse, but the orchestra per-
formed lustily—"as if playing at a ball"—and the curtain rose precisely
on time. Originally entitled *New York Burglars; or, a Wedding by Moonlight* by poplar playwright Charles Hubbs Foster (1833–95), *The Wildcat* had been renamed for western audiences and now starred Marietta
Ravel, the French actress, pantomime artist, dancer, and tightrope per-
former, in the principal role of Florence Ellwood. The improbably complicated plot of the play was pure melodrama, involving the machina-
tions of the "genteely dressed villain," Bob Stanley, who, having lost his
beloved to his rival, William Ellwood, seeks his revenge on the children
of this union, starting with the attempted drowning of infant Florence,
who is saved and subsequently raised by a gang of New York burglars,
thus transforming her into the wildcat of the title. The rest of the play
consists of Florence systematically foiling Stanley's increasingly das-
tardly plots, including a blackmailed marriage in the dead of night and,
in the pièce de resistance, the attempted murder of Florence's drunken

brother by means of a pile driver set to crush his skull at the stroke of seven—the audience breathlessly counted out the strokes. One can easily guess how it ended.

"It was," as Thayer put it to Sophy, "a real bowery boy performance — entirely decent, but spiced highly and full of blood and thunder." And "not the least amusing thing of all was to see the interested half amused look of Mr. Emerson as all this passed before him. A funny situation was it not! He quite enjoyed it." Although Emerson did tend to be a snob when it came to popular culture (witness his utter disdain of the likes of P. T. Barnum), he nevertheless had once claimed, "Everything that is popular . . . , deserves the attention of the philosopher: and this for the obvious reason, that although it may not be of any worth in itself, yet it characterizes the people." So perhaps *The Wildcat* appealed to Emerson as a window into the soul of the American common man, just as he had said that the popular plays of Shakespeare's day flowed with "the rude warm blood" of Elizabethan England. Or perhaps, too, it appealed to him simply because it was a ripping good time at the theater. Whatever the source of his pleasure at this performance, this time would not be the last on this trip that, much to his companions' surprise, Emerson would seek out forms of popular entertainment that many considered quite low.

It was near midnight when the theater party returned to the Huron, well satisfied and ready for a good night's sleep. While they were gone, the remaining Forbeses had entertained a newspaperman from the *Salt Lake Herald-Republican* who wished to record John Murray Forbes's "impressions of the west." Sarah Forbes, who always admired her father's common touch, wrote later that the reporter "was received very pleasantly; but to our great amusement we soon found the reporter giving *his* own views of the West, and my father listening with interest and attention, and continuing to ply him with questions till the end of the interview. The gentleman of the press went away much pleased, but without having discovered that we had the 'Seer of Concord' with us, and quite in the dark as to Mr. Forbes's views on any subject." A small article duly appeared the next day under the innocuous headline "Excursion Party," recording that "a party of ladies and gentlemen from Boston, who left the city about a week ago, 'on a pleasure bent,' arrived last night in a special Pullman palace car." Ninth in the list of names, the Seer of Concord was noted simply as "Mr. Emerson."

PEACHES AND POLYGAMY

As usual the next morning, Thayer was up well before the others and set out a little after six o'clock to stroll the streets of Salt Lake City. A snow-rain mix had fallen the night before, and the streets were "a shallow slosh." The day itself was overcast, and rain still threatened from northern clouds, but "west and south, snowy mountain ranges were shining in the sun." Thayer admired the many large trees that lined the streets, their roots watered by gurgling irrigation ditches. He also noted that the green ended abruptly outside the limits of the city and that the surrounding plains and foothills were completely treeless and bare.

Walking west, Thayer passed many small adobe houses with their blooming orchards of apricots and peaches, until finally coming to a small adobe house with a proper "burnt brick" chimney on the very edge of the prairie. Here he met up with a good-looking young man coming in from a morning of duck hunting on the marshes. The two struck up a conversation, which, as such conversations between tourists and residents were wont to go in Salt Lake City, naturally gravitated to polygamy. Since the doctrine of plural marriage had been revealed to Joseph Smith Jr. in Nauvoo, Illinois, in 1843, it had attracted the outraged attention of the Mormons' Gentile (i.e., non-Mormon) neighbors. Now that polygamy was established in Utah under Brigham Young, it had become an issue of national importance, especially because the federal government saw it as a convenient way to attack Mormon power in the region. Beyond simply its political and moral implications, Mormon polygamy also fascinated Victorian Americans for less high-minded reasons, which probably accounts for why sensationalistic discussions of polygamy were often prominently featured in the newspapers and magazines of the day, although only about a quarter of all Mormon households ever adopted the practice.

Thayer's new friend, it turned out, was the nephew of Daniel H. Wells, a high-ranking Mormon who was one of the original immigrants to Salt Lake City and a close adviser to Brigham Young. Wells, he reported, had six wives and twenty-five children, which was considered a small family in those parts. President Young himself had several wives, all "fine, lady-like women," and innumerable children. Pressed by Thayer for details about this way of life, the boy assured him that each wife lived "very pleasantly" in their own "separate establishment" with "a separate kitchen and other apartments" and that "each looks after her own children." Surprisingly, Thayer's interlocutor admitted that he was "not *exactly* a Mormon," although he was obviously a supporter of the church and castigated those Gentiles "who want to interfere with everything."

Growing cold in the morning air, the two soon went their separate ways, and Thayer returned to the station. He continued asking probing questions about polygamy, this time chatting up the grizzled stationmaster, an elderly English Mormon who had lived and preached the faith in Boston for several years before heading to Utah. No one was forced to practice polygamy, the stationmaster assured Thayer; he himself had only one wife. Those who did practice polygamy, however, did so not because of "lust of the flesh" but because, as the Bible says, Abraham, Isaac, and Moses took many wives "to raise up a mighty seed to God and to obey the command to Adam to multiply and replenish the earth." Thayer accepted the old man as sincere, but like many Americans of the day, he couldn't quite make sense of the fact that sane and orderly people would willingly practice what he considered a relic of barbarism. Later, when a young plural wife tried to convince Mrs. Forbes that the New Testament taught that Jesus had many wives, Thayer was perhaps comforted by the fact that the "wild eager look about" her "showed a fanatic." Yet the other plural wives he saw at the station had "a sober quiet way" about them and "seemed affectionate to one another" and to all their children. All in all, despite polygamy and what he considered the Mormons' general antinomianism, Thayer had to grudgingly admit that most of the Mormons he had met so far "seemed serious and well-meaning." In fact, "all through this town, even in the shops, one found in the people a certain flavor of religion,—a subdued and virtuous air, as of those who felt themselves to be own brothers to the early Christians."

After a substantial breakfast on the Huron, the party, armed with *Crofutt's New Map of Salt Lake City* (included as a foldout in the guidebook), set out to see the sights in two hired carriages. A fixed tourist itinerary of the city's attractions could be found in any guidebook, including Crofutt's. In addition to the Salt Lake Theatre, attractions included Temple Square, which contained the Tabernacle and the foundations of the future Temple (not completed until 1893); Brigham Young's Lion and Beehive Houses; and the Deseret Museum. Also popular were excursions to bathe in the Great Salt Lake or to soak in the local hot springs located on the "bench" one mile north of downtown. Given that John Murray Forbes was nursing a sore arm from a riding accident in Milton, the group decided to do some quick shopping downtown for jewelry (specifically, Utah agates) and then drive to the hot springs to see if the medicinal saline sulphur waters would afford Forbes any relief (we are not informed as to whether it was effective). After that visit, Emerson asked that the next stop be the Lion and Beehive Houses. The guidebooks said that President Young often consented to meet with visitors. Emerson said he would very much like to meet him.

BRIGHAM YOUNG

Born in Vermont two years before Emerson, Brigham Young was one of the early readers of the *Book of Mormon* and became a member of the Church of Jesus Christ of Latter-day Saints (LDS) in 1832. Shortly after, he traveled to Kirtland, Ohio, where the Mormons had relocated, to meet Joseph Smith Jr., with whom he had a great deal in common. They quickly formed a fast friendship. Smith trusted Young from the first, appreciating both his fervor and his bluff common sense. He appointed him as one of the original Quorum of Twelve Apostles and entrusted him with missions to the Northeast and to England, which Young carried out with a fair degree of success. It was while Young was on a mission to Boston in 1844 that Smith was murdered outside Nauvoo, Illinois, and upon his return to that Mormon town, Young quickly prepared for its defense and was recognized by many as the natural successor to the assassinated prophet. By 1846, it was clear to the Mormons that continued residence in Illinois was untenable, so Young organized the massive exodus west, first to Council Bluffs in Iowa and Winter Quarters in Nebraska, and then to the Salt Lake Valley a year later.

From his arrival in Salt Lake to his death thirty years later, Brigham Young ruled his coreligionists with a firm, autocratic grip, gathering up immense political, economic, and religious power in the process. The Salt Lake region was still Mexican territory in 1847, so the Mormons took it upon themselves to organize a state, which they called Deseret, and electing Young as their governor. When the region was annexed in 1850 by the United States in the wake of Mexican War, Young for a time served as U.S. territorial governor, a position that allowed him to mediate between the church and the federal government. It is a measure of his prestige that even after his removal from this position by James Buchanan in 1857, Young's popular political power only continued to grow, despite increasing federal pressure to check Mormon influence in the region, especially after the Civil War. Meanwhile, Young had a significant hand in the development of Salt Lake City. Since the forty-niners and other immigrants came streaming through in need of provisions, Young took an active and sometimes interventionist interest in commerce, which, along with the tithes of the faithful, made the church—and the Young family—extremely wealthy. Young, for the most part, invested his personal wealth in agriculture, mining, communications, and transportation, which again allowed him a great deal of sway in how these resources were exploited and managed. It was Young, for example, who shrewdly negotiated for the creation of the Utah Central Railroad that connected Salt Lake City with the Union Pacific in Ogden.

Even more important, Young was first president and prophet of the LDS Church, preaching to the faithful every Sunday in the Tabernacle, promulgating and debating doctrine, reforming ritual, reorganizing the Mormon hierarchy, fending off heretics, and spearheading a massive building campaign, including ward chapels, the Tabernacle, and four temples, one being that rising in Temple Square, which was built according to his own architectural design. And, of course, Young was also by far the most famous promoter of polygamy in America, of which his multiple homes, twenty wives, and fifty-seven children were proof. Feared and despised on the one hand, but widely admired and envied on the other, Young was a figure to be reckoned with. Even Crofutt's *Guide*, whose policy it was not "to indorse or condemn any man," nevertheless proclaimed that Brigham Young stood "prominently forward as one of the most remarkable men of the 19th century."

As the Emerson party's carriage approached the southeast corner of Temple Square, they would have seen on the next block two substantial mansions connected by a covered walkway. The Gothic Revival Lion House, so named for the crouched lion statue above its crenellated entrance, was the private home for many of Young's wives and children and was off-limits to visitors, signaled by the fact that it was surrounded by a stout adobe wall segmented with formidable conical columns. To the right of the Lion House was the Beehive House, a two-story Federal-style home with Greek Revival elements and a long veranda along its front on both stories. Prominent on the roof of the house was a tall, square observatory of Egyptian Revival design, surmounted by a large hemp beehive from which the house derived its name (the beehive, in addition to being an ancient symbol of industry, was associated with the name Deseret, said to mean "honey bee" in the reformed Egyptian language of the *Book of Mormon*). Other members of Young's extended family resided here, but the president also maintained a public room on the second floor. Brigham Young, like Emerson, was a national celebrity, and just as nineteenth-century tourists to Concord were in habit of dropping in on Emerson unannounced, so, too, tourists in Salt Lake City felt free to do likewise with Young. This was a practice that had increased exponentially since the completion of the transcontinental railroad. Young had some fifteen hundred such meetings in the first two years alone. These meetings took time away from Young's busy schedule, but he found them "too valuable a means of correcting false ideas and removing prejudice to be discontinued."

Leaving the women in the carriage (Emerson later remarked that everything that had to do with Mormonism gave the ladies a "subacid," or heartburning, feeling), the men entered the front door of the Beehive House and were greeted by one of Brigham Young's secretaries, "a thin, pallid man," according to Thayer. Young's carriage was waiting outside, and it was apparent that he was just about the leave, but the secretary took Emerson's card in to Young. Meanwhile, the group was ushered upstairs to the public room. The travel writer Bayard Taylor wrote about such an interview the year before, and he described this space as "a handsome well furnished room, divided by a wooden screen from a dim back-office. The floor was carpeted, a circular table, with a great globe of gold-fish, was in the center, sofas and chairs were on either side, and the walls were covered with pictures—portraits of Joseph and Hyrum Smith, Alpine landscapes, and a chromotint of Bierstadt's 'Sunshine and Shadow,' which the artist had sent to Brigham Young." Soon, Young himself appeared, dressed for his drive in a long coat and hat in hand. John Murray Forbes later remarked that when it came to Emerson and Young, "nothing could be stronger than the contrast between the two men," as Young "was a bull-necked, coarse-looking, hard-headed man of affairs." Thayer was no more complimentary in his description, remarking that the president was "a man of not over medium height, full-blooded, and with the look of some stout stage-driver who had prospered and been used to authority." Not a little snobbish when it came to many things, Thayer went so far as to be offended that Young's thin, reddish hair, wet from washing, was combed over from the back like a "teamster at a ball, or on a teamster's child that had just left the hands of its mother." Nevertheless, Young's "manner [was] good and steady," and after shaking hands with "a stolid sort of dignity," they all sat down. As always, Young was ready to field questions in defense of the Mormon faith and Mormon way of life.

Although it was Emerson who instigated the meeting, he was always more comfortable listening than he was interrogating, so he left it to John Murray Forbes to ask questions, which he was more than happy to do. Forbes opened by rather artlessly observing that it was amazing what could be achieved when a large pool of labor was under the control of "one-man power." This was a particular sore spot for Young, who had preached against just such characterizations of his leadership in the Tabernacle only eleven days before. "Yes, the one-man power," he replied, clearly annoyed, "it's easy to talk about that! We have no more of it than they have elsewhere!" This faux pas, however, "was smoothed over" and Young redirected the conversation to the development of mining in Utah and to the dangers it posed for the church, considering the kind of people mining always attracted—"locusts," he called them, perhaps a sly reference to actual locusts that were an agricultural bane in the first year of the Mormon residence in the valley until, seemingly miraculously, they had been eaten by a flock of seagulls.

At this point, Emerson, less interested in commerce and more in religion, finally piped up and asked if there were a book Young would recommend that gave a fair account of Mormon beliefs and practices. Young at first demurred, saying there was nothing available, but then the secretary suggested a pamphlet that had been created for just such a purpose called "Answers to Questions." "Yes," said Young, "that was good; as good as anything." As Thayer later wrote, it was clear that Brigham Young was "in profound ignorance of Mr. Emerson's fame" and had no idea who he was, probably thinking him just another tourist. However, the pallid secretary knew who he was, and when the conversation flagged again, he pointedly asked Thayer in a loud voice, "Is this the justly celebrated Ralph Waldo Emerson?" When this was confirmed, he then addressed Emerson himself, saying, "I have read a great many of your books." It is not known what impression this made on Brigham Young, but apparently not much, for the interview was soon over. The secretary asked each person to sign the guest register, and the party was then shown the door.

Rejoining the ladies, the party continued their tour of the city from the Beehive House, walking the short distance to the Tabernacle, which dominated the skyline of Salt Lake City with its great, oblong dome. Two hundred and forty feet long and 150 feet in width, the Tabernacle, which was based on sketches by Brigham Young, seated ten thousand people in a completely unobstructed interior space, its ceiling supported by forty-six exterior sandstone piers making up the wall of the building. At the west end of the interior was a four-tiered podium and ranks of choir seats, in the middle of which was a large pipe organ, beetled over by some 2,638 pipes. Built between 1864 and 1867, the Tabernacle was intended primarily for worship services but could also be used for cultural performances or business and other administrative meetings that required gathering together large numbers of church members. It was even a place where ministers of other Protestant churches were invited to preach on occasion or to engage in public debate with Mormon elders, for unlike Mormon temples, the Tabernacle was meant to be open to all. Even Thayer was impressed by the edifice, fascinated by its near perfect acoustics. He and Wilkie played at conversing with each other in "ordinary tones" across its length. Next they inspected the nearby foundations of the temple, which had been under construction since 1853. Workmen were "hammering leisurely away on it," Thayer observed, prophesying that "the Lord in his 19th century or his 20th, will have undertaken and destroyed [the Mormons] long before they have done it probably." This prophecy, of course, proved entirely wrong, as the completed temple was dedicated in 1893 and dominates Temple Square to this day.

Last on the tour was the grandly named Deseret Museum, located in a tiny adobe house directly across from the Tabernacle on South Temple Street. Brainchild of John W. Young, one of the president's sons, and curated with zeal by the naturalist Joseph L. Barfoot, the museum displayed a remarkable jumble of materials, mostly, but not exclusively, from

Utah. These ranged from local rocks and minerals and samples of home-spun cloth to stuffed birds, shells, and animal skulls. Since the Indigenous peoples of the Americas were believed by the Mormons to be the remnants of one of the lost tribes of Israel (the Lamanites, according to the *Book of Mormon*), much space featured Native American artifacts, including blankets, baskets, and "a scalp from the head of a dead Indian," as well as "various articles from the Sandwich Islands." It is hard to tell what the Emerson party made of all this, but like most visitors, Thayer was excited by the live animals on display in cages in the museum's yard. "Tell the boys," he wrote to his wife that night, "that I saw a bald eagle in a cage this morning . . . and a wolverine and a sage hen and a prairie hen and a wolf and ever so many other creatures." He promised to write "to the little shavers" more about what he saw when he got to California.

Now it was getting late, nearly two-o'clock and almost time to board the Huron for the trip back to Ogden. They made a quick stop at James Dwyer's bookstore in the McCormick Bank Building on Main Street. While not typically on the tourist itinerary, Dwyer's was nevertheless a Salt Lake City institution and a place where the name Ralph Waldo Emerson was definitely known. Dwyer (1831–1915), an Irish convert to Mormonism, had come overland to the city in 1860, where he operated a series of bookstores "that served as bureau of information, dispensary of Mormon publications, and unofficial headquarters for the 'intellectuals' of Salt Lake Valley." Eastern newspapers and magazines such as the *Atlantic Monthly* could be had, and stationary and school supplies purchased. Its main attraction, however, was a reading room and lending library, which offered the citizens of Salt Lake City the latest publications from eastern publishers, including Houghton-Mifflin, Scribner's, and Harper's. Dwyer himself was a progressive thinker, well known for promoting free education and women's rights (he would eventually become notorious for defending homosexuality, perhaps because his daughter, the famous actress Ada Dwyer Russell, lived in an open lesbian relationship with the Boston poet Amy Lowell—an early example of what came to be called a "Boston marriage"). Here in Dwyer's reading room, Thayer scratched out a quick letter to Sophia, bought a compass, and both he and Edith Emerson Forbes browsed for souvenir postcards depicting the city and Brigham Young. Edith also treated herself to a pair of new gloves. Emerson himself bought that day's edition of the

Deseret News, which had the text of Brigham Young's "One-Man Power" Tabernacle sermon of April 8. He also found a copy of the pamphlet recommended by Young's secretary, the full title of which turned out to be *The Rise, Progress and Travels of the Church of Jesus Christ of Latter-Day Saints Being a Series of Answers to Questions* (1869) by George A. Smith. This would make for interesting reading on the train.

With the party now aboard, the Huron, newly coupled to the end of a Utah Central locomotive, left the Salt Lake Depot on West Third Street, heading back north to Ogden. There the Huron was transferred to a train of the Central Pacific Railroad, finally getting under way sometime after 8:00 p.m. San Francisco was now less than one thousand miles away according to the *Guide*, and Thayer wrote excitedly to his wife, "Forty eight hours now will bring us to our furthest point west, the firm land will carry us no farther." From Ogden to Promontory, where the last spike was driven connecting east and west, the train hurried on, "scudding" close to the northern edge of the Great Salt Lake. Thayer was mesmerized by the scene outside the car's windows: "Ducks in profusion were flying and settling on the water, purple mountains were in the distance, and behind these the sun was setting in majesty." Soon the train was "running along under a snow-covered range of mountains," most likely the Grouse Creek Range. "The soft tints and changes of light on these engaged every one's attention," even Emerson's, who to this point had been absorbed writing a letter across the desk from Thayer. Putting away his implements, perhaps after a gentle nudge from Thayer, he, too, stared raptly at the chromatic splendors of the rapidly darkening landscape. When it was over and night had fallen, Emerson turned to Mrs. Forbes and asked, "Well, what are you going to *do* about this,—all this beauty?" Always quick with a pert reply, she said, "You say somewhere that it is better to die for beauty than to live for bread." Emerson, again not knowing whether he was being teased, "murmured a little, good-naturedly, and was silent."

EMERSON AND THE MORMONS

As the train chugged into the darkness, Emerson sat ruminating on the Mormons and their beliefs. He had had a chance to read Brigham Young's "One-Man Power" in the *Deseret News*, and Thayer reported that Emerson "was exceedingly interested in it and greatly liked it." He may have also had a chance to dip into *Answers to Questions*. At forty-nine pages, it would have taken little time to read but much longer to absorb, because it contained, in no particular order, a brief history of the Mormon exodus to the Great Salt Lake; an overview of the institutional structure of the church and the civil government of the Utah Territory; a gazetteer of the territory; a review of conflicts with American Indians; the progress of Mormon missions overseas; and finally an epitome of passages on polygamy in the Old Testament. Perhaps more interesting to Emerson were the specimens of Joseph Smith's own genius that were included in the pamphlet: his autobiography and creed, reprinted from an 1842 issue of the *Chicago Democrat*, and his revelation and defense of "celestial marriage" or polygamy. After a while, Emerson came and sat on one of the swivel chairs opposite Thayer and asked him what he thought of the Mormons. Thayer responded that "certainly Brigham Young is to be credited with a great deal more than is commonly allowed him at the East," but he felt that the Tabernacle sermon "was a strange discourse, —patriarchal, giving much homely good advice, marked by quaint sense, and yet flavored also with a revolting mixture of religious fanaticism and vulgar dishonesty." He was especially incensed by Mormon attempts to "impress the imaginations of ignorant persons by their use of biblical names and imagery." Emerson, on the other hand, "was a good deal interested by a certain power in the address, and a certain homespun sense," although he had to agree that Mormonism was "an after-clap of Puritanism," adding archly, "One would think that after this Father Abraham could go no further."

Upon his return to Concord later that June, Emerson would respond to a letter from Carlyle who asked if he had met Brigham Young. Emerson wrote back that he had and enclosed a small "engraving" of President Young as token of his bona fides (perhaps one of the postcards from Dwyer's). Emerson summed up his own take on the meeting as follows: "On our way out we left the Pacific RR for 24 hours to visit Salt Lake: called on Brigham Young—just 70 years old—who received us with quiet uncommitting courtesy, at first—a strong-built, self-possessed, sufficient man with plain manners, He took early occasion to remark that 'the one-man-power really meant all-mens-power.' Our interview was peaceable enough, & rather mended my impression of the man; & after our visit, I read in the Deseret newspaper his Speech to his people on the previous Sunday. It avoided religion, but was full of Franklinian good sense. . . . He is clearly a sufficient ruler & perhaps civilizer of his kingdom of blockheads *ad interim*; but I found that the San Franciscans believe that this exceptional power cannot survive Brigham." Again, like Thayer's prophecy, Emerson's, too, fell well wide of the mark, as the church, despite manifold obstacles and continuing federal harassment, would go on to consolidate its influence in the region and grow to have an international presence with millions of members.

Years later, in his biography of Emerson, Oliver Wendell Holmes Sr. would remark that although Brigham Young "did not seem to appreciate who his visitor was, at any rate gave no sign of so doing," the meeting was still of great interest because of "the wide contrast between these leaders of spiritual and of material forces." It is indeed interesting that these two Yankees, rough contemporaries of each other, would go on to found such diametrically opposed religious movements: one that championed "self-reliance" and became the basis of American individualism, and the other championing a rigorous, theocratic communitarianism that was designed to last into eternity. In some respects, however, they were on the same page. Both, for example, believed that man was a god in the making. Since Joseph Smith Jr. had preached in the King Follett Discourse (1844) that "God himself was once as we are now, and is an exalted man," the notion of theosis has been a cornerstone of the Mormon faith. In this, Emerson heartily concurred, writing three years before in "The Over-Soul" that there is a "union of man and God in every act of the soul," such that "the simplest person, who in his integrity worships God, becomes God." The means of achieving this theosis, of course, was different in each tradition. Smith and Young taught that it comes only through the eternal preservation of the family in the hereafter, whereas Emerson contended that it could be achieved in the here and now by recognizing the "infinitude of the private man." Nevertheless, they both shared an unwavering belief in human deification, making them equally blasphemous in the eyes of the orthodox. What's more, the later Smith doctrine of the postmortem colonization of other planets by deified Mormons has something of the echo of Transcendentalism. "Every spirit builds itself a house; and beyond its house, a world; and beyond its world a heaven," Emerson had written in *Nature*. "Know then, that the world exists for you. . . . Build, therefore, your own world."

Thus, while they may have been radically different in terms of their spiritual methods, it is perhaps not an overstatement to say that Emerson, Smith, and Young shared a penchant for a kind of cosmic grandiosity that seemed to lurk at the back of many a Yankee soul.

After their colloquy on Brigham Young and the Mormons, Thayer went back to letter writing, although he had to borrow more stationary from Emerson, having improvidently forgotten to lay in a fresh supply at Dwyer's Bookstore. Tea was served, after which Emerson, Will, and Edith sat at a table looking over the guidebook, while Mr. Forbes, Sarah, and Mrs. Russell played cards. The four young people, Alice, Annie, Wilkie, and Holdrege, all sat together at another table engaged in their own card game. Meanwhile, Mrs. Forbes came to chat with Thayer, who listened to her distractedly as he tried to finish his letter home. "Orion looks in on our left hand and Venus very bright," he wrote to Sophy. "Meantime we tear ahead and nearly two days of this furious pace are still needed to carry us over the rest of this immense land of ours."

THE GREAT AMERICAN DESERT

By the time the Emerson party awoke the next day, the train had entered into the Territory of Nevada with its forbidding landscape, which the *Guide* called "the Great American Desert." All around them spread "a desolate, barren country" of sand, gravel, and broken limestone, studded with the "everlasting sage-brush" that so interested Thayer, as well as a few stunted cedars. Off in the distance on both sides of the car could be seen the "rough blocks" of snowy mountains glinting in the sunrise. Up first as usual, Thayer stretched his legs during a water stop at the signal station of Tulasco. The air was chilly and ice still lingered on the ditches by the side of the track, but Thayer found the sunlight warm and invigorating and was charmed by the note of a single meadowlark singing nearby. He also noticed a group of Chinese workers playing with a white dog, which for some reason he found unexpected, as though an American dog could not possibly understand them or they it: "The language of good-will, at any rate, was understood between them," he later wrote.

Reboarding the train, Thayer found that the ladies had still not risen, so breakfast was again delayed. In the interim, he entertained himself by noting the change in scenery as the train entered the valley of the Humboldt River, with its narrow gorges, tiny green meadows, and miniature willow trees. On one side of the track, sheer cliffs reared up hundreds of feet, "broken into columns in some places and so jagged and twisted and gnarled as to suggest volcanoes and the action of fire." Recalling to his mind the Nahant rocks on the coast of Massachusetts, the massive cliffs set Thayer to ruminating about their immense age, "worn and rubbed and discolored as if by the action of a thousand centuries of lightning and storm." Weirdly awesome, "one may almost be said to 'experience religion' as he goes along," Thayer said, a Transcendentalist sentiment expressed by more than one traveler through this region and even repeated in summary fashion in Crofutt's *Guide*: "The whole sum of man's existence does not consist in mines, mills, merchandise and money. There are other ways of employing the mind besides bending its energies to the accumulation of wealth; there is still another God, mightier than Mammon, worshipped by the few. Among the works of His hands these barren plains, brown hills and curious lakes—the seeker after knowledge can find ample opportunities to gratify his taste." Emerson's own reaction to the Great American Desert was that it reminded him "of the Bible and Asia," to which Thayer readily concurred, himself comparing the Great Salt Lake to the Dead Sea. There was, it seems, an irresistible attraction to such comparisons to Bible-steeped Americans of the time, and within a few years at least one railroad would publish a publicity map that, through some minor contortions, made the topography of the Great Basin mirror that of Palestine.

Since leaving Salt Lake City, the party saw numerous American Indians at each of the station stops. The *Guide* identified them as Shoshones or Paiutes, but Thayer simply dismissed them, with the racism typical of tourists of the time, as "short and dirty creatures." Whole families "stood about at the stations, idly looking on, or asking for money and food; some were in blankets, red or gray; some had their faces stained with red earth, all over or in stripes." Next to the stations could frequently be seen clusters of skin wigwams, their tops stained with smoke. Thayer was fascinated by the physiognomy of these Indigenous people, who, though sharing some features with the Chinese they saw, were even more alien to him. He found them "ugly and wild in their look," the men's beardlessness off-putting, as was their hair, which "was like horsehair, —heavy, long, coarse, black, lying thick above their low

foreheads and hanging about their heads, and held in their teeth sometimes to keep it still." Only some of the young girls he found appealing,
with their "smooth and full cheeks . . . even pretty, what with a sort of
shy and modest look they had and the freshness of youth."

At Elko, where Thayer was finishing breakfast with Mr. Forbes
and Mrs. Russell, a group of small Shoshone children, "nice little fat
innocent, happy little chaps," approached the Huron with hands out-
stretched and were rewarded with oranges, sugar, and nuts thrown from
the window. "One was struck by the picture and contrast," Thayer wrote
to Sophy, between "these ignorant creatures *at the bottom* of uncultivated humanity looking up at the locomotive and a Pullman car where
we sleep and eat and live as we do; and then think of Mr. Emerson and
Mrs. Russell; could one well emphasize the matter more?" George Holdrege's contempt was even more blunt: "Why don't they go to work,"
he complained, "like the Chinese?" It is interesting to note that while
people like Thayer and Holdrege saw only lethargy among the Indians
they encountered in the Great Basin, percolating beneath the surface at
this time and place were the makings of a highly influential revitalization movement that would eventually help unite Native Americans far
beyond Nevada. Catalyzed by the Paiute prophet Wodziwob (died ca.
1872), whose 1869 apocalyptic visions revealed to him the ritual of the
Ghost Dance, the movement would be promoted in the 1880s by another
prophet of the region, Wovoka (1856–1932). Soon the Ghost Dance would
spread to tribes to the east, most notably the Lakota, who adopted it as a
powerful symbol of defiance against the assimilationist pressures of the
federal government. As "uncultivated" as they may have appeared to the
tourists, the religious imagination of the Paiutes was no less active than
that of anyone aboard the Huron.

Near midday, west of Argenta, Nevada, where Thayer posted a letter
to an eastbound train, the party passed into a flat country, thick with
white alkali dust. At the next stop, and much against the protestations
of the porters and the cook, both Emerson and Thayer felt compelled to
sample the dust because it looked like the salt rime left behind when the
roads back home were sprayed with brine. As they had been warned,
however, it left a powerful taste in their mouths, not of salt but of potash,
much to their discomfort and chagrin. Throughout the rest of the day,
the train passed through many miles of flat alkali country, treeless for

the most part but studded with sagebrush, some kind of prickly shrub, and another plant Thayer likened to Scotch broom. Every now and then, the steam from hot springs could be seen rising in wisps in the middle distance, and far away, bright against the blue sky, snowy ranges of mountains were constantly in view. The day continued monotonous, station after station—Battle Mountain, Side Track ("a flag station, unimportant and uninteresting," sniffed the *Guide*), Winnemucca, Lovelock. Supper at five must have been a welcome diversion. By dusk, the train had entered the Great Nevada Desert or Forty Mile Desert, a region even more alkali than before, and now all "were troubled by the alkali dust until sleep came."

Chapter 3

EMERSON IN CALIFORNIA

(APRIL 21 TO APRIL 23, 1871)

Suffice it for the joy of the universe, that we have not arrived at a wall,
but at interminable oceans.

—Ralph Waldo Emerson, "Experience" (1844)

The next morning, April 21, Thayer went out to the Huron's back platform and found it thickly covered with alkali dust picked up the previous day. The scenery, however, had completely changed. Now they were
finally in California. During the night, the train, with the help of an extra
locomotive, had climbed nearly 3,000 feet to Summit Station, which sits
squarely in the middle of the Sierra Nevada, some 7,042 feet above sea
level. All around him, Thayer could see snow-covered granite peaks glis-
tening in the sun, and nearer the track, several streams flowed across
the broken granite. Tall stands of firs and spruce trees were frequent.
After the Great American Desert, Thayer observed, "it was good for New
England eyes to see trees once more." Summit Station was the highest
point in the Sierra Nevada reached by Central Pacific tracks, and during
the next hundred miles down the western slope to Sacramento, the train
would descend approximately seven thousand feet, in some places over
a one hundred feet per mile. As the rest of the party emerged from their
berths, the train entered a series of dark snowsheds, which necessitated
lighting the lamps in the car to keep everyone from bumping into one
another, as, uncharacteristically, all had risen early to take in the scenery. So lengthy were some of these sheds that a few stations were built
into the middle of them. Other sheds were open to the rock face on one
of their sides such that the bare granite was illuminated by the head-
lamps of the locomotives, an uncomfortable reminder that the train was
whizzing along suspended on the side of a mountain.

As the train began its descent into the great Central Valley of California, Bennett the conductor urgently whispered to Thayer a grave concern: given that the train was long and heavy and the Pullman car itself extremely heavy, it was not typically included on this run—the train, in his opinion, was moving too fast! According to Bennett, the regular Central Pacific (CP) conductor did not like running Pullman carriages on this route, and he would deliberately allow the train's speed to rise to the point where the occupants of the Pullman car, which had twelve wheels instead of eight, would be jerked about in a most uncomfortable manner. Bennett had already remonstrated with the regular conductor about this issue, but the CP man had "turned him off rather roughly and continued along as before." As Bennett's growing anxiety communicated itself to the rest of the Huron's passengers, especially as they neared Cape Horn, the treacherous mountain curve that George Pullman had warned them about, the young men in the party "told him that they would back him up in taking control of the train if he thought it proper—with their pistols if necessary." Bennett, however, hit on a less violent solution: he would threaten to have the Huron sidetracked at the next station and would telegraph the road's superintendent in Mr. Forbes's name demanding that the recalcitrant conductor be replaced. This did the trick. The CP conductor grudgingly communicated with the engineer, who slowed the train's speed, and the remaining journey down the Sierra was comfortable and smooth. Rather too blandly, Thayer concluded from this incident that "Bennett is an obliging, good fellow."

At 7:00 a.m. at Emigrant Gap, an observation car was added to the train. Thayer described it as "much like an open horse car," and indeed it was little more than a flatcar fitted out with low walls and benches so that passengers could better see the mountain scenery. Thayer was enraptured by what he saw: "We passed the most wonderful scenery; one cannot describe it but he can never forget it: the air was soft and spring like and the sun struck down across the tops of the trees in the great gorges that we looked into, *drenching* these tree tops with light and leaving soft misty shadows below; and so you would look down into a ravine of a thousand feet with a mountain on the other side coming towards you like a buttress, all covered with trees and with a gorge on each side of each." Finally, they rounded Cape Horn, and it turned out to be as fully terrifying as advertised: "The train is carried by a road cut into the mountain, along the side of it, away up near its top. You look straight down off the car a depth of fourteen hundred feet, a fearful distance, into the valley of the American River." And yet "one quite gives up in wonder and delight for in the midst of all that is grand in such a sight there is set at the bottom straight under us, a beautiful little valley, smooth, grass covered with peach trees in blossom and purple flowers and the ground fairly gilded in spots with yellow flowers." All of this terror and wonder quickly passed by, however, reminding Thayer of "Mr. Emerson's own lines on such transitory glories, where he speaks, in the 'Threnody,' of what 'rainbows show and sunsets teach'; we could not detain" them even if we wanted to.

The train stopped next at Colfax to allow those passengers not in a hotel car to eat breakfast at the station. Here the observation car was removed, and Thayer noted that, surfeited by mountain scenery "there was a general falling back" of the party to the Huron for their own morning meal. Colfax was enjoying June-like weather, with bright sun, green grass, roses and trees in bloom, "and every one was happy in the mere delight of living." In honor of the occasion, Thayer repeated over and over a line from Emerson's "Divinity School Address": "In this refulgent summer, it is a luxury to draw the breath of life."

After breakfast, with the train again under way, Thayer and Emerson retreated to the rear platform, surveying the passing scenery, silent except for Emerson's occasional "mere utterance of delight." "It was the only time in the whole journey," Thayer confided to Sophy, "when one would have hated to have the silence broken, even by him." As they descended from the Sierra foothills into the vast Central Valley, Thayer was amazed by the profusion of flowers, listing them off to Sophia: "lupine, larkspur, buttercups, a little dandelion, an orange collared poppy, a little reddish purple flower, a small deep yellow daisy without any petals—a sort of yellow *button*, another flower of a light yellow like the evening primrose, a little light blue fellow of the shade of a Star of Bethlehem and others without number." He also remarked the damage to the landscape as they passed through the gold districts, "where the earth had been all dug over into fantastic shapes" and hydraulic mining had turned the clear mountain waters into a "yellow broth." Nevertheless, so buoyant was his mood, the entire descent enchanted him: "I never passed a morning of greater delight in my life than that, as we ran on down the mountains to Sacramento."

It took four more hours by train from Sacramento to cross the dry prairie-like western valley and pass over the Coast Range—"all was greenness and beauty" with "great fields of flowers"—to reach Oakland, the western terminus of the Central Pacific Railroad. Here, each member of the party gave Bennett and the rest of the Huron's crew their final tips (typically from twenty-five to fifty cents per travel day). As arranged in advance by Mr. Forbes, they were then taken by carriage to the ferry and, once across the bay, to the Occidental Hotel. Thus, late in the afternoon of April 21, after eleven days on the cars, Emerson and the rest of the party finally found themselves in the heart of the "Queen City of the Pacific," San Francisco.

SAN FRANCISCO

San Francisco in 1871 was a city in transition. Founded in 1776 as a Franciscan mission and small garrison outpost of the Spanish Empire, the tiny village began in the 1830s to attract a small contingent of permanent American settlers, mainly traders in hides and tallow. By 1848, it was still little more than a town. The population stood at 850 living in some two hundred houses, a few of frame but mostly adobe, and all perched precariously on the sandy hills of a perpetually windswept peninsula. With the discovery of gold and its public announcement in the streets of San Francisco by the Mormon Sam Brannan (1819–99), the population exploded. As Bayard Taylor observed, the once tiny village had improbably become almost overnight "an actual metropolis." Fires periodically devastated the city, and the constant presence of rowdy miners and other toughs created waves of social chaos during the early 1850s. "Villainy flourished," the publisher A. L. Bancroft reported, and "drinking, gambling, robbery and murder held high carnival." This in turn led to waves of vigilante violence, which suppressed the worst of the outrage but at a cost of perpetrating its own. Despite this, the gold flowing in made San Francisco rich, and its population continued to grow, attracted both by the ready wealth and because, given its prime location on the West Coast's most magnificent bay, it was destined to become California's most important entrepôt. As Josiah Royce succinctly put it, the "progress of San Francisco was to be largely identical to the progress of the whole of the new state."

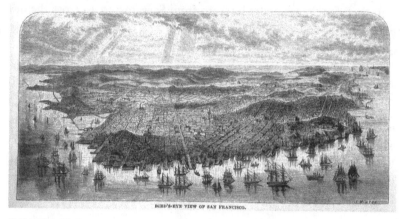

BIRD'S-EYE VIEW OF SAN FRANCISCO.

FIGURE 6. *Bird's-eye View of San Francisco*, engraving by J. Minton from Henry T. Williams, *The Pacific Tourist*, 1876. —Author's collection.

By the end of the 1850s, San Francisco had become calmer and less frenzied. Its population stood at some fifty thousand, but the miners and the chaotic element that followed in their wake were largely gone, off to other goldfields, other frontiers. Mining in California had become industrialized, as the hydraulic operations Thayer spied from the train attested, and gold still flowed into the city. So, too, did the silver of Nevada's newly discovered Comstock Lode, making entrepreneurs such as William Ralston (1826–75) of the Bank of California fabulously rich. Ralston and those like him were inveterate city boosters, investing heavily in the San Francisco's infrastructure, building massive hotels, theaters, opera houses, and office buildings, as well as public amenities such as schools, churches, libraries, and parks, including Golden Gate Park, planned in part according to the advice and designs of Frederick Law Olmstead. It was during the 1860s that San Francisco first developed its artistic and literary culture, the latter primarily through the medium of the city's dozen or so daily newspapers. San Francisco's growing cultural scene would attract the likes of Mark Twain and encourage homegrown talent, such as the short-story writer Bret Harte and the poet Charles Warren Stoddard, whose work Emerson enjoyed, telling him so in an appreciative letter in 1867. A new era in San Francisco's history began with the completion in 1869 of the transcontinental railroad, which finally connected the city directly to the financial, commodity, and cultural markets of the East. This event spurred even greater expansion and infrastructural development, thus boosting the tourist trade, which now brought the likes of John Murray Forbes and Ralph Waldo Emerson to the burgeoning city.

The Occidental Hotel into which John Murray Forbes booked the party was an excellent example of the heights of luxury and comfort now available in this Far West outpost. "Verily the Occidental Hotel is Heaven on the half shell," crowed Mark Twain, adding that he "may even secretly consider it to be heaven on the entire shell, but his religion teaches a sound Washoe Christian that it would be sacrilege to say it." Begun in 1861 and only fully completed eight years later just in time for the arrival of the railroad, the Occidental Hotel was well positioned to accommodate demanding visitors from the East. Running the length of an entire city block on the east side of Montgomery Street and nearly half a block up both side streets of Bush and Sutter, it was one of the largest in the city, boasting, according to *Bancroft's Tourist's Guide*, that "four hundred and twelve elegant single and double rooms, with numerous suites having ample bathing and other accommodations, besides ladies' parlors, dining-halls, billiard-hall, convenient offices, broad stairways, spacious halls, and roomy passages, make up this truly magnificent mammoth establishment. The carpets and furniture are of the most elegant and costly description. A large and beautifully-fitted patent safety elevator adjoins the grand staircase near the main hall, and reading-room at the Montgomery street entrance. Near the main entrance is a telegraph-office— hacks stand always in front, and four leading lines of horse-cars pass the three entrances. A newspaper and periodical stand, with post-office letter-box, complete the conveniences of the reading-room." And, in case one was concerned about earthquakes, the advertisement also specified that "the walls are braced with iron, and securely anchored, besides being connected across the building by heavy iron ties on every story." Thayer, for one, was well pleased with his room, its luxurious appointments and amenities; he also liked it because, as he wrote to his children, on the roof of the mercantile across the street he could see a "*great grizzly bear!*" with "long claws and . . . very savage [looks] and if one didn't know he was wooden, he would scare one, as he looks so savage and sly." Such was San Francisco in 1871: costly luxury of the cosmopolitan future looking out over crude hucksterism of the fading frontier past.

It was six o'clock by the time everyone was checked into the Occidental. After a quick dinner in the dining room, all but Thayer retired to bed. Thayer had arranged in advance to have his letters delivered to Captain Oliver Eldridge, a retired ship captain and Civil War hero from Massachusetts, now one of San Francisco's leading citizens and an agent of the Pacific Mail Steamship Company. He therefore walked the several blocks to Eldridge's office on the wharf at the corner of First and Brannan Streets in search of letters, but much to his frustration—having a "raving thirst for news"—it was closed. He trudged back to the hotel, arriving around nine o'clock. He sat down in the reading room to pen a brief letter to Sophy, telling her to now send her letters to the Occidental, at least until May 2. So far, he added, "We have had a wonderfully easy and agreeable trip," and although Mr. Emerson and Mrs. Russell were suffering from inflamed eyes because of the alkali dust and the cold, they were both in "reasonable condition." He ended with a PS asking Sophy to tell Mrs. Russell's son Henry "that I count it a special providence which gave me the opportunity of seeing so much of so lovely a person as his mother."

THOMAS STARR KING AND CALIFORNIA UNITARIANISM

Thayer was up the next morning at eight, having slept a "superb night." Soon, Captain Eldridge appeared, but he brought no letters, so he and Thayer trooped off to his office, and finding none there, Thayer continued on to the post office, again to no avail. Back at the Occidental, Thayer found that word had already spread of John Murray Forbes's presence in the city. Invitations for dinner and sightseeing were arriving from the likes of the banker Ralston, "who placed a fine saddle horse at Mr. Forbes' disposal," and John Felton, the Harvard-educated lawyer who had gained fame for negotiating the Oakland right-of-way for the transcontinental railroad. The presence of Emerson, too, was soon noticed, and even before breakfast, while Emerson and Thayer were "loafing around" in the Occidental's magnificent lobby, in strode the equally magnificent figure of the Reverend Horatio Stebbins (1821–1902), acclaimed minister of the First Unitarian Church of San Francisco. The Reverend Stebbins, whom Emerson had known since at least the 1850s, wasted no time in enlisting him to lecture to his congregation. To no one's surprise, Emerson instantly agreed, and the talk was hastily scheduled for Sunday evening, April 23.

Considering his fraught relationship with Unitarianism over the years, Emerson may have been gratified by the celerity of the request to speak. As a formal denomination, Unitarianism dated only to 1825, having been created after it became clear that the theological divisions between evangelical Trinitarians and rationalist Unitarians within New England Congregationalism had become too rancorous for comfortable coexistence. Thus, the American Unitarian Association (AUA) was born a scant four years before Emerson accepted ordination as a minister in that denomination. However, even with this schism, there remained within the Unitarian Church radical elements that threatened to divide the nascent AUA even further. These ministers were all Transcendentalists. The most radical of these, of course, was Emerson himself, who, even after leaving the church in 1832, continued to unsettle the new denomination with his writings, especially the 1838 "Divinity School Address." As we have noted, Emerson's hyper-individualistic strain of Transcendentalism provoked a tremendous response, most notably from the conservative "pope of Unitarianism," Andrews Norton, who sought to preserve the AUA's Christian character and defend the denomination against Transcendentalist heresies. Emerson, as already mentioned, was banned from Harvard for his views; he also found conservative Unitarian pulpits increasingly closed to him.

Not all Transcendentalist ministers left Unitarianism, however. Indeed, such Unitarian ministers as Theodore Parker and George Ripley ably defended the Transcendentalist position from within the church, a position that engendered a theological debate between those who wished to preserve the primacy of Jesus and his miracles and those who wished to jettison Christianity altogether. This argument would continue in one form or another within the Unitarian Church for decades to come. Given the strictly congregational structure of the AUA, it was impossible for either side to overwhelm the other and impose its particular theological views on the entire church. Tensions between the two factions remained high throughout the 1840s and 1850s. Moreover, the problem was exacerbated with the formation of the Western Unitarian Association (WUA) in the wake of Unitarian missionary efforts in the Midwest. Here, ministers with strong Transcendentalist leanings fought tirelessly against any form of creedalism and frequently called into question not simply Christianity but also any form of theism. As it turned out, the First Unitarian Church of San Francisco, although an AUA member, was nevertheless firmly within the Transcendentalist camp—Horatio Stebbins's recent predecessor in the pulpit had been the ardent Transcendentalist minister Thomas Starr King (1824–64), one of the most celebrated Unitarians of his day.

Born to a father who was a Universalist minister in New England, King was destined to be a minister too, although his father's death when King was fifteen made realizing this goal difficult. However, he was both precocious and persistent, and his intellectual qualities were quickly recognized by giants in the field, including the Universalist Hosea Ballou II and the Unitarian Theodore Parker, who later facilitated his private studies and eventual ordination. At twenty-one, King accepted a call from the Charlestown Universalist Church in 1846 and then the Hollis Street Unitarian Church in Boston a little later. At five feet tall, a slight 120 pounds, and perpetually boyish, King was often underestimated by his parishioners and others, but he rapidly distinguished himself as a charismatic orator in a city that prized these gifts. He soon found himself much in demand throughout the Northeast, occupying both pulpits and the lecterns of Lyceum halls, where he spoke on religious, philosophical, and literary topics. Indeed, Emerson himself envied King his easy manner and confidence before an audience, as Emerson himself had never managed to be as naturally comfortable as King was speaking in public.

After eleven successful years at Hollis Street, King, never a robust man, felt the need for a change. After mulling several options, he accepted a call to the First Unitarian Church of San Francisco in 1860. Unitarianism had been on the ground early in California. The First Unitarian Church of San Francisco was incorporated in 1850, but even while the congregation grew, the church was hampered by the short tenure of its ministers—four in its first decade, with long vacancies in between, as it was hard to recruit for the distant West. Thus, when King and his family arrived, the minister had his work cut out for him. He needed to retire the debts of the church, begin fund-raising for a new building, and reorganize the Sunday school, not to mention preaching a new sermon every week. He was also drawn into the politics of the day. King spent weeks traveling up and down the Pacific Coast stumping for Abraham Lincoln and the Republican Party, and with the outbreak of the Civil War, he furiously and effectively campaigned against California's succession from the Union. Inevitably, all of this activity took its toll on his fragile health, and he died of a combination of diphtheria and pneumonia on March 4, 1864, at the age of only thirty-nine. It is a measure of his immense popularity in California that his funeral was treated as a state occasion: flags flew at half-staff, businesses and government offices were shuttered, and guns were fired in salute. King's new church building, known thereafter simply as Starr King's church, hosted the obsequies, which were attended by twenty thousand people. In the audience were the governor, the mayor, ministers from the Methodist and Presbyterian churches, and local literary luminaries such as Charles Warren Stoddard, Bret Harte, and Ina Coolbrith, the poet who would later become Jack London's muse.

Today, Thomas Starr King is remembered as "the Apostle of Liberty" who helped "save California for the Union." From 1931 to 2006, a statue of him as a representative Californian could be found in the U.S. Congress's Statuary Hall (it was replaced by a statue of Ronald Reagan). King's other, equally important legacy, however, was as a transmitter of Transcendentalist spirituality to the state's evolving religious culture. King was steeped in the varieties of New England Transcendentalism, including that of Ralph Waldo Emerson, whom he knew fairly well: it is reported that King preferred to be called by his middle name "Starr" in imitation of Emerson, who preferred "Waldo" to "Ralph." While we don't know exactly when the two first met, we do know that King attended some of Emerson's public lectures in the late 1840s and he was Emerson's guest to tea after preaching in Concord in 1850 (here King did a wickedly amusing imitation of the preaching style of Henry Ward Beecher, which Emerson quite appreciated). What's more, Emerson was in the audience in 1854 when King gave his most famous sermon, "Substance and Show," and although terrified by the older man's presence, King gratefully reported afterward that Emerson was "quite eloquent with compliment and joy." The two corresponded on occasion, and in 1862, after King had relocated to San Francisco, Emerson wrote asking him to look after his son Edward when he arrived in the city; he did, and Edward was suitably impressed by him, enthusing to his father that King was the "salvation & future" of California. In return, King became Emerson's greatest booster in California, recommending his works to friends, including Jessie Benton Frémont, the wife of the great western explorer, John C. Frémont, whose travel narratives had been such an inspiration to Emerson.

That King had drunk deeply at the well of Emerson is evident in many of his writings. In the sermon "Spiritual Christianity" (1858), for example, King, influenced by Emerson's "Divinity School Address," rejected the absolute necessity of institutions, clergy, or doctrine, since God as

"Infinite Spirit" was everywhere available and his grace was like the rain: "It falls on the mountain slopes; it collects in the rills, it combines into streams and rivers; it hides underground, and bubbles in fountains." These words suggest that the emblematic symbolism of nature also came easily to King. Such views can best be seen in some of his California sermons, such as "Living Waters from Lake Tahoe" (1863), which teaches that to recognize the beauty of this mountain lake and its surroundings was to enter into "the glory of sympathy" with the mind of God, or in "The Lessons of the Sierra Nevada" (1863), in which King preached that "the mountains are measures by which we may form conceptions of Omnipotence. They lead us up from matter to mind. They teach faith in an invisible force." King's observations of California's natural scenery were made firsthand. Shortly after landing in San Francisco in 1860, he took an extended tour of the Sierra Nevada at the behest of John and Jessie Frémont, visiting the Yosemite Valley, the Mariposa Grove of Big Trees, and Lake Tahoe. Soon after, King began writing a series of exceedingly well-received articles about this trip for the *Boston Evening Transcript*, which for many in the East was their first introduction to the wonders of Yosemite and the giant sequoias. Even before coming west, King had already written a popular, Transcendentalist-inspired guidebook to the White Mountains of New Hampshire—*The White Hills: Their Legends, Landscape, and Poetry* (1859)—and several of the Boston literati, including the poet John Greenleaf Whittier, encouraged him to do likewise for California. Sadly, King's political activism took priority, and he died before he could realize this project. Nevertheless, by this time his brand of Transcendentalism had already sunk deep roots into California's soil.

Thomas Starr King's passing was undoubtedly a major blow to California Unitarianism, but given the robustness of his replacement, Horatio Stebbins, the First Unitarian Church of San Francisco found itself in good hands. As Mark Twain put it, the Reverend Stebbins was "a regular brick." A native of South Wilbraham, Massachusetts, Stebbins, like King, came from humble circumstances, but by dint of perseverance and forceful personality, he made his way to Harvard, where he graduated from the Divinity School in 1851. Stebbins had actually declined the San Francisco pastorate in 1852, but in the wake of King's death twelve years later, he didn't hesitate to make the move west, remaining there for thirty-five years. During that time, he not only solidified the presence of Unitarianism in San Francisco but also helped create churches in Los Angeles, Santa Barbara, San Diego, and Portland, Oregon.

"Dr. Stebbins once met was never forgotten," wrote his biographer, as "his erect, towering form, his dignified bearing, his strong face, his expressive eyes, his polished manner arrested attention." And while he didn't quite have the charismatic presence of King as an orator, he did have a style all his own that attracted and kept parishioners. What's more, while not as politically active as his predecessor, he nonetheless was a fearless defender of the rights of the Chinese and African Americans, as well as a champion of higher education, serving as a trustee of both the University of California and Stanford. Theologically, Stebbins was more of a liberal Christian than a radical Transcendentalist like King and more interested in human nature than nature generally: it is reported that although Stebbins found Yosemite "tremendously impressive," he actually had more fun talking horses with the stage driver. Nevertheless, Stebbins was noted for his belief in the "freedom of the pulpit" and thus was happy and eager to invite such a celebrity as Ralph Waldo Emerson to occupy his. Stebbins knew that, regardless of what he might lecture on, the simple fact of Emerson's presence would be of great significance to his many parishioners still mourning the loss of Thomas Starr King.

TO THE PACIFIC AT LAST

As much as Emerson seemed determined to turn his vacation into a busman's holiday, a vacation it was to be. Most of his days during the first week in San Francisco were spent sightseeing. When the Reverend Stebbins had asked Emerson to speak at his church, he sweetened the request by offering a carriage ride with him out to the Cliff House that day. Emerson was eager to see the Pacific Ocean, and Thayer and Edith were happy to be included in the outing. After breakfast at 9:30 a.m., Stebbins came to collect them in a "beach wagon" pulled by two horses. A cool breeze blew in from the west, which necessitated their wearing coats, but the sun was out and the day bright and clear. The journey took them directly through Chinatown. Emerson was fascinated by the "China-men" in their blue robes and "long queues reaching almost to their feet," whereas Thayer noted the abundance of tea shops, open-air butchers with whole cooked hogs hanging in front, and the ubiquitous laundries advertising their services in English on horizontal signboards and in Chinese on vertical ribbons.

At the end of Geary Street, a wide toll road named Point Lobos Avenue extended westward through the dunes to the Pacific shore. This was
a popular drive for San Franciscans, and according to *Bancroft's Tourist's
Guide*, the avenue was often "filled from side to side with smooth-rolling
or friendly racing teams, from the natty single buggy to the elegant coach,
or the stately four-in-hand." Once out of the city, few trees were to be seen,
but Thayer reported that the sandy, grassy hills were "covered with blue
and yellow lupine and a hundred delightful flowers." Soon they, too, like
"Cortez" at Darien, "stared at the Pacific," its blue horizon broken only by
the small points of the Farallon Islands far out to sea. Stebbins drove them
along the beach for a little ways, watching the waves roll in—a "reviving
sight," according to Thayer, who noted that "Mr. Emerson was delighted"
by the bright, expansive scene. Driving north along the beach, they arrived
at their destination, the Cliff House, where Stebbins, after having the carriage parked in a long shed to shield the horses from the constant wind,
led the group to the front veranda of the establishment.

FIGURE 7. *At the Cliff House*, photograph by Carleton Watkins, 1873. —Courtesy
of the Miriam and Ira D. Wallach Division of Art, Prints and Photographs: Photography Collection, New York Public Library, https://digitalcollections.nypl.org/
items/510d47e0-41df-a3d9-e040-e00a18064a99.

Constructed as a restaurant in 1863 and managed by Captain Junius G. Foster, Cliff House was a large, rectangular, vaguely Greek Revival building constructed over a rocky cliff to take advantage of the famed Seal Rocks, which jutted up from the ocean a hundred feet offshore. The most important feature of the Cliff House was its wide veranda on the ocean side of the building, where the fashionable could be seated at outdoor tables and take tea and other refreshments while watching the antics of the seals and sea lions basking below. "Smooth and shiny" as they were, Thayer thought they looked like giant leeches. Emerson, fulfilling a promise to Edith, wrote a charming letter about Seal Rock to his grandson, Ralph Emerson Forbes, one of the few of his letters from the trip to survive. He first described the ride through Chinatown and then the road to Ocean Beach:

> Pretty soon [we] came in sight of the Pacific Ocean, and keeping on till we came to the shore we did not stop till we arrived at a handsome white house where the ostler [sic] took charge of our horses and we went up the stairs to a balcony which went all round the house and going to the back of the house we saw under us and before us the Ocean and not far in front of us a rocky island. The top of the rocks on it was covered with sea-birds which looked like ducks, but lower down we presently saw the sea-lions, long creatures as large as bears, and much longer than bears. Some of them are twelve feet long, that is, if they could stand upright on their hind-feet they would be twice as tall as I am. They were lying about on the rocks and some of them all the time trying to crawl up on to the rocks from the water and sometimes a big one would lie on a low rock partly in the water and push every sea-lion off that tried to get up on it. Now and then they roar loudly as if they would make more noise than the waves rushing up the rocks do and as if they wished to be heard by the people on the Cliff House balcony who [sit] gazing at them through spy glasses. We talked loud but they did not seem to mind what we said about them[.] I don't think they understand English.

Emerson ended the letter by assuring Ralph that California had banned the hunting of sea lions, "so these are safe and wailing for you to come and see them."

From Ocean Beach, Stebbins pointed the carriage back down Point Lobos Avenue and wended his way south to the venerable Mission San

Francisco de Asís from which the city took its name. Locally, the mission was more commonly known as Mission Dolores due to the nearby Arroyo de Nuestra Señora de los Dolores (Our Lady of Sorrows Creek). Built in 1776 by Father Francisco Palóu, a member of Junípero Serra's company of Franciscan missionaries, it was the sixth in the mission chain, which by the early nineteenth century had become a bustling center of agriculture and trade. The Mexican secularization of the California missions in 1834 hit Dolores hard, and most of its outbuildings and land were sold off. However, much of the original church building continued intact, especially its distinctive facade, and as the oldest surviving structure in San Francisco, it had become an important tourist attraction by the late nineteenth century. Despite the fact that Anglos had spent much of the 1850s and 1860s attempting to extirpate—often violently—Californio influence in the state, by the 1870s it was no longer seen as much of a threat, and Anglos were just beginning to wax nostalgic about California's Hispanic past, especially the mission system (it wasn't until 1884, when Emerson's friend and fellow Transcendentalist Helen Hunt Jackson published her bestselling novel *Ramona*, that the mission craze really blossomed). Thayer accordingly found Mission Dolores "quaint, covered with tiles with a little grave yard attached where roses are in full bloom in profusion." Emerson was much taken with the interior of the church, "particularly the decoration of the ceiling which was made up of the plainest boards and rafters, but had been so painted or colored with a wash in the form of a zigzag with four colors, red, brown, white, and grayish blue, that the effect was quite fine." So pleased was he that after lunch at the Occidental, Emerson took a horsecar back out to Mission Dolores with Alice, Sarah, Annie Anthony, and Holdrege. Indeed, just about everything of that day's touring in San Francisco seemed to please him. "I never saw Mr. Emerson so fresh and radiant as he seems now," Thayer wrote to Sophy, adding in a later letter that "He is greatly interested in all that is peculiar out here, [and] reads up the local history."

The next day, April 23, was a Sunday, but it was soon apparent that the Sabbath in San Francisco was kept a bit differently from that in Boston. Thayer was surprised that the city was a lively place even on the Lord's Day, with many shops open and doing business. An Irish brass band in military uniforms (most likely the local Fenian Brotherhood) marched noisily down the street in front of the Occidental on route to a picnic in San Jose. John Murray and Will Forbes took the morning to go out to the Cliff House, while Thayer accompanied Edith Emerson to First Unitarian to hear Reverend Stebbins preach. They were disappointed, however, because the pulpit was being filled that day by "a young sprout from the East, a Mr. Lewis who was poor enough." Apparently Emerson was to come as well but arrived late and "was canny enough to ask at the door whether Mr. Stebbins would preach and so went back and saved himself." Meanwhile, Mrs. Russell remained confined to the hotel with her inflamed eyes, waiting for a doctor; she was later joined after lunch by Edith, who spent the afternoon writing letters and receiving guests. Thayer, too, spent much of the rest of the day writing letters and visiting a succession of friends and acquaintances from Boston—San Francisco seemed full of them. At 5:30, they all dressed for dinner, after which it was back to Stebbins's church for Emerson's first talk, "Immortality."

"IMMORTALITY"

Since his talk was to be in lieu of the evening service, Emerson probably felt his essay, "Immortality," would be a suitable offering, and Stebbins accepted it without quibble. At six that Sunday evening after dinner at the Occidental, Emerson's party walked the five blocks to the church, which was located on Geary Street near Stockton. Built at considerable expense, First Unitarian featured a High Gothic style with a facade boasting a large rose window flanked by eight pillars topped by pinnacles with crockets. Before entering, the group would have undoubtedly stopped to pay their respects at King's gothic white marble sarcophagus, which sat primly in the middle of a small open courtyard to the left of the church. It was a measure of the minister's immense popularity that the ban on city burials had been waived in just this one case.

The church was filled to capacity when Emerson and his group entered. Because the invitation to speak was last minute, newspapers had advertised that the Reverend Stebbins was to preach that evening on "Methodism," but apparently the change had been announced at the morning service, which was enough to fill the church. At precisely seven thirty, after a brief introduction by Stebbins, Emerson ascended to the desk at the front of the dais and, after a moment's hesitation to shuffle his manuscript, began speaking. Dressed in his usual ill-fitting black broadcloth suit, Emerson made few gestures while speaking, letting his clasped hands hang before him except to turn a page. He would, however, rock on his feet ever so slightly to the left and right as he spoke and occasionally look up to make eye contact with his audience, often beaming with a "luminous expression" that many found mesmerizing. However, what people most noticed was either his voice, which Oliver Wendell Holmes Sr. characterized as "never loud, never shrill, but singularly penetrating," or his tendency "to hesitate in the course of a sentence, so as to be sure of the exact word he wanted; picking his way through his vocabulary, to get at the best expression of his thought, as a well-dressed woman crosses the muddy pavement to reach the opposite sidewalk." Holmes also observed that "this natural slight and not unpleasant semicolon pausing of the memory . . . grew upon him in his years of decline," and so we can imagine, after the long journey across the continent, this mannerism was on full display that night.

"Immortality," which would eventually be published in Emerson's *Letters and Social Aims*, begins with a brief survey of afterlife beliefs from the ancient world through Christianity to their latter developments in Calvinism and Swedenborgianism. All, of course, presuppose the immortality of the soul, but perversely, all have tended to highlight the terror of death rather than the joy of life and the hope for the hereafter. For the "healthy mind," the philosophical approach of Marcus Aurelius or Schiller is better: death is a natural transition, and if we are meant by God to live forever after, then so be it, and if not, then this must be for the best. In the end, "the healthy state of mind is the love of life," and to this end Goethe had carved on his tomb, "Think on Living." This does not mean that contemplating the question of immortality is not worthwhile, if only one does not expect to reason oneself to certainty on the point. What certainty we can have comes only intuitively, through contemplation of God's design of nature, which demonstrates beyond doubt his goodwill. What's more, "the mind delights in immense time; delights in rocks, in metals, in mountain chains, and in the evidence of vast geologic periods which these give; in the age of trees, say of the sequoias, a few of which will span the whole history of mankind." Such longevity suggests eternity and is symbolic of our own immortality, of which this life is just preparation. Finally, because the soul has been implanted by its creator with a burning desire to know all and the presence of such a desire implies the possibility of its fulfillment, which cannot possibly be achieved in one lifetime—or even many lifetimes—then, again, immortality is a given. Likewise, the desire for virtue, so hard in this life, is obtainable nevertheless. Indeed, the desire to learn the secrets of the cosmos and to grow virtuous is life itself, and as long as these desires remain, life remains. Of course, the ignorant will wish for more concrete doctrines, but even Jesus and the gods of the ancient Hindus refused to reveal the subtle details of the afterlife. These cannot be known, only experienced, either through our own personal moments of transcendence or through the poetry of the likes of Plato, Shakespeare, and Swedenborg.

Although his audience that night was enthusiastic, the assessment of Emerson's lecture in the next day's papers was decidedly mixed. All remarked on the size of the audience despite the short notice, but the *Chronicle* was not above a little lampooning: "Ralph Waldo Emerson, the most original, profound and incomprehensible American essayist, lecturer and philosopher, is at present sojourning in San Francisco—the guest of Rev. Horatio Stebbins. He has already lectured on 'The Immortality of the Soul' and will probably soon deliver another of his characteristic imponderable dissertations." Others were more straightforwardly complimentary, if not effusive. Featured on the front page of the *Daily Alta California*, right below an article on the killing of "a mad dog" ("Narrow Escape of Several Parties—Heroic Extinction of the Brute"), under the heading of "An Intellectual Treat," it was reported that Emerson's "discourse, although an hour long, was listened to with breathless attention, every one feeling as they left the Church that an elegant tribute had been paid to the creative genius of the Great First Cause, and that a masterly use of the English language had contributed to this end." Thayer found this overblown encomium very funny, as did Emerson, who "was greatly entertained and laughed over it with that quiet *ground swell* laugh of his." Nevertheless, Thayer was impressed by the talk, which he had not heard before, and thought the lecture "was most admirable and it seemed to me as great and excellent in its way as all the great things we have been seeing." "It is pleasant enough to hear the subject treated without any theological or technical talk," Thayer continued, "and the hints and suggestions all stated so to confirm one's belief in immortality and then the firm and cordial expression of his own belief in it." So she wouldn't feel left out, Emerson made a point of reading the lecture to Mrs. Russell back at the hotel.

The fact that Emerson managed to draw such a large crowd on the spur of the moment is a good indication of just how bright his charisma still shined, especially considering that San Francisco was not lacking in entertainment, both of the spiritually uplifting kind and otherwise. As for the former, during the weeks that Emerson was in town, audiences could choose to attend, for example, talks of the famous temperance lecturer John B. Gough—"Without being as erudite as Emerson, he will please where that scholar would not interest," predicted the *Chronicle*—or the revivalist preaching of Dwight L. Moody. There could not have been two New Englanders more theologically distinct than Moody and Emerson, with the Christian revivalist Moody preaching an old-fashioned fire-and-brimstone theology as opposed to Emerson's urbane and oblique Transcendentalism. However, given California's laissez-faire attitude toward religion, both found appreciative audiences.

Less serious forms of entertainment were equally abundant in San Francisco, ranging from "the great comic pantomime, Wee Willie Winkie," in rehearsals at Maguire's Opera House, to the Great Emerson Minstrels at the Alhambra—the Emerson in question here being Billy Emerson, whose blackface routines were all the rage. What's more, on returning to the hotel after his lecture, Emerson (Ralph Waldo, not Billy) found tickets waiting for him from Miss Carrie Moore, the "Skatorial Queen," who was then performing at the Pavilion Rink at Woodward's Gardens. In this case, Caroline "Carrie" Augusta Moore (1840–92) was already well known to Emerson, for she was the daughter of Concord's deputy sheriff, John B. Moore, and granddaughter of Abel Moore, whose famous 1846 arrest of Thoreau for tax evasion inspired the essay "Civil Disobedience." Carrie had gotten her start at the annual ice-skating carnival on Walden Pond in the 1850s. After demonstrating her skills in Boston, Moore went on to skate professionally in cities across the United States and Europe, where she astonished her audiences not only with the difficulty of her moves, executed on specially designed smooth skates, but also with her flamboyant costumes, which included, according to the *Sacramento Daily Union*, "a basque of blue velvet, and scarlet skirt trimmed with ermine fur and gold lace, the entire dress being spangled with small gold stars." Moore was equally adept on roller skates, which was how she was performing her flying routines in San Francisco. Emerson had already sent her tickets to his upcoming lecture, but unfortunately they were both scheduled for the same evenings. Nevertheless, Moore told Emerson that she would be happy to repeat her performance if he came late, and Emerson promised that "he meant to see her yet." Sadly, it appears that Emerson never made one of Moore's performances, for it was the kind of homey entertainment he liked. "We live among surfaces," he had written in "Experience," "and the true art of life is to skate well on them." That was something at which his fellow Concordian was truly an expert.

Chapter 4
TOURING SAN FRANCISCO AND THE BAY AREA

(APRIL 24 TO MAY 1, 1871)

Poor country boys of Vermont and Connecticut formerly owed what knowledge they had to their peddling trips to the Southern States. California and the Pacific Coast is [sic] now the university of this class.

—Ralph Waldo Emerson, "Culture" (1860)

Monday, April 24, marked the beginning of the Emerson party's first full week in San Francisco, and each member was determined not to waste a minute of it. That morning, the entire party with the exception of Wilkie took an early drive back out to the Cliff House for breakfast, more seal watching, and a leisurely stroll on the beach, where they collected shells and other flotsam. It was a warm, cloudless day, and Thayer complained that the ride back "was really *hot*." In town before noon, Emerson spent the afternoon at the hotel receiving a steady troop of callers. Thayer, meanwhile, whose wedding anniversary it was, went to a jewelry store where he bought "California gold quartz" buttons as a present for Sophy, after which he "fell in with" John Codman Ropes, a friend from Boston who was the senior partner in the law firm of Ropes & Gray. Ropes, a close friend of the Forbes family, had been active with Emerson on a number of Harvard committees during the 1860s. After lunch, Thayer next visited Julia Sumner Hastings, the sister of the Massachusetts senator Charles Sumner, famous for his fiery abolitionist rhetoric, which led to his being beaten senseless with a cane by a slave-owning Southern senator on the floor of the U.S. Senate in 1856. Mrs. Hastings lived in San Francisco with a young daughter and her husband, John Hastings, a physician who had made his fortune in the gold rush and had decided to settle in the city to live like a lord. During a later visit to the Hastings home, Thayer was accompanied by Emerson. John Hastings proudly showed off three of his Italian Renaissance paintings, two Cimabues, and a Giotto, which he "asserted to be originals," Thayer reported dubiously. Emerson, who had seen his share of Italian masters during his 1833 trip to Italy, also gave a less-than-enthusiastic assessment: whatever else they were, he said, they were indeed "*vastly* old." Paintings apparently weren't the only things the good doctor collected: after his retirement from the U.S. Marine Hospital, where he pioneered treatments for gonorrhea, he would run the dodgy Pacific Anatomical Museum on Market Street, which contained, among many other collectibles, the pickled head of California's most famous bandit, Joaquín Murrieta, a brutal relic of the Anglo war against the Californios in the 1850s.

For that evening's entertainment, Thayer approached the Occidental's manager, Captain Cragin (a good New Bedford man, he noted), to ask whether he and his house detectives would be available to accompany him, Emerson, and John Murray Forbes on a tour of Chinatown. Such Chinatown expeditions with bodyguards were commonplace in most big American cities of the time and could be arranged with a small fee and suitable tips afterward. Captain Cragin was happy to oblige, as he and his detectives were old hands at these tours. Wilkie had gone on one the night before and spoke glowingly of the Chinese theater and a new Chinese temple, which he described as a "'Joss House,' full of idols with a couple of big 'Boss Josses,' as they call them, in front." Chinatown, of course, was already a key tourist attraction in the city, and tourists' guides such as *Bancroft's* devoted several pages to describing its exotic, mazy delights.

CHINATOWN

The first stop on the tour of Chinatown was a Chinese theater on Jackson Street, perhaps the Royal China (also known as Hing Chuen Yuen). Here the party was treated to "the most singular performance." The theater was entered through a long hallway with fruit and cake vendors' tables to one side. This led to a gaslit auditorium consisting of rows of benches seating some six hundred, above which a large curving gallery seated five hundred more. At the front of the theater, an off-center platform served as a stage, which was bare except for a door to the wings at stage left. As the party entered, a woman and a long-bearded man were engaged in a dialogue, mostly speaking in high nasal voices. Occasionally, however, they would break into song accompanied by an orchestra, which "thumped and beat on a caterwauling set of instruments," seated on stage behind them. Thayer was amused that when the members of the orchestra were not playing, they "eat peanuts and look about in a cool uninterested way." The audience was equally casual, drifting in and out of the theater, seemingly at random. Needless to say, given the language barrier, none in the party could make sense of the spectacle and perhaps left believing this was representative of all Chinese theater, although what they witnessed was Cantonese opera, considered to be a lowly regional form in China proper and actually banned there since 1856 owing to its association with political subversion. Nevertheless, given the enthusiastic patronage of the local Chinese community, most of whom were Cantonese immigrants, as well as to the equally reliable white tourist trade, Chinese theaters like the Royal China were to be some of the most profitable theaters in nineteenth-century San Francisco.

Captain Cragin then led the gentlemen through a Chinese gambling parlor specializing in Fan Tan ("a sort of Faro game," according to Thayer), and then descended into a series of opium dens, which were always a highlight of Chinatown tours. In a succession of dark rooms fetid with opium smoke, Emerson, Thayer, and Forbes encountered rows of narrow, low bunks with two smokers to a bunk with a small lamp to light the pipes between them. It looked like berths on a ship or the sleeping car of a train, except that below the berths, hidden by a ragged curtain, men of less means would lay directly on the ground, "stowed away like dogs." His wife Lidian being a habitual user of laudanum for her chronic maladies, Emerson understood opium addiction; he also understood the visionary lure of the drug: "Dreams and drunkenness, the use of opium and alcohol," he once wrote, "are the semblance and counterfeit of . . . oracular genius, and hence their dangerous attraction to men." Watching the wreaths of smoke as they arose periodically from the mouths of the insensate figures, Emerson must have been both profoundly appalled and profoundly sympathetic to the scene before him. Thayer, on the other hand, was fascinated simply by the mechanics of opium smoking, later describing in detail to Sophy how the pellet of opium was prepared on the point of a needle and smeared on the inside of the pipe's bowl, which was then heated over the lamp flame to produce the smoke. The customer then took a long, long drag on the pipe, allowing little of the smoke to escape his lungs, and then laid back to enjoy the ecstatic stupor.

From the opium dens, Cragin proposed taking the party to see a house of prostitution, where, unlike American bordellos, "one may see the women stripped and on exhibition," but "Mr. Forbes thought it would hardly be agreeable to Mr. Emerson." They contented themselves by passing through the alleys where these establishments were tucked away, gazing at the women lounging at the houses' front doors, some playing games: "They were for the most part repulsive enough," Thayer reported back to Sophy, "and in this way much like what one sees when one passes along North St. in Boston." The new Joss House on Clay Street held a more uplifting interest. Climbing a set of steep stairs and passing "a great paper devil" scheduled for burning that night, the party entered an upper room, which led to more rooms with "a number of Josses . . . in each, with lamps burning before them." Other images could be seen as well, and Thayer likened these to fighters in a tournament, "beautifully lifelike, graceful, and well done." The rooms were crowded, with Chinese passing in and out, stopping briefly before the images and lighting candles and sticks of incense. Thayer was generally impressed by the Joss House's opulence and calculated the thousands of dollars that it took to "fit up this place," especially since all the images and ornaments had been brought from China.

Dinner at a Chinese restaurant followed, and again Thayer was impressed, this time by the fact that cooking was done in the open, people ate dexterously with chopsticks, and the clerk swiftly wrote up their order in precise Chinese characters with a brush dipped in India ink. They dined on "heaps" of rice, vegetables, and pork but for some reason didn't sample the smoked geese that hung from the ceiling around them, split and pressed "just like our dried codfish." Finally, the party returned to the theater at nine for the tumbling, which was the highlight of the evening: "A set of strangely dressed creatures flourish about and have a sort of war with each other, and then others appear and turn somersaults over a table, jumping up at the end and turning a clean, beautiful somersault in the air, jumping from the ground turning clean head over heels in the air and landing square on their feet." An "inexplicable piece of acting followed," so the group took the opportunity to leave and headed back to the more familiar surroundings of the Occidental Hotel.

For John Murray Forbes, the tour of Chinatown proved nostalgic, having witnessed many similar scenes while working in China thirty years before. What proved even more remarkable for Forbes, though, was how calmly Emerson seemed to take it all in. Years later, Forbes wrote in his memoirs, "If I could tell the whole of our visit in San Francisco, to the midnight orgies of the Chinese opium smokers and other bad characters, it would be interesting. But who can describe the poetic blindness, or perhaps far-seeing insight, of the Sage, looking, as he did, dreamily on or over these creatures who seemed half-way between the animal and the human race?—the drug smokers laid on tiers like the bunks of a crowded forecastle, the painted women, the theatrical performances. All this in the Chinese quarter. No sign ever came from Emerson that these made any impression on his mental vision." Perhaps this assessment resulted from the blurring of time and the power of the growing Emersonian myth of implacable stoicism. Thayer, for his part, told a markedly different story. On the whole, according to Thayer, far from being indifferent to what he was seeing, "Mr. Emerson seemed interested in it all," albeit with a critical eye. Thayer found parts of the tour extremely dispiriting and said so to Emerson, who agreed, remarking that "there is not much aspiration there,—or inspiration." What's more, Emerson wondered, not a little obtusely, "at the strange way in which our civilization seemed to fail to take hold of" the Chinese, "and at their persistence in herding and huddling together, when there was such vast room all about them." (The history of animosity against the Chinese in California would lead to a full-scale pogrom in Los Angeles a few months later that resulted in the lynchings of fifteen men.) Thayer, too, had his own set of prejudices to deal with: as with the Native Americans playing with the dog in Nevada, he was surprised by the fundamental humanity of the Chinese. Captivated by "the little China boys playing about,—little fellows even, just able to toddle, having a pig tail and shaved head," he was heartened by the fact that "Chinese mothers and fathers seem to hug and dandle their babies and crane out their heads at them and kiss them, just like a Christian! There is hope for them yet!"

Over the next two days, the Emerson party continued their exploration of San Francisco and its environs. On Tuesday, April 25, Emerson, Edith, and Will took the ferry across the Bay to San Rafael to visit Lidian's niece Elizabeth Barber and her family, who, Emerson reported, "all shone with hospitality & health" and whose seventy-one-acre estate at the foot of Mt. Tamalpais was filled with trees "almost all new to us, live oak, madrona, redwood, & other pines than ours; & our garden flowers wild in all the fields." Emerson's excursion left Thayer free to roam about San Francisco, tramping up Telegraph Hill with John Ropes and then off to the Mission Woolen Mills with a young Boston friend, Clarence Denny. In a letter to Sophy, Thayer waxed enthusiastic about not only the quality of blankets produced by the Woolen Mills (although too expensive at thirty dollars) but also the efficiency of the Chinese labor force, who in everything were, in his opinion, far superior to the Irish. Next Thayer went to the mint to exchange for paper money the heavy silver dollars he had been forced to carry on the trip out and then on to the post office, looking again for letters from home. In the post office lobby, lists of unclaimed letters were posted, which Thayer saw as a microcosm of polyglot San Francisco: "After the American list . . . comes the heading 'Lettres Francaises,' about 50; then 'Lettrer Italiani,' about 50 more: then 'Cartas Españolas,'—5; then 'Cartas Portugezas,'—5 more; and then 'Chinese Letters,'" and here he carefully recorded the English transliterations of fifteen Chinese names:

YOU WOP	YE TYE	KWONG CHING KEE
QUONG SANG	HONG YUNE & CO.	HOP GUNG
YETO	TY CHUNG	ANKE
MONG SING & CO.	LING GUON CHUNG	LOON CHUNG
KIM WING & CO.	LIO HELEY	TAY LOG

The following morning, Wednesday, April 26, Emerson returned from San Rafael around nine, and Thayer was delighted to have him the whole day for sightseeing. They walked down to the fish market, admiring the large salmon which could be bought whole for only forty cents, and then on to a champagne cellar, most likely that of Isidor Landsberger and Arpad Haraszthy, the son of Agoston Haraszthy. Here they were shown the wine-making process and did some late morning tasting, which Emerson quite liked: "Wine is not adulterated" in California, Emerson would later speculate, "because grapes at one cent a pound are cheaper than any substitute." Next came a browse of the newspapers at the Merchants' Exchange Building reading room, and then on to the Mercantile Library. Thayer thought the library "a capital one of 20 odd thousand volumes" with two librarians, "both graduates of Amherst." Opened in

1853 with the bequest of Vermont-born brigadier general Ethan Allen Hitchcock, the Mercantile was the first public library in the city and was generously supported by its subscribers. Thayer marveled that the library had "a magnificent edition of Shakespeare of which there appears to be no copy in any public library in Massachusetts." When Emerson asked if they had a copy of the collected works of Keats's poetry, one was quickly produced, and both men found it a "peculiar pleasure" to be on the rim of the great western ocean and still be able to verify that the poet had indeed erroneously identified Cortez and not Balboa as the discoverer of the Pacific.

ARRANGING A LECTURE SERIES

Emerson's Sunday lecture, "Immortality," had been a big hit with Stebbins's congregation, and the next day the *San Francisco Bulletin*, which described Emerson as "the most profound and original thinker America has ever produced," noted that "large numbers of our people would be delighted if other opportunities were offered to see and hear him." The *San Francisco Examiner* concurred. Already, the Monday edition of the *Daily Evening Herald* had announced that a committee of Unitarian laymen would try to buttonhole Emerson at his hotel that afternoon, and on Tuesday, both the *Bulletin* and the *Daily Alta California* ran squibs announcing that Emerson would indeed give a course of lectures during his stay in San Francisco—"New Englanders rejoice," wrote the *Bulletin*.

All of this was news to Emerson, however. It was only on Wednesday morning that a pair of Unitarian laymen actually approached him about a lecture series. These two were Horace Davis, whom Emerson knew from Concord, and Charles A. Murdock, who knew Emerson from the Lyceum circuit back east. In his 1921 autobiography, Murdock would write fondly about his San Francisco encounter, remembering Emerson as "the most approachable of men —as simple and kindly in his manner as could be imagined, and putting one at ease with that happy faculty which only a true gentleman possesses." Davis and Murdock began their visit by inquiring about his trip so far. Emerson replied that he was very impressed by the scenery, remarking further that, "When one crosses your mountains and sees their wonderful arches, one discovers how architecture came to be invented," a sentiment straight out of the "Commodity" chapter in *Nature*. The two next broached the possibility of further lectures, perhaps even a series, for which Emerson would be paid $500 in gold. "Well," Emerson replied, "my daughter thought you might want something of that kind and put a few [manuscripts] in my trunk, in case of an emergency." Then could he do one that evening, they asked? "Oh, yes, . . . but in Boston we could not expect to get an audience on such short notice." Not to worry, they assured him: they would get notices in the newspapers that afternoon and have an army of news-boys distribute fliers throughout the business district. Dates were then discussed for three more lectures that would accommodate Emerson's travel plans: April 29 and May 1, after he got back from an excursion to the Napa Valley and Calistoga, and one more, May 17, when he returned from Yosemite.

Thus, despite the fact that he was supposed to be traveling for plea-sure and not for business, Emerson could not pass up more opportuni-ties to lecture in San Francisco, just as his daughter Ellen had predicted. Always bashful of charity, perhaps this was a means of paying his own way on the trip. Or perhaps Emerson couldn't resist being lionized in this bustling outpost of the Far West. Whatever the case, the die was cast, and articles duly appeared in that afternoon's *Examiner* and *Bulletin* announcing that Emerson had committed to four more lectures at the First Unitarian Church.

Late that Wednesday afternoon, Emerson and Thayer paid a visit to the Reverend Stebbins and Charles Murdock, who took them on a full tour of the physical plant of First Unitarian. Both men were impressed by the grandness of the edifice, but Emerson was particularly taken by the study that King had built for himself in the attic so as to escape "the over-persistent," as Murdock put it. "I think I should like a study beyond the orbit of the chambermaid," Emerson said with a smile, paraphras-ing a line from his lecture "Resources." Stebbins was especially proud of the Sunday school, run by fellow Bay Stater Horace Davis, who "*bosses the teachers and meets them every week.*" Some five hundred children attended the school weekly, mostly from other parishes, but because the "main point about the Sunday school was to have a pleasant *social* centre for the children," Stebbins was pleased with the large turnout even if they never became members of his particular church. Thayer, however, thought this was actually a savvy recruiting tool, whatever the minister said. At this point, mindful that Emerson's second talk, so hastily negotiated by Davis and Murdock just that morning, was scheduled for that evening, Emerson and Thayer bid their good-byes and returned to the hotel for a quick dinner and a change of clothes before returning to First Unitarian.

"SOCIETY IN AMERICA"

Despite the fifty-cent fee for tickets (Sunday's lecture had been free), attendance was good, and the audience enthusiastically awaited Emerson's talk, "Society in America." In his introduction, the Reverend Stebbins attributed the few empty seats to the last-minute nature of the event, given that Emerson had "stolen in upon us by surprise even as his thoughts steal in and astonish our minds." The talk itself was a vintage Emerson performance. According to Murdock's recollections, "His peculiar manner of reading a few pages, and then shuffling his papers, as though they were inextricably mixed, was embarrassing at first, but when it was found that he was not disturbed by it and that it was not the result of an accident, but a characteristic manner of delivery, the audience withheld its sympathy and rather enjoyed the novelty and the feeling of uncertainty as to what would come next." At one point, Emerson even managed to knock off the reading desk a small vase of flowers, which fell onto the floor. "Not at all disconcerted," Murdock remembered, "he skipped nimbly out of the pulpit, picked up the flowers, put them back in the vase, replaced it on the desk, and went on with the lecture as though nothing had happened." Such an incident so calmly handled, "occasioned an admiring smile" and applause from one and all.

But what exactly did Emerson talk about that night? Based on news reports, the lecture was a version of the essay published as "Social Aims" and if so was dense and complex, although the gist was easily summarized by the newspapers. Emerson began by observing that American manners were often criticized, which should be heeded, because fine manners are a mirror of true character. Nature, however, has endowed all people of good character with the rudiments of such manners, although outward circumstances did not always allow us to develop them fully. Indeed, throughout most of its short history, the frontier condition of American society had not been conducive to fine manners, and those of the previous generation who did possess them—Washington, Adams, Hamilton—were the product of English precedents. Happily, though, Emerson had long noted that wherever he traveled in the country, he found men and women whose force of character naturally expressed itself in fine manners, the essence of which was courtesy, self-control, and public spiritedness (Emerson at this point in the talk launched into an encomium of one such "American to be proud of," who, though not named, was none other than John Murray Forbes). The presence of such men and women, coupled with the fact that postbellum America had turned its attention away from Europe and exclusively onto itself, boded well, in Emerson's estimation, for the development of a "civil and polite society," a truly "American civilization" that "will penetrate every square mile" of the continent. "We have much to regret, much to mend, in our society," Emerson concluded, "but I believe that with all liberal and hopeful men there is a firm faith in the beneficent results which we really enjoy; that intelligence, manly enterprise, good education, virtuous life and elegant manners have been and are found here, and, we hope, in the next generation will still more abound."

The reaction to the talk in the next day's newspapers was wildly mixed. Almost all of the *San Francisco Chronicle*'s coverage of Emerson would be consistently snarky, and the review of "Society in America" simply set the tone. The reporter dwelt on descriptions of Emerson's appearance: "his figure is slight and his face almost Wellingtonian in the prominence of its features"; demeanor: his "expression is one of benevolence, of one who rises above the petty annoyances of life, and finds pleasure in dwelling on pleasing abstractions and discovering the beauties of the infinite"; and oratorical style: "colloquial, unassuming and deliberate—so deliberate and interlarded with so many hesitations after unimportant words, that the style of the indifferent English public speaker is unavoidably suggested to the mind of the auditor." The content was "a disappointment to at least one who delights in the reading of his essays," since "although full of those curt, telling sentences in which each word expresses so much, and are so perfect in themselves that the slightest attempt at emphasis would have destroyed their symmetry, the ideas were not harmoniously blended, and the transitions were often abrupt." "As a whole," the *Chronicle* reporter summarized, "although abounding in beautiful thoughts and aphorisms, pertinent illustration and apt quotation, the lecture failed in producing the effect, the impression which it may fairly have been expected from a spoken essay by so great a man." The other daily papers, however, couldn't have disagreed more. In the estimation of the reporter for the *Daily Alta California*, "The lecture was a masterpiece of talent and research, showing a depth of thought in keeping with the reputation of the lecturer" who possesses "a peculiar facility of combining words to express plainly but forcibly his most sublime ideas." After summarizing the talk in a long column, the *Bulletin* reporter concurred: "The lecturer relied entirely upon his perception and sentiment of beauty and truth in addressing the audience, making no attempts at oratorical display," and although his "style is entirely colloquial, . . . the dainty intellectual sweetmeats lose none of their delicacy by his manipulation; and his wit is so irresistibly clear that the dullest mind can comprehend and admire it."

These latter sentiments were undoubtedly shared by the majority of Stebbins's parishioners, who were more than gratified to find this Transcendentalist celebrity in their midst, whatever he said. At the reception after the talk, Emerson continued to charm his audience, first by marveling at the twenty-dollar gold pieces with which he was paid—apparently the first he had ever seen—and second because "his encouraging friendliness of manner quite removed any feeling that the great man's time was being wasted through one's intercourse." Indeed, Murdock added, "He gossiped pleasantly of men and things as though talking with an equal." Murdock had actually been married earlier that day, and Emerson, aware of this, insisted on meeting his new bride, and when he did, "he chatted with her familiarly, asking where she had lived before coming to California, and placing her wholly at ease." Regardless of what he actually said in the pulpit, Emerson's "gentleness of manner" and "beauty in conduct" exerted a charismatic power over all who met him that night. Many were eager to repeat the experience at Emerson's third talk, but that would have to wait until Saturday after he returned from the North Bay and Calistoga.

CALISTOGA AND THE GEYSERS

Setting out early the next day from the Washington Street wharf on a California Pacific Line ferry, Emerson, Edith, Will Forbes, and Thayer journeyed up the Bay to Vallejo, where they caught the California Pacific

Railroad to take them the sixteen miles to the lush Napa Valley and then by carriage to the hot springs and spa town of Calistoga, situated in the shadow of Mt. St. Helena. Founded by Brigham Young's quondam colleague, Sam Brannan, who, after the gold rush he helped start, had made a fortune in real estate and other enterprises, Calistoga was intended to be the "Saratoga of California," hence the portmanteau name. Beginning in the 1860s, Brannan built a large hotel surrounded by palm, cactus, and rose gardens, along with a series of white duplex Carpenter Gothic cottages and a great barnlike bathhouse. Soon, it became one of the most popular attractions north of San Francisco Bay.

Arriving at Calistoga at one in the afternoon, the Emerson party was assigned to the Occidental Cottage, with Will and Edith occupying one wing and Emerson and Thayer the other, all sharing a common parlor in the middle. Since John Murray Forbes apparently really liked soaking in hot springs, he and the rest of the group had already been in Calistoga for two days, although when Emerson arrived, Mr. and Mrs. Forbes were absent from the town, having traveled to see the nearby Petrified Forest, only to return later that afternoon. In the meantime, Thayer "loafed about in the sun" with Wilkie and then took Emerson to the bathhouse to inspect the sulfur springs, which could be enjoyed, according to the ad copy on the hotel's stationery, by means of "Chemical, Steam, Vapor, Tub, Mud, and Shower bath[s]." Dinner at the hotel followed, and the evening was spent in the common parlor before a roaring fire, with Edith and Thayer writing letters and Emerson reading a book. "It is quite cozy," Thayer wrote Sophy.

Sometime during the day, Emerson wrote one of his longest surviving letters from California. Addressed to Lidian but obviously designed to be shared with friends and family, it is a chatty letter, alternating between the descriptive and the personal. "We live today & every day," he begins, "in the loveliest climate," adding a bit later, "Our company is, as you know, New England's best, . . . & we fare sumptuously every day." He described Calistoga as "a village of sulphur springs, with baths to swim in, & healing waters to drink, for all such as need such medicaments," which he was not: "You may judge how religiously I use such a privilege,—as that word *wont* has two meanings." The Napa Valley was lovely, however, "and if we were all young,—as some of us are not,—we might each claim his quarter-section of the Government, & plant grapes

& oranges, & and never come back to your east winds & cold summers,—
only remembering to send home a few tickets of the Pacific Railroad to
one or two or three pale natives of Massachusetts Bay, & half-tickets
to as many minors." Years before, Emerson had written facetiously that
had the West been discovered first, New England would have remained
unpopulated to his day; now, having actually experienced California, he
realized this was no joke.

Emerson also reported that Edith was "well & wise & brilliant all the
way in house & on the road" and that both he and she were constantly
busy with visits from friends and family who had relocated to California; he promised to write to others of their acquaintance in the Bay Area.
Emerson especially asked Lidian to "thank Ellen for filling my trunk &
valise so richly & skillfully," perhaps thinking mainly of the manuscript
essays she had packed, as he had indeed been asked to lecture as predicted, "for even in the vales of Enna & Olympian ranges, every creature
sticks to his habit." Emerson's only concern was that the Forbeses a few
days before had received a telegram stating that Emerson's son Edward
"was better," but Emerson "had not heard that he was worse, or bad or
sick at all." "Comfort me," he pleaded with Lidian, "by writing that the
rash boy takes more care of himself, & is not rash & a tempter of Providence." Emerson would have to wait a week before Edith received a letter
from Ellen for this mystery to be solved.

The next morning dawned bright and warm, with meadowlarks and
red-winged blackbirds singing in the trees. After breakfast about seven
o'clock, Thayer and most of the party set out on a trip to the geysers some
thirty miles to the north. The caravan consisted of three open wagons,
each seating ten or eleven people, and was captained by Clark T. Foss
(1825–85), the Maine-born teamster extraordinaire whose driving skills
with a six-horse team were legendary (Thayer instructed Sophy to look
him up in Samuel Bowles's *Across the Continent* [1865], extant in the family library). At the beginning of the trip, Thayer sat on the back seat of the
wagon with two undertakers from East Cambridge, Massachusetts, both
of whom, despite their profession, were "intelligent and cheerful."

Soon they were passing through a landscape of "fine grassy ranches
with hills and mountains about" and "broad meadows covered with
bright yellow flowers and sometimes open groups of handsome oak
trees" that "look like groves or parks that have been cultivated." Stopping

Foss at the Geysers, Sonoma County, California.

FIGURE 8. *Foss at the Geysers,* woodcut from Laura De Force Gordon, *The Great Geysers of California and How to Reach Them,* 1877. —Courtesy of the San Francisco Public Library.

at Foss's house, the travelers were served lunch at "a table of model cleanness and with great pitchers of nice cream, the best of bread, butter, and milk etc." Dining with them was a group just returning from the Geysers, who gave "portentous accounts of the rest of the road," occasioning some second thoughts. Edith Emerson and Mrs. Forbes decided the journey would be too rough for them, and because Emerson himself had to be back in San Francisco by Saturday for his next lecture, Will Forbes volunteered to take the three on "an easier jaunt . . . through Sonoma Valley" and get them back to the city by Saturday morning. The rest set out with Foss, with Mr. Forbes on horseback, and George Holdrege, Alice Forbes, and Annie Anthony alone in the second wagon.

The journey was indeed as rough and as exciting as presented, and the drivers earned every penny of the round-trip fare of fifty dollars. The "Foss Road," as it was called, followed McDonnell Creek for a ways to the hamlets of Schoolhouse and Pine Flats and then up and over Geyser Peak by means of a series of steep and dangerous ridges known as the Hog's Back and the Rattlesnake. At this point, the road was barely the width of the wagon, which had to negotiate thirty-five sharp turns before it ended at Geyser Canyon, where, as Thayer put, one was "plumped down right out of the mountains" into the yard of the Geysers Hotel. Foss had adopted a flamboyant persona, wearing a Stetson hat and duster jacket, and flicking his fourteen-foot horse whip with vociferous glee, he drove as fast as he possibly could to demonstrate his prowess in managing the "six-in-hand." Thayer found the ride exhilarating as much for the scenery as for the horsemanship. From Geyser Peak, one could see "a snowy peak of the Sierra Nevada on one side and the line of vapor that rose from the ocean beyond the Coast Range on the other." On the Hog's Back, where the road "fell off steep on both sides just under us, . . . we had superb views on each side." And then "down and down continually so steep that you were amazed at carrying a stage over such a road and yet a curve would be added right in the middle of the steepness, . . . curved a little less than a right angle and these six horses went gently trotting down like dogs." "The driving," he concluded with typical understatement, "was wonderfully good." John Murray Forbes, too, was amazed by the performance. Years later, when asked by Oliver Wendell Holmes Sr. about his memories of the trip, one of the first things he mentioned was the drive to the Geysers with Foss, "the famous Vermont [sic] coachman."

Arriving at four, Thayer and the rest checked into the Geysers Hotel, a spacious two-story wooden structure with wide wraparound verandas on both floors. A strong scent of sulfur permeated the air at the hotel, and from the veranda, wisps and puffs of vapor could clearly be seen rising between the hills that formed Geyser Canyon. Given the lateness of the hour and not wishing to spend precious daylight time on dinner, the group quickly hired a guide and set off to the Pluton River, which ran along the bottom of Geyser Canyon. The goal was a tributary of the river—Pluton Creek—whose rising streambed was studded on both sides with bubbling mud pots, boiling springs, and jets of steam (because none actually featured jets of water erupting on a regular basis, "geyser" was a misnomer—the correct term for these features was "fumarole"). The short hike from the hotel down a narrow, grassy footpath to the small bridge across Pluton River gave little indication of the remarkable sights that awaited the group. As Laura De Force Gordon pointed out in her guidebook, *The Great Geysers of California and How to Reach Them* (1877), all that could be seen at this point was the "beautiful green of luxuriant trees, whose thick foliage embowers Geyser Cañon, and . . . hedge in Pluton River." However, the landscape changed abruptly at Pluton Creek canyon, which displayed "on either side a charred and burnt surface, as if a huge lime-kiln had at some time found lodgment there in, leaving its smouldering fires to complete the terrible picture of perfect desolation."

As the group climbed the canyon of Pluton Creek—the "Ascent into Tartarus," Gordon's guidebook called it—everywhere could be heard subterranean gurgling, hissing, whistling, and puffing, and the ground grew increasing warm and soft and the air more pungent with the hot smell of sulfur that stung one's nostrils and permeated one's clothes. All about, the rocks were stained with crystalized sulfur, alum, copper and iron sulfate, and a variety of other minerals, yellow, white, red, green, and black. Thayer was especially taken by "the spiky little crystals of bright yellow sulphur that the hot vapor deposited about some of the holes." As the group advanced, they were introduced to the seemingly endless series of weirdly shaped features, each with such hellish names as the Devil's Kitchen, the Devil's Inkstand, and Pluto's Punchbowl, this last being a rocky basin in which thick, black water boiled and tossed ceaselessly. Next was the Witches' Cauldron, where "steam-jets spurt out, hissing and puffing on every side, the air . . . thick with vapors from every chemical combination possible to imagine." The whole atmosphere radiated danger and instability, although the guide blithely reassured everyone that no major explosion had occurred in the canyon since 1860. Thayer's response to the scene was typical of tourists: "We could not but sympathize with what the Indians must have thought, that all this was of the devil."

Climbing even higher, the trail was completely obscured by thick, mephitic clouds, and only by passing through them could one reach the highest point on the tour, the foot of Devil's Pulpit, "a rocky promontory . . . from which issue clouds of steam in small puffs, great waves, or occasional jets, from base to summit, seventy-five feet or more above" the trail's end. Here Thayer and company looked back over the entirety of the blasted canyon and could plainly see the Geysers Hotel calmly perched on the now incongruously green and wooded hillside across the Pluton River. Here, too, Thayer serendipitously encountered a friend, Arnold Henry Guyot (1807–84), the Swiss-born Princeton geology professor whose famous lectures at Boston's Lowell Technological Institute resulted in *Earth and Man* (1849), an early work on human geography that influenced both Emerson and Thoreau. Both were surprised to find the other there, but Guyot was soon lecturing Thayer that the "geysers" were due to chemical action, not volcanism, as proposed by the state geologist Josiah Whitney. Good scientist that he was, however, Guyot told Thayer he would not be dogmatic on the point (and a good thing, too, as in this case Whitney was correct).

Now exhausted by the day's activities, the group retreated back to the Geysers Hotel to enjoy a hearty meal of "royal mountain fare," including "brook trout, venison, fresh eggs, cream, and fresh ranch butter." Although they could still hear the distant, diabolical rumblings from Pluton Creek, they were all blessedly too tired to let it invade their dreams. The next morning, after a similarly hearty breakfast, Thayer and Holdrege set off walking before the arrival of the wagons, which eventually caught up to them seven miles along. At Calistoga, most of the group stayed another night at Brannan's hotel, but Thayer, keen for mail, pushed on by rail and ferry, arriving back at the Occidental in San Francisco that evening only to be frustrated in his objective; Emerson, Edith, and Will, having arrived back from Sonoma the day before, had thoughtlessly "seized and carried off all letters." Now Thayer would have to wait to get his letters until they returned from Emerson's talk that evening.

"RESOURCES" AND "CHARACTER"

Emerson was greeted by another full house at Stebbins's church for the third of his scheduled talks, "Resources." Apparently feeling in fine fettle and inspired by all the sights he had seen, Emerson improvised a short introduction to his talk especially for his California audience. He began by noting that "in communities so exceptional to the course of history as your own, so recent in its formation, containing such unparalleled advantages of climate and geographic position, with its productions of fruit trees, of animals, of minerals; with its commerce, its plantations, rising manufactures, the new observer cannot but believe that the inhabitants have been more occupied than elsewhere on the laws of progress. Perhaps it is not so, but no one can come hither without unexampled spirit of growth forcing that conclusion on his mind." The lecture proper began with some of Emerson's most optimistic prose: "Men are made up of potencies" and "the world is all gates,—all opportunities,—strings of tension waiting to be struck." History is the history of progress, invention, and discovery, he pronounced, all because man is "a plastic little creature . . . making himself comfortable in every climate, in every condition." And for every problem he encounters, nature provides the solution just at the time it is needed. The colonization of America by the "Saxon race" and its spread west is the latest example of this, led on by "the inexhaustible wealth of Nature" and the promptings of spirit. The material resources of America and the spiritual resources of its people are great indeed and spreading globally, through markets and ideas. "The disgust of California has not been able to drive nor kick out the Chinaman back to his home; and now it turns out, that he has sent home to China American food, and tools, and luxuries, until he has taught his people to use them, and a new market has grown up for our commerce." As for spiritual resources, history abounds in anecdotes of the ingenuity and presence of mind, heroism and courage, of the "energetic man," all of which connote power over nature and the mob. Of course, all of this comes from the energetic resources of the mind, which must be husbanded through variety and recreation, for if not, inspiration, which is episodic at the best of times, will fail completely. Thus it is necessary to look to one's health and sleep; to have solitary converse with nature; to create a workspace free of distractions; to read poetry, natural science, history, and biography; and to make time for serious conversation with friends.

Newspaper coverage of Emerson's third San Francisco lecture was limited to the long column on the front page of the *Bulletin*, which was respectful but not uncritical. The *Bulletin* reporter again made much of Emerson's calmness at the podium but remarked less charitably about Emerson's habit of shuffling his manuscript: "He fingers them over backwards and forwards as if at a loss whether to commence on the first page or the middle; and finally selecting a good starting point, he begins in a conversational tone of voice to read." Because of this method of lecturing, "the intelligent audience (for he draws none other) hang [sic] on his words with eagerness as if fearful of losing a single one," for "indeed, they need to give close attention to catch the force of his ideas, for all who are familiar with the style of his published writings, which really require close thought and a well disciplined mind to appreciate, can picture to themselves the difficulty they would have in comprehending, if they were to hear those works from the lips of a poor reader." And as if to leave no doubt what kind of reader Emerson was, the reporter concluded by saying that "the difference between hearing him read his works and reading them one's self is certainly in favor of the latter."

Two days later, on Monday, May 1, Thayer, returning from his trip to San Rafael to visit the Barbers, accompanied Wilkie James and Will Forbes to hear the fourth of Emerson's talks, "Character." "Character," like "Resources," had been given many times by Emerson on the Lyceum circuit, and Thayer, for one, had already heard it three years before. Emerson began by stipulating that the highest end anyone can aim for is the achievement of greatness or "completeness," which is "the fulfillment of a natural tendency in each man" to be true to one's own character. We have a tendency to think of greatness in terms of "Alexander and Bonaparte," but in reality true greatness can be found only in the scholar or intellectual whose "wisdom and civility" leads to "the creation of laws, institutions, letters and art" and all that we call "the *humanities*." To be great, one must trust in the truth of one's own ideas and pursue the calling to which one is best fitted, for "every individual man has a bias which he must obey, and that it is only as he feels and obeys this that he rightly develops and attains his legitimate power in the world." Indeed, this bias is the "practical perception of the Deity in man." To develop one's greatness takes not only hard work and concentration but also receptivity to genius wherever one finds it, even the unjust Napoleon or the Devil himself, for "it is difficult to find greatness pure." Indeed, "Bret Harte has pleased himself with noting and recording the sudden virtue blazing in the wild reprobates of the ranches and mines of California." Of course, it is the virtue not the wickedness of the great that is of interest to us, for in time "the air of the world shall be purified by nobler society, when the measure of greatness shall be usefulness in the highest sense, greatness consisting in truth, reverence and good will." And one must not think they need to travel far to find examples of greatness; instances are everywhere if one seeks to find them, for "wit is a magnet to find wit, and character to find character." Emerson ended the lecture with some apparently off-the-cuff observations on civil rights, especially women's rights, and another encomium on California.

It is hard to tell from the differing newspaper reports how well attended the fourth lecture was. The *Daily Alta California* said that it was "largely attended" and "was full of the most valuable thoughts and reflections." The reporter was especially pleased that Emerson "concluded with an allusion to the wonderful capabilities and possibilities of California life and the advantages we should take of it—the noble men of California should and will produce." The *Bulletin*, too, was complimentary as usual: "Mr. Emerson delivered a lecture last night at Starr King's Church to a large audience. The subject of his discourse was *Character*, and an epitome can scarcely do it justice." The rest of the long column was precisely such an epitome, however, and like the *Alta* ended by citing Emerson's "glowing tribute to the resources and capabilities of California, which, if properly husbanded and developed, will give her a standing second to no other state in the Union." The *Chronicle*, on the other hand, merely reported that "Ralph Waldo Emerson lectured last night at Dr. Stebbins' church, on 'Character.' The attendance was not large."

In all likelihood, despite the *Alta*'s and *Bulletin*'s positive assessments of the size of the audience, the *Chronicle*'s laconic reporting was probably accurate. The audiences at the first three lectures were indeed large, but apparently curiosity had been the leading motive for attendance. Murdock later reported that toward the end of the series the audiences dropped off. Of course, the various options for entertainment with which the city always abounded probably pulled away some of the original audiences who had gone to see a celebrity and, once satisfied, did not come back for the difficult content. Indeed, Stebbins had remarked that he was afraid "the people would tire in the sockets of their wings, if they tried to follow him," and apparently they did. What's more, Emerson still hadn't been able to shake the cold he had contracted on the train, and it is clear that he was becoming overtired, which was now affecting his mental state. In a letter to Sophy, Thayer mentioned that while

Emerson was "kind and wise and funny," nevertheless "he seems to me to be growing old a little; he loses his memory somewhat; and attaches his memory of some event to the wrong person or the wrong time sometimes; but this is slight perhaps." What Emerson needed at this point was a break from his "vacation." Happily, this is precisely what he would get next week when the party started off for Yosemite.

Chapter 5

YOSEMITE

(MAY 2 TO MAY 8, 1871)

In Yosemite, grandeur of these mountains perhaps unmatched in the
globe; for here they strip themselves like athletes for exhibition, and
stand perpendicular granite walls, showing their entire height, and wearing a liberty cap of snow on their head.

—Ralph Waldo Emerson, *Journals* (May 1871)

At 7:45 a.m. on Tuesday, May 2, Emerson and his party set off for Yosemite, a trip that everyone was looking forward to eagerly. The week before,
John Murray Forbes had carefully planned out the trip with the help of
a "Mr. Coulter," presumably George W. Coulter (1818–1902), founder of
Coulterville and, in his capacity as one of the first state commissioners of
Yosemite, a tireless booster of tourism who built one of the first improved
roads into the valley. The trip, by no means an easy one, would take the
party four days to reach the valley floor, requiring travel by ferry, railroad,
stagecoach, wagon, and finally horseback. Having to travel light, Thayer
found it difficult to pack: "My bag had to sweat in order to hold all I
wanted to put in and as it was I had to omit the big shoes and my slippers
and my Wordsworth, all of which were sore trials." The only one of the
party who would not be going to Yosemite was Edith Emerson, who, perhaps unbeknownst to everyone else but Will, was five months pregnant.
After seeing everyone off on the ferry, Edith took the nine o'clock ferry
to San Rafael to stay with the Barbers. Over the next week, she would
spend her time resting, sewing "on the piazza," arranging flowers, visiting
with such family friends as Annie Mailliard (sister of the poet Julia Ward
Howe), and taking short trips to see the state prison at St. Quentin and
the trees at nearby Redwood Canyon (today's Muir Woods).

Edith also spent time in San Rafael answering letters to Ellen Emerson, who, since the beginning of the trip, had been sending her a regular series of missives describing her amusement—and grandmother Lidian's bemusement—at the bratty antics of Will and Edith's children back in Concord. During this time, Will and Edith also exchanged letters, with Edith asking Will especially not to forget to bring her back some bark from the Mariposa Big Trees to make pincushions. (Apparently this indeed was a fad, according to the travel writer Charles Nordhoff: "At the Calaveras Grove Hotel they will sell you, for a trifle, pieces of the bark of the *sequoia*, formed into pincushions, which make an agreeable souvenir of the journey.") On a more serious note, she finally found out from Ellen what was wrong with Edward Emerson—he had contracted chicken pox, although he was improving. She asked that Will not "frighten Father with the news—nor your mother," but that he not "stay in the valley longer than you intended if you can help" it, thinking they might have to cut their trip short depending on the news from home.

The ferry from San Francisco dropped the Emerson party off at Martinez, where they caught the train to Modesto in the San Joaquin Valley. The cars were hot and there was a two-hour delay at the town of Lathrop, but happily a good hotel provided an acceptable dinner before they finally left at 2:15. Only twenty miles south, they soon reached Modesto; true to its name, it reminded Thayer of a little prairie town in Iowa, still raw in its newness and sparsely populated. The party transferred to a pair of four-in-hand wagons to continue the journey west to Coulterville. For most of the day, Thayer sat up front with the driver of the first wagon, with Mrs. Forbes and Emerson on the bench behind, and Mrs. Russell and John Murray Forbes behind them. All the young people rode in the second wagon, which brought up the rear.

Drought was on the land, and the road was hot, dry, and dusty—only the overhead canopies on the wagons protected occupants from the full fury of the sun. However, the full majesty of the Sierra Nevada could clearly be seen, with the road running due east along the Tuolumne River, discernible on the right by a band of trees and grass, the only green to be seen for miles around. Wildlife abounded. Thayer loved the abundance of "jackass rabbits" and ground squirrels that seemed to be scampering in all directions at once, unlike the pygmy owls that "sat gravely" at the openings of their underground burrows, "dapper, gray little gentry, with wings that closed in front like a Quaker's shad-belly coat." Other birds were abundant, especially magpies and Yellow-breasted Chats that flew in tight flocks, landing for a time on the branches of the oaks or on the tops of fence posts. Further up into the foothills, they would hear the "sweet, plaintive note" of the Western Meadowlark. "Staging," Thayer concluded, was "a wholly delightful mode of traveling."

Throughout the day, John Murray Forbes was amazed at Emerson's stoicism. Even "with the thermometer at 100°," he later told Oliver Wendell Holmes Sr., Emerson "would sometimes drive with the buffalo robes drawn up over his knees, apparently indifferent to the weather, gazing on the new and grand scenes of mountain and valley through which we journeyed." Mrs. Forbes, who according to Thayer had "great gifts" for drawing Emerson out, often managed to pull him out of his reveries and engage him in conversation on the drive, for which he was "always affable and ready and always as benignant as in his own parlor at Concord," and this despite the heat and the dust. On one occasion, Mrs. Forbes questioned him closely on his recent talk "Immortality," confronting him

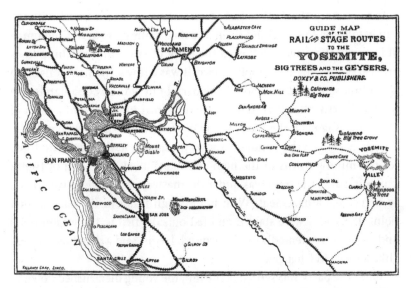

FIGURE 9. *Guide Map of the Rail and Stage Routes to the Yosemite, Big Trees and the Geysers,* engraving originally created by Doxey & Co. Publishers, reprinted in *Specimen Book of Electrotypes comprising Pacific Coast Scenery, General Illustrations, Trade Cuts, Advertising Novelties, &c* (Oakland, CA: Pacific Press, 1885). —Courtesy of the Library of Congress, Washington, D.C., Z250 .P14.

with Darwin and the negative evidence of science. Emerson patiently responded that the soul had its own evidences for its immortality: "It feels that it is in communication with the Source and it *knows*," perhaps because during peak spiritual experiences, time passes completely away and one is left with a feeling of eternity. What's more, the soul has an "insatiable desire to know and to learn," and we would feel "in a manner wronged if there was nothing more" to explore after death. Here he quoted lines from his talk taken from Goethe, who shared this sentiment: "To me, the eternal existence of my soul is proved from my idea of activity. If I work incessantly till my death, Nature is bound to give me another form of existence, when the present can no longer sustain my spirit." Goethe's hopes for an infinite life to satisfy an infinite curiosity were well founded, Emerson believed, since the future held as much as the past, and indeed, he imagined that heaven would be so full of new things that, even in eternity, there would be time to see each thing only once. And with that bit of pithy wisdom, the conversation lapsed and Emerson went back to admiring the Tuolumne River and the surrounding countryside.

After twenty-three miles and several hours of bumpy travel, with the sun beginning to set behind them, the road came close to the Tuolumne at last, and the wagons followed the bank of river until reaching Roberts Ferry, that night's stopping place. It was a tiny settlement consisting of an inn, some houses, and a huge barn built with 105,000 handmade bricks. Shortly after they arrived, there turned into the yard a train of two huge wagons linked together and overloaded with merchandise—"chests of tea, scythe-handles, crockery, chairs, and the like"—destined for the mining towns in the high country. Pulled by a team of twelve mules in pairs, the train was under the mastery of a single driver, much to everyone's amazement. With not enough room in the barn at that point, the mules were stabled and fed outside, tied to the wagon poles and left to lie contentedly on the ground. It was, said a delighted Thayer, "like a scene in Chaucer."

Once the party was settled at the inn, the young men rushed down to inspect the Tuolumne River, whose snowmelt water was swift and cold but of a frothy yellow or chocolate color owing to placer mining farther up in the mountains. Only on Mondays did transparency return to the water. "The miners keep Sunday," Roberts told Thayer, "and on Monday mornings the river certifies their virtue, and runs clear." Taking advantage of the ferryboat, which was drawn across the river by means of a cable, Will, Wilkie, and Holdrege used it as a swimming platform, winching it to the middle, stripping off their clothes to their underwear, and plunging into the icy water. Will and Wilkie managed to grab hold of a trailing rope, but Wilkie, losing his grip, was quickly taken down the river by the current and had to suffer the indignity of walking back to the ferry in his sopping long johns. After their "splendid bath in water cold from the Sierra" and drying out in the sun, the three men were ready for a hot meal and headed back to Roberts's Inn.

The Roberts of Roberts Ferry "turned out to be a Boston boy," both Thayer and Will Forbes proudly remarked, and had been living on the banks of the Tuolumne River for twenty-one years. Here he had thrived by serving miners, merchants, and now tourists on their way to the mountains. "His wife," on the other hand, noted Thayer somewhat sourly, "was a Western woman" and so their supper consisted of "a profusion of liver and pork and saleratus hot biscuits etc. as well as some good things" (Thayer was obviously not a fan of typical Western fare). The party were waited on at table by a "hideous wizened" Chinese man and a young serving girl, whose fresh good looks caught the eyes of both Will Forbes and Emerson. Emerson "gravely praised" her for her beauty to her face and then, taking an old man's liberty, continued to comment on her all through supper, likely much to the poor girl's embarrassment. After the meal, the group retreated to the inn's inviting "piazza," or front porch, where the breezeless evening continued warm and all drank glasses of the local wine. When Will Forbes announced he was tired and off to bed, Emerson said he would stay a while longer: "To me, *this* is delightful: I enjoy the passing hour." Soon, however, it was dark, and all were in bed, falling quickly into exhausted sleep. Some slept well, while others tossed and turned in the valley heat.

The next morning at 7:30, the party loaded themselves and their luggage back into the two wagons and set out for Coulterville, some forty miles distant in the Sierra foothills. They had to wait until the tremendous mule team was ferried across the Tuolumne; the road was then clear, and they started higher into the mountains. Thayer again noted the profusion of owls, "jackass rabbits," and squirrels, which seemed to be especially numerous and active that day. For a time, the party traveled over rounded hills that John Murray Forbes likened to the "swellings of a piecrust," but then the landscape changed abruptly, and great slate-like rocks covered with multicolored lichen "stood upright and stuck out of the ground over the fields like the oldest weather-eaten grave stone in a county graveyard." In many places, they saw the destructive evidence of gold mining: holes and tailings in abundance and great tracks of land dug over and the surface soil washed away by placer mining such that "only rocks remained."

During the early part of this journey, it was John Murray Forbes who drew Emerson into conversation, and as they rolled through the pines, Emerson talked extensively of Goethe, Schiller, Voltaire, Rousseau, and Tom Paine, pointing out that the latter two were not his favorites because he felt their critiques of Christianity were unfair. Twice during the day, these conversations were interrupted when the wagons stopped for a respite, first at a place named Morley's Well, which carried a large sign reading "Water for Horses. None for Old Wagons." Mr. Morley explained that sometimes wagoneers used as much as five buckets of water to cool an axel and that was too much; if a wagon axle needed cooling, then the driver should just give it time to cool down and not wantonly waste his precious water just to save a few minutes. The party then stopped at a cabin for milk, and Thayer was proud to record that even in this rude place the inhabitants knew who Ralph Waldo Emerson was. They arrived in Coulterville late in the afternoon around 4:30.

Coulterville was then a dying mining town, with many empty buildings and "something of the look of decay that one notices at Salem," according to Thayer, who noted that many of the remaining miners were Chinese, as they seemed to be the only ones with the skill and patience to glean gold from worked-over claims. The party checked into Wagner's Hotel, which, in the proprietor's absence in Stockton, was being run by two New Bedford men, David Clark ("a Franklin medal scholar in the Boston schools," boasted Thayer) and his assistant, Mr. Swain, who used to work in the Boston countinghouse of a Thayer family friend. As was fast becoming a ritual, Thayer, Will Forbes, Holdrege, and Wilkie all stripped off their clothes and had an invigorating bath, this time in a large water tank behind the hotel. Used for irrigation, the tank was filled by means of a large wooden wheel powered by a dog running on a treadmill for five to ten minutes at a time ("he looked happy," Thayer claimed). The owners of the tank, an Italian and a Chinese named Ah Pan, had apparently not thought to use the tank as a bathtub, but no complaint was registered. Dinner was at 5:30, which Thayer pronounced decidedly better than the fare they received at Roberts Ferry, perhaps in part because it was complemented by an "excellent red wine" that cost only "fifty cents a *gallon*."

After tea later that evening, the three men of the group who smoked— Thayer, Wilkie James, and Emerson—repaired with Mr. Clark to the hotel's piazza to enjoy the cool of the evening, listen to the sound of crickets, and have their postprandial cigar. Much to Thayer's delight, Emerson proceeded to apostrophize his cigar, reflecting that at home he could rarely finish a whole one, but in company he enjoyed it greatly. Concurring with Hawthorne, Emerson said that cigars were so "agreeable" because, for those who don't make friends easily, "one who is smoking may be as silent as he likes, and yet be good company." Thayer had observed that while traveling, Emerson would smoke either after lunch or after tea, and even occasionally after both, which "was multiplying, several times over, anything that was usual with him at home." In the wake of this homey performance, Thayer was moved to say, "One's respect for him grows constantly."

INTO THE SIERRA

Passing a pleasant night at Wagner's Hotel—it was much cooler at night in the upper foothills than in the valley—the party breakfasted and made ready to travel twenty-six miles to Hazel Green. Most of the men and all the women loaded up into the two wagons, but a couple of the men mounted for the day's journey what Will Forbes could only describe as "sorry looking horses." The road, which roughly paralleled the North Fork of the Merced River, became steeper outside of Coulterville, and the pine forests denser and more magnificent. Thayer enthused about the sheer size of the pines and firs, "four feet, six feet, and even eight or ten feet in diameter and rising, straight as an arrow, two hundred feet or more." He was especially taken with the "alligator skin" of the sugar pine, whose "great smooth stems, having no branches for a great height, were very noble." Emerson, too, was entranced with the scenery, addressing the great trees as "you *gentlemen* pines" and fancying that a mushroom rock was shaped that way because it had indeed once been a mushroom, but one that stank so much that a passing "benevolent demi-god" transformed it into stone to end its misery.

After pausing briefly for water at the house of a Mr. Dexter, originally of Bangor and well known to Maine friends of Thayer, the party stopped to explore Bower Cave, which Bancroft in his guidebook deemed "a picturesque and unique locality . . . well worth a visit." Entered through a large sinkhole that was created when a face of a limestone mountain fell away, the cave proper could be reached only by passing through a wooden door marked "Open Sesame" and then descending a wooden staircase a hundred feet down. Mature maple trees grew up and out into the light from the bottom of the gloomy sinkhole, and a series of benches had been built around their bases. Near the bottom, one of the sheer sides of the cave curved inward, forming a covered space that extended deep into the mountain. A natural auditorium, this area was large enough for church services or, as Bancroft admitted, more often for dances and pic-nics. The floor of the sinkhole was also partially flooded by "a small but singularly beautiful lake, rendered somewhat ghostly and mysterious by the overhanging rocky wall." It could be traversed in "a small boat, in which the imaginative visitor may easily fancy himself crossing the Styx, with himself as his own Charon." Like most limestone caves, Bower had had its share of galleries filled with stalactites and other features, but even in 1871 those had long been despoiled by the "ruthless hand of van-dal visitors" searching for souvenirs. Nevertheless, Thayer was pleased by the detour, thinking the whole thing looked like "a cave and grotto on the stage," and everyone quite enjoyed taking turns paddling the "poor old flat bottomed boat" on the lake, marveling at its "beautiful clearness, green and in the deeper parts of a lovely blue," complete with tame fish that came at a whistle.

At Hazel Green, an altitude of 6,679 feet above sea level, the stage-coaches were left behind, and everyone mounted horses for the remain-der of the trip. They were joined by three guides, one to manage three packhorses and two, one ahead and one behind, to guide the party. At this elevation there were still some patches of snow on the ground in the shadier parts of the forest, and the air was noticeably cooler. Riding for an hour and a half more, mainly downhill, they arrived at Crane Flat late in the afternoon. "A 'Flat,'" Thayer helpfully explained to Sophy, "is a level spot among the hills,—and so 'Dow's Flat' you know among Bret Harte's poems." Here the group was to spend the night at Gobin's Ranch but found the "hotel" ill prepared to receive them. The proprietors were absent in search of supplies, the rooms had yet to be plastered, there were no bedsteads, nor were there any silverware and towels. Nevertheless, the travelers were in good humor and decided to make the best of it. There were plenty of candles and new blankets, and beds were made up on the floors of the unfinished rooms. What's more, the old English cook managed to whip up "a really sumptuous dinner of canned oysters, corn, tomatoes, bread and butter and coffee and tea." The party had brought along a few knives and forks, and others used their "jackknives and soda biscuits to eat with and to scoop out our sugar."

After dinner, the night being cool, Emerson, Thayer, and Wilkie commandeered a room in which to smoke, but when Mrs. Russell came in to chat with Emerson, the two younger men retired to the kitchen, which had a large fire roaring in the hearth and tended by the English cook. Here they lounged in comfort on the cook's bed and finished their cigars, and soon Emerson appeared to finish his own cigar, hailing them all jovially with, "These are the only philosophers!" Sitting down with his shawl wrapped tightly around his shoulders, Emerson was soon deep in conversation with the cook about the Englishman's experiences serving on Panama steamers. "The uses of travel are occasional and short," Emerson had once written, "but the best fruits it finds, when it finds it, is conversation," even if it be in the smoky confines of a rustic California kitchen.

The evening weather started out fine and clear, with a full moon that inspired the myriad frogs in the pond by the hotel to sing for hours. Will Forbes and Holdrege decided it was too nice a night to be cooped up (even by unfinished walls), so they built a large bonfire and bedded down in the open air on what Will described as a "luxurious couch of boughs." It was not destined to be a comfortable night, however: Will had drunk "two strong cups of coffee and one of tea" that kept him awake, and just after midnight, as he was falling asleep, it began to rain, finally driving the two men indoors, now dripping wet. Only the horses, tethered to the trunk of a giant fallen pine, had to weather the worst of the storm.

The next morning, the "solid gray rain" of the night before had settled into drizzle and fog. The party took the opportunity to walk the mile to the Tuolumne Grove of Big Trees, the first giant sequoias anybody in the party had yet seen. Emerson was stunned, remarking that they "had a monster talent for being tall"! The twenty-three big trees in the grove provided only a taste of the vegetable grandeur they would see later on, but the sight was still impressive. It was around eight when the party finally mounted up the pack train to make the last, relatively short push into the Yosemite Valley.

YOSEMITE

The entry on "Yosemite Valley" in *Bancroft's Tourist's Guide* begins simply: "The name is Indian. Pronounce it in four syllables, accenting the second. It means 'Great Grizzly Bear.'" Bancroft then goes on to situate the valley as lying in the very heart of the Sierra Nevada and running nearly east and west for about seven and a half miles along the course of the Merced River. Precipitous walls of granite, capped with spectacular peaks and domes, enclose it, and from these heights, during the spring flood, equally spectacular waterfalls project themselves, their flow crashing to the talus escarpment at the walls' feet and draining into the densely wooded, nearly level valley floor. Although long inhabited by the Miwok, Yosemite was only "discovered" by whites in 1851 when the infamous Mariposa Battalion of the state militia entered the valley, bent on destruction of the Indians. By 1855, the Miwok now decimated and dispossessed, the first tourists were visiting the valley. In 1864, its fame as an unparalleled natural wonder having been spread nationally by newspaper reports, magazine articles, books, and photographs, the valley was preserved by Abraham Lincoln, who turned it over the state of California as a park "for public use, resort, and recreation . . . inalienable for all time." This preservation came none too soon, for with the completion of the transcontinental railroad in 1869, the number of visitors rose from 600 the previous year to 1,122. Still, even by 1871, the journey to the valley was relatively difficult, and as Emerson and his party were soon to find out, the accommodations remained rudimentary at best.

The rest of the day continued to be foggy and drizzly after the Emerson party left Crane Flat, and the mountain air was so cold that all wore heavy shirts and overcoats. Snow still blocked the regular route into the valley; they were forced to take a detour that took them a couple of miles out of their way. Although their guides had told them that the trail would be hard, Thayer thought that, although "the climb and the descent into the valley [was] *good* mountain work," it was "not especially difficult." They did, however, miss several good views of the valley because of the fog, although at the very edge of the valley, the day cleared and they could finally look down into the "immense rocky gorge" for the first time. The scene reminded Thayer of the White Mountain Notch in New Hampshire, "but the vast depth and the grandeur of the great iron-gray cliffs of solid rock was more impressive" in the Yosemite Valley. Indeed, "the valley has a wild untamed look that I hope it would never lose."

The pack train slowly wended its way down a series of switchbacks alongside the Merced River, eventually arriving at the parklike meadow of the valley floor. With John Murray Forbes in the vanguard, the train, according to Thayer, "barring some want of tinsel and splendor," could have been "De Soto and his troop passing along the grassy meadow or under the open grove or over the gravelly plain." Forbes, for his part, was mightily impressed that "the two elder ladies of the party [Mrs. Forbes and Mrs. Russell], who had not been in the saddle before for a great many years, rode without apparent fatigue," likely "due to the extraordinary air and to their entire enjoyment of the grand scenery." At some point, Mrs. Russell did suffer a minor accident when her saddle turned on her, but "she came safely to the ground before any one could rescue her," apparently no worse for wear. Soon the party passed Bridalveil Fall ("a silly name for a beautiful thing," opined Thayer) and Cathedral Rocks. Further on, they could see the "magnificent huge buttress" of El Capitan looming on their left. Crossing a toll bridge over the swift current of the crystal-clear Merced, which, at seventy-five cents a head, Thayer thought excessive, the party arrived at its destination, Leidig's Hotel. It was a quarter past two in the afternoon; they'd been in the saddle a steady six hours.

Leidig's was one of three hotels in the valley at the time, located midway between Black's "Lower" Hotel and Hutchings "Upper" Hotel. George F. Leidig (1839–1902) had arrived in Yosemite with his family in 1866 to manage the Lower Hotel, but he eventually built his own establishment three years later, carefully siting it in the shadow of the seven-thousand-foot Sentinel Rock with a view of Yosemite Falls from its front. At three dollars a night, the hotel was a decidedly primitive affair: two stories with twelve rooms, six on a side, with the upper rooms accessible only by outside stairways that led to a "piazza," or veranda, that ran around three sides of the building. Beds were constructed of slats with mattresses stuffed with pulu, a tree fern produced commercially in Hawaii and imported to California as a cheap form of furniture stuffing. None of the rooms had permanent ceilings but were covered with stretched canvas, which, according to Thayer, meant "we all have to exert our discretion all the time so as not to be heard by everybody else." Leidig himself was absent when the party arrived, but Mrs. Leidig and her brother-in-law, the hotel's clerk, quickly got them all situated in their rooms. The hotel was empty at the time, so the party had its pick:

FIGURE 10. *Sentinel Rock, 3270 ft. high, and Cataract, 3850 ft. high. View from Leidig's Hotel,* photograph by Thomas C. Roche, *Glories of the Yosemite Stereoview No. 153* (NY: E. & H. T. Anthony & Co., 1871). —Author's collection.

Emerson, Mrs. Russell, and Alice Forbes all had single rooms on the first floor front, while the twosomes Mr. and Mrs. Forbes, Sarah Forbes and Annie Anthony, and Will Forbes and Thayer all shared rooms on the second floor front off the piazza. Wilkie and Holdrege, meanwhile, occupied a second-story room on the Sentinel Rock side of the hotel.

It had started to rain hard as soon as they arrived at Leidig's. Some turned in for naps, while others sat on the lower porch. Mrs. Russell tended to Mrs. Leidig's baby while "our sturdy little landlady," as Thayer called her, went about the endless tasks necessary for running an inn in the wilderness. The only members of the party to venture out immediately were Will Forbes and Holdrege, who decided to try to get in some fishing before dinner (unsuccessfully). Exhausted, Thayer himself slept, and when he didn't appear for dinner, Will had to roused him from slumber for the evening meal. Supper was served outdoors under the veranda. The fare was simple—meat, potatoes, and vegetables—but Mrs. Leidig's culinary skills were such that Leidig's was noted for having the best food in the valley, despite its plainness and lack of variety (as one contemporary wag put it, "After traveling a few months in California, a person is liable to think less of variety and more of quality"). Afterward, as was their wont, Emerson, Wilkie, and Thayer indulged in a smoke on the upstairs piazza. The weather having cleared by this time, the three spent the waning hours before bed lazily contemplating the landscape and, as it grew dark, following the course of bright Venus as it dipped slowly and disappeared behind the towering cliff walls opposite the hotel.

TOURING THE VALLEY

Even before breakfast the next day, many of the party were up and about seeing the sights, not wishing to waste a moment of their time in the valley. Thayer hadn't spent a very peaceful night, having been awoken after midnight by a rockslide near Sentinel Rock, and at dawn he found a hen trying to roost in his bed. Despite this, he was still of good cheer, and he spared no detail in describing to Sophy the area immediately around the hotel:

> [Leidig's] stands right under 'Sentinel Rock'; the valley is a mile wide here (so they say, but it doesn't seem so wide) and in front, rises a high enormous wall of rock; at the right (due north) is the Yo Semite Fall, as I said in full sight. The valley here is quite level—like a table—running up each side to these perpendicular

walls; it is made up of gravel, the debris of the mountains and is covered mostly with starveling scatted growth of grass and weeds and small bushes and a thin jungle of trees, oaks, and maples (as they seem) and pines and balsams; some of the pines are noble fellows; at other places there is more grass and meadow. Something at every turn impresses you with the greatness of the objects about you, especially the smallness of your companions as you see them walking about. Evidently, one's senses and instinctive judgments need readjusting here.

What impressed Thayer most was the magnificent Sentinel Rock, which seemed always to command his attention: "It rises straight up into a peak and lifts you ever before; you feel as your eyes rest at the top, something as when you have followed a shooting rocket, that goes higher and higher, when at last it stops and breaks. You will see by the card that I enclose, that this rises 3270 feet above the valley; that means ten Bunker Hill Monuments, on top of another." As for the "great Yo Semite Fall" two miles distant, "it does not seem so large as it is, or as one expects, and yet it is pretty large to the eye. It falls, as you see by the card sixteen hundred feet straight down at its first fall. As you watch the descending sheets of water it takes them long to come down and there is a *crash* now and then in the falls—a shattering sound, like heavy cannon heard at a distance that brings home to one the nature of the drop."

As there was so much to see and process in Yosemite Valley, Bancroft's guidebook strongly recommended that tourists "spend at least two weeks in the valley" because of all places in California, it was the one that demanded "deliberation and leisure." Only then could one "intelligently enjoy and heartily appreciate the least of its wonder" and finally grow to know "the true scale of [its] grandeur." "Even Niagara requires two or three days before one begins to fully realize or truly appreciate its greatness," Bancroft noted, so "how much more, then, Yosemite, compared with which Niagara is but a very little thing!" Bancroft mercilessly lampooned the New York newspaper editor Horace Greeley, who during his visit in 1859 "staid about as long as it would take him to rush off one of his patent chain-lightning, hieroglyphic Tribune editorials. He rode in at midnight, reached his lodging at one o'clock in the morning, too tired to eat, and too sore to tell of it; went to bed, sick, sore and disgusted. Up late next morning, so lame he could hardly sit in his saddle, hobbled hurriedly around three or four hours, and was on his way out again at a little after noon." Not only did Greeley have the effrontery to devote only five pages to the valley in his subsequent 238-page book, *An Overland Journey* (1860), but he even went so far as to suggest that Yosemite Falls was a "humbug." "The soul that can see and feel as little as thine did in Yosemite," concluded Bancroft, "provokes no anger, but only sorrow and compassion." Thomas Starr King, on the other hand, visiting the valley a year later, was duly impressed by everything he saw and pronounced it "the grandest piece of rock-and-water scenery in the world," the natural equivalent of Beethoven's Ninth Symphony. Perhaps this difference in opinion resulted from King's Transcendentalist leanings predisposing him to respond this way, but perhaps it was also because his stay lasted five full days. Emerson and his party, while not budgeting the two weeks called for by Bancroft, at least did King one better: they were to remain for six days.

In addition to Bancroft, the party was also carrying the 1869 edition of Josiah Whitney's *Yosemite Guide-Book,* the best-informed and most comprehensive guide then available. It is even possible that Whitney, holder of the Sturgis-Hooper Chair of Geology at Harvard since 1865, had himself personally brought the volume to Thayer's attention. Hailing from Northampton, Massachusetts, Whitney was the California state geologist from 1860 to 1865, during which time he and his colleagues logged hundreds of miles of arduous travel up and down California (the state's highest peak, Mt. Whitney, was named in his honor). The result of this work were the six massive volumes of the *Geological Survey of California* (1864–70), out of which Whitney distilled a practical and readable guide to the valley covering its history, geography, geology, and flora, as well as carefully naming and describing its most prominent features and laying out a clear itinerary for its exploration by tourists. The book also contained an excellent foldout map, making it easy to orient oneself amid the various landmarks and natural splendors. Given Thayer's letters from the valley and later quotations in his *Western Journey* from the *Yosemite Guide-Book,* he clearly found the book indispensable.

The day after they arrived, Saturday, May 6, Emerson and most of the rest of the party set off on horseback to Mirror Lake, a journey of several miles up Tenaya Creek. As they rode, Emerson conversed with Mrs. Forbes, and together they recited snatches of Sir Walter Scott back and forth, with Thayer trailing behind, listening intently. The group approached Mirror Lake by way of a "broad grassy meadow, the soil rich and black," which led Thayer to speculate that this was the vantage point from which Bierstadt created his famous 1864 painting of the scene. Unfortunately, the party arrived too late to get the full effect of the mirroring of Mt. Watkins and the northwest face of Half Dome, since after a certain hour the mountain winds unsettled the lake's surface. Despite their disappointment, it was still a "magnificent array of hills on each hand." Half Dome, especially, with its sheer face rising some 5,000 feet mesmerized the group, and Thayer was fascinated by the way streams of water flowed over the precipitous sides of canyon walls. "Sometimes they would drop over a shelf of rock and disperse in a vapor before they found the Earth," he wrote, "and in one place a sheet of water or a broad ribbon or a succession of threads came falling down in this way and was blown away as if it were the puffing of a frosty breath; and yet this does not describe the gentle pretty wavering of it, this way and that, and the slow decent of some of the delicate veil upon the rock below." While most of the party idled on the shores of Mirror Lake, Will Forbes and Thayer ventured up the canyon even further, hoping to reach another waterfall, but it was too far, and they had to content themselves with the changing aspects of the swift flowing Merced. Arriving back at the lake, they found Emerson waxing enthusiastic about all he saw: "This valley is the only place that comes up to the brag about it, and exceeds it!" he exclaimed.

Back at the hotel in the afternoon, Emerson, Wilkie, and Thayer paced off a "prostrate Sugar Pine," and according to Emerson's notes, they estimated its height when living at 210 feet. Thayer told Sophy that these "are not the 'Big Trees'" —"only the common trees of the country." Another oddity noted by the three was the way the local woodpeckers "riddle the bark of the pines here, making it look just like the top of [a] thimble, and then stuff an acorn in each hole." Emerson was skeptical that the birds actually used the holes in this way and insisted that it was the squirrels that made use of the holes for storage. The debate continued on back and forth, as the three climbed up the talus slope behind Leidig's Hotel to indulge in their afternoon smoke.

The next morning, both Wilkie's and Emerson's colds had flared up again, and Thayer privately groused to Sophy that he wished the women of the party would look after Emerson more: "I wish the chiefs of our party had something more of your thoughtfulness. There are twenty ways in which he could be made more comfortable every day without knowing it. Will looks after him a great deal but he is not a woman" (Emerson himself, of course, was not complaining: "there is one topic peremptorily forbidden to all well-bred," he had opined in his essay "Behavior," "namely, their distempers"). That day's excursion would take the party eight miles up the Main Fork of the Merced River, which, unlike the Tenaya Fork, rose in a series of steps, making for two sets of waterfalls, the Vernal and Nevada Falls. Both were spectacular and their tops accessible. Wilkie decided to stay behind at Leidig's to nurse his cold, but Emerson, fain to miss any of the sights of the valley, set off with the rest on horseback at 8:30. They rode through a lush meadow past Hutchings' Hotel, admiring the Royal Arches and North Dome across the valley. At some point, Mr. Forbes's horse slipped while crossing a stream, and he couldn't keep himself in the saddle, in part because his right arm was in sling due to a sprain suffered in a riding accident back home. In he went, soaking his only suit of clothes. He debated returning to the hotel to change, but the day was too fine to turn back now, so he pressed on with the party and dried out in the saddle.

Curving southeast around Glacier Point through a dense forest, the party was rewarded by the perpetual rainbow at the base of Vernal Fall. Here, at Register Rock, they tied up the horses and stared in silence at the way the Merced River came "pouring straight over the rock in a beautiful broad mass of foam," falling thence in "fleecy lines." This reminded Thayer of lines from Longfellow's "Wreck of the Hesperus"—"She stuck where the white and fleecy waves / Looked *soft as carded wool*"—which he quoted to Emerson, who nodded with approval and repeated them to himself over and over for the rest of the day.

With the women on horseback and the men on foot, there came a long, steep climb up to the foot of Nevada Fall by means of what Will Forbes described as "a zig zag trail as steep as can be made for horses," which as a rule were ridden for only three minutes at a stretch and then rested. Reaching the top, they were surprised to find the new and as yet unpainted hotel of transplanted Vermonter F. Albert Snow, called La Casa Nevada. The party stopped for lunch, served by Albert's wife, Emily, "a real kind, genuine Yankee up country woman, who knows how to feed you well and to talk real Yankee," Thayer enthused. After a dessert of apple pie and doughnuts, Emerson and some of the group wandered over to the foot of Nevada Fall to luxuriate in its spray and marvel at the complete rainbow that emerged there. Thayer noticed that halfway up the falls there was an outcrop of rock, sending the foaming water shooting out "like rockets, with a head and a long tail," which for some reason reminded him of the horses in a painting by William Morris Hunt called *The Horses of Anahita, Persian Goddess of the Moon*, although he admitted that the association was rather fanciful.

Now wet with spray, Emerson and Thayer parked themselves in the sun on the porch of La Casa Nevada and smoked, while Sarah Forbes sat near and listened, soaking up their learned chatter. With Nevada Fall thundering in the background, Thayer attempted to convince Emerson of the fineness of the Italian character, especially when it came to their feelings about women. Emerson was dubious, and when Thayer quoted Dante on the subject, Emerson replied, "'Yes, oh yes, Dante,' . . . as if he were exceptional, and not to be counted." Undaunted, Thayer rattled off Ruffini, Michelangelo, Vittoria Colonna, and Tasso, to which Emerson did admit that he enjoyed Madame Arconati and Alessandro Manzoni but drew the line at Machiavelli: "'Machiavelli,' he said, in his slow, paus-ing way, 'wrote—like—the Devil; uttering his devilish sentiments with so much sweetness and coolness,—as if they were all summer air!'" Finally, signaling his overall lack of sympathy with the Italian authors, Emerson, as he often did, brought Goethe into the conversation, citing the German author's "maxim of a literary man": "Spend not a moment's time with people to whom you do not belong and who do not belong to you."

A little after three o'clock, most of the party gathered to leave, and on the trail down, they stopped to peer over the ledge of Vernal Fall and watch the sheet of milky white water roll effortlessly into space, trans-forming itself into "fleecy sheets and folds" and giving off "clouds of delicate mist . . . like the vapor of silver." Emerson had once written in "The Method of Nature" that "the wholeness we admire in the order of the world, is the result of infinite distribution. Its smoothness is the smoothness of the pitch of a cataract. Its permanence is in perpetual inchoation," a perfect description of the action of the fall. Meanwhile, George Holdrege, who had met a young German guide named Hickman at La Casa Nevada, convinced Will Forbes to join them on a climb of the Liberty Cap, a nearby 1,700-foot peak so named, it was said, because

California governor Leland Stanford thought it looked like the liberty cap then featured on the American half-dollar. Despite having packed only a single pair of pants, Forbes decided to risk it and go, much to Emerson's consternation: "Why will those madcap boys do that? And what is the use of *teasing* the mind? It can only receive a certain number of impressions"! Undeterred by his protests, Forbes, Holdrege, and Hickman "had some stiff work getting up," according to Will, who "found his wind rather inadequate for the occasion." Nevertheless, in an hour and twenty minutes, the three found themselves at the top of the peak. As he feared, Will had indeed ruined his pants, "but from the top we saw enough to make us glad of the trip." Returning at a run to the La Casa Nevada in half the time they took to climb up, and stopping long enough to accept a "treat of ale from the landlord who seemed to be much pleased with our performance," Forbes and Holdrege "overhauled" the rest of the party, probably much to Emerson's relief, and all returned in good time for tea back at Leidig's Hotel.

All in all, Emerson had greatly enjoyed their Sunday outing to Vernal and Nevada Falls, and Thayer recorded that on the ride back to Leidig's, he had said "with quiet happiness" that "this we must call the *Lord's day*: we seldom read such leaves in the Bible." And indeed, later that evening, Emerson would pencil into his notebook that it had been "a day of wonders ... our best day yet." Earlier, back at the Casa Nevada, talking with Thayer, Emerson had quoted Goethe's tomb inscription, which he had cited in his lecture "Immortality": "Think on Living." Apparently, being in Yosemite made this easy to do.

JAMES MASON HUTCHINGS

Thoroughly tired by their expedition, Mr. and Mrs. Forbes and Sarah decided to rest at the hotel the next day, while Wilkie, disappointed he missed the trip to Vernal and Nevada Falls, would hire a guide and make the trip himself. The rest, Emerson included, would be lured back to Mirror Lake, anxious to try again to catch the landscape's magnificent but elusive reflection on the water's surface.

Woken the next day by the singing of robins near the hotel, the party assembled very early for breakfast, which, much to Emerson's delight, included pie, his favorite breakfast food. As Oliver Wendell Holmes Sr.

would later write, "Emerson's mode of living was very simple: coffee in the morning, tea in the evening, animal food by choice only once a day, wine only when with others using it, but always *pie* at breakfast." It wasn't everyone's favorite so early in the morning, however, and as Emerson offered an extra slice of one of Mrs. Leidig's pies around the table, everyone declined, including Mr. Forbes. "'But Mr. Forbes!' Mr. Emerson remonstrated, with humorous emphasis, thrusting the knife under a piece of the pie, and putting the entire weight of his character into his manner,—'but Mr. Forbes, *what is pie for?*'"

Soon after breakfast, all those who wished to go were mounted up for the ride back up Tenaya Canyon. The early morning ride was much to Emerson's enjoyment. "One thinks here of the Arab proverb, 'Allah does not count the days spent in the chase,'" he said to Thayer as they cantered along. As they arrived at the lakeshore at eight thirty, with the sun still behind Half Dome, the wind was just beginning to rise, but "still we saw fine effects": "The inverted cañon looked [like] the opening of a great cave out of which we were looking. By getting round under the South Dome and poking your head out and looking back at the water near the line of the shore, one saw the upper edge of that superb wall and it was like magic to see the increasing light and then the blaze of the sun as it rose *under your feet* above the line of the mountains, and all in an inch or two of water with a muddy bottom." From such sights, "One saw where fables of caves of sea nymphs and ocean gods might come from."

At this point, the younger members of the group wanted to keep going and explore the canyon further up, but it was clear to Thayer that Emerson was eager to return, so they headed back toward Leidig's Hotel. Along the way, after crossing two bridges over the Merced, Emerson and Thayer stopped at the tent of an itinerant photographer to buy some "views" as souvenirs. The photographer turned out to be Thomas C. Roche, who was in the valley taking photos for his immensely popular series of stereograph cards, "The Glories of Yosemite," published by the E. & H. T. Anthony & Co. of New York. Apparently Roche recognized Emerson and made him a present of six of his best, and later Emerson would also buy two more photographs from J. J. Reilly, another noted photographer, who maintained a studio in the valley. The two decided on a whim to ride over and inspect more closely the crashing waters at the base of Yosemite Falls, which was nearby Roche's tent. The falls were an especially favorite subject for photographers, despite Bancroft's claim that "not even the photogram itself can reproduce one tithe the grandeur here enthroned." Happily drenched by its spray as they gazed upward, watching the wind whip the water into "foam and vapor," Thayer had a hard time convincing Emerson that these lower falls were some six hundred feet high—such were the impossibilities of scale in the valley. Of course, as Bancroft wisely counseled, "When a man is overwhelmed with the sublime, don't plunge him into statistics," but Thayer kept at it to no avail. Whether it be woodpecker holes or the heights of waterfalls, there were some facts of nature Emerson was not prepared to accept based on perception alone.

Continuing on to Leidig's, Thayer stopped by Hutchings' House Hotel to lay in a supply of fresh cigars. James Mason Hutchings (1820–1902), who would become one of the leading, if controversial figures in Yosemite's history, had owned and operated his hotel since 1864. English by birth, he had been attracted to California by the gold rush, but his mining days were brief, and he went on to greater success as a journalist. Having heard from members of the Mariposa Battalion that a waterfall of fabulous height could be found in the Sierra, Hutchings hired two guides and entered the valley in 1855. He was overwhelmed by what he saw, and his articles about the valley in the San Francisco newspapers were so popular that he created *Hutchings' California Magazine* to publicize the natural wonders of Yosemite. The magazine ran for sixty issues between 1856 and 1861 and has the distinction of carrying the first published pictures of Yosemite Valley. Entrepreneurial by nature, Hutchings saw potential in operating a good hotel in the valley, so he relocated his family there and slowly built Hutchings' House into a going concern (it is reported that what success the place had was due to the iron administration of his mother-in-law, Florantha T. Sproat, whom the sources invariably describe as "no nonsense"). Unfortunately for Hutchings, when Lincoln signed into law the act making Yosemite a park, his claim to his property was called into question. As Emerson had famously observed in *Nature*, even with deeds and warrants of sale, no one really "owns the landscape," and that would be especially true in the case of a national park. Nevertheless, Hutchings spent the next decade making himself unpopular by his uncompromising fight to retain his Yosemite land.

Despite his ongoing legal troubles, Hutchings remained a gregarious and genial host, with a fund of Yosemite stories that tourists found irresistible. Hearing that Ralph Waldo Emerson was idling outside his hotel waiting for his companion, Hutchings, who knew Emerson's works well, insisted that the pair stay for a while. He produced some wine and cake for their refreshment and gave Emerson an immense Sugar Pine cone as a souvenir. He also regaled them with the lore of the once indigenous Miwok Indians that Emerson found fascinating, especially about their diet of "dried grubs and the chrysalis of flies" and the mush of acorns, the laborious preparation of which Hutchings was only too happy to describe at great length. Such a coup was it to have Ralph Waldo Emerson at his hotel that in later years Hutchings put it about that the great man had actually been a guest at Hutchings' House and not Leidig's.

AN EVENING COLLOQUY

After dinner that night, Thayer noted that "several of us sat on the shady side of the house and smoked and I had a charming talk with Mr. Emerson." Literary themes were on Emerson's mind as usual, and he talked about the Elizabethan poet Fulke Greville, the biographer of Philip Sidney; about Boccaccio, who, despite Thayer's objection to the *Decameron*'s "excessive coarseness," Emerson defended because of his faithfulness to "Italian life and manners" (a reversal from the morning); and about the poetry of George MacDonald, a Scot who would later be better known for his fantasy stories. Emerson interjected here a funny story about a Harvard undergraduate from Concord named Henry Joel Walcott, who had recently asked Emerson if he had met Spinoza on his travels to Europe, to which Emerson replied that he did not since "Spinoza must now be pretty old, since he was born in 1632." At this point, Thayer rather insensitively asked why he had named his late lecture series at Harvard "The Natural History of the Intellect." Apparently unfazed, Emerson replied that it wasn't because he was interested in metaphysics and for that matter thought that Harvard's resident metaphysician, Francis Bowen, was "a mere block." Rather, "he thought that as a man grows he observes certain facts about his own mind,—about memory, for example. These he had set down from time to time." This is what he wished to express in his Harvard lectures. The mention of memory then triggered an anecdote that Thayer recalled from Emerson's lecture "Memory." As a young man, Emerson had gone to Charleston by boat, and to while away the time, he surprised himself to find that he could recall all the lines of Milton's poem, "Lycidas." "'What a range ... memory gives to a man,'" Emerson concluded, "'so small a creature!'"

By now it was nine and the sun had set and the air was beginning to cool rapidly as it does at such elevations. It had been an eventful three days in the valley, yet there was more to explore and more people to meet. Indeed, as Thayer rather coyly recorded in *A Western Journey*, "That evening (Monday) there came an admiring, enthusiastic letter for Mr. Emerson from M., a young man living in the valley, and tending a sawmill there. He was a Scotchman by birth, who had come to this country at the age of eleven, and was a graduate at Madison University, in Wisconsin. Some friends near San Francisco had written him that Mr. Emerson was coming, and they had also told Mr. Emerson about him. He had read Mr. Emerson's books, but had never seen him, and wrote now with enthusiasm, wishing for an opportunity to come to him." With such an enthusiastic invitation in hand, Emerson and Thayer quickly decided that the first thing they would do next morning was to pay a visit to "M."

Chapter 6
THE MARIPOSA BIG TREES
(MAY 9 TO MAY 15, 1871)

The greatest wonder is that we can see these trees and not wonder more.

—Ralph Waldo Emerson, quoted in J. B. Thayer, *A Western Journey with Mr. Emerson* (1884)

"M" was John Muir (1838–1914), although at this point the thirty-three-year-old Scot was still a rather callow youth, and it would be a long time before he achieved national fame. Muir had been herding sheep in the Sierra when he was hired in 1869 by James Mason Hutchings to build and operate a sawmill in Yosemite Valley (using only fallen trees, we are told). A mechanical genius, Muir soon had the mill up and running, leaving him plenty of free time to do the botany he so enjoyed. He also guided tourists through the valley and indulged his interest in geological exploration in the backcountry, looking for examples of glaciation. As Muir himself put it in his typical high-flown Victorian language, "I was then living in Yosemite Valley as a convenient and grand vestibule of the Sierra from which I could make excursions into the adjacent mountains."

Born in Dunbar, Scotland, John Muir had immigrated with his family in 1849 to a farm outside Portage, Wisconsin. Muir's father was a puritanical evangelical and harsh disciplinarian, so John's childhood was one of unremitting work and not a little privation. Nevertheless, he was a determined autodidact, reading widely, and as a budding naturalist, he was attuned to the changing seasons of the Wisconsin countryside. Muir was also a talented inventor, and when he took some of his inventions to the Wisconsin State Fair in Madison in 1860, he also enrolled in the University of Wisconsin. He studied there for three years before leaving to avoid the Civil War draft. Wandering for a time in Canada, where he botanized extensively in Ontario, he eventually returned to the United States to take a job in a carriage factory in Indianapolis. Here, in 1867, he suffered an eye injury that left him temporarily blind. When he'd recovered sufficiently, he decided never again to be cooped up in a factory and chose to develop his vocation as a naturalist. Doing so entailed a thousand-mile walk to the Gulf of Mexico, where he planned to take ship to Brazil and discover the headwaters of the Amazon. A

FIGURE 11. *John Muir,* photograph by Carleton Watkins, San Francisco, ca. 1875. —Courtesy of the John Muir Papers, Holt-Atherton Special Collections and Archives, University of the Pacific Library. © 1984 Muir Hanna Trust.

near-fatal bout with a tropical fever dissuaded him of this goal, so he instead set his sights on California, arriving in San Francisco by Panama steamer in 1868. Spending as little time in the city as possible, Muir headed for the interior of the state, first catching sight of the Sierra from atop Pacheco Pass at the southern end of Santa Clara Valley. His first view of this "luminous wall of the mountains," as he was to write later, was an epiphany: "Then it seemed to me the Sierra should be called not the Nevada, or Snowy Range, but the Range of Light," as it was "the most divinely beautiful of all the mountain chains I have ever seen." From then on, the Sierra Nevada would always be Muir's spiritual home.

Both Muir and Emerson were apprised of the presence of the other in the valley by letters from Jeanne Carr (1825–1903). She knew Muir from his student days at the University of Wisconsin and Emerson from his periodic visits to the Madison Lyceum. Now living in Oakland, Carr had written to Emerson in San Francisco, telling him that if he journeyed to Yosemite (which she knew he must), he should be on the lookout for the young Scotsman as someone to meet. She had already sent a letter to Muir on Monday, May 1: "I am feeling as glad for you as possible since Mr. Emerson will be in the Valley in a few days—and in your hands I hope and trust, the dear old singer of places where we have sung his song. I have not seen him yet, but shall after his return. Have been so driven with work and company no spiritual influence could be felt. Else I could have gone straight to him with my eyes shut." Even before receiving Carr's letter, however, Muir had already "heard the hotel people say with solemn emphasis, Emerson is here." This electrified Muir, who had read some of Emerson's writings and learned even more about the "Sage of Concord" from Mrs. Carr, who knew his entire oeuvre. "I was as excited as I had never been excited before," he wrote long after the event, "and my heart throbbed as if an angel direct from heaven had alighted on the Sierran rocks. But so great was my awe and reverence, I did not dare go to him or speak to him. I hovered on the outside of the crowd of people that were pressing forward to be introduced to him and shaking hands with him." Then, the day Carr's letter arrived on May 8, Muir learned that Emerson was to be off in a few days, so "in the course of sheer desperation I wrote him a note and carried it to his hotel":

YOSEMITE VALLEY,
Monday night

MR. R. W. EMERSON

Dear Sir

I received today a letter from Mrs. Professor Ezra Carr of Oakland, California stating that you were in the Valley and that she
expected to see you on your return. Also she promised that she
would write you here and send you to me. I was delighted at the
thought of meeting you but have just learned that you contem-
plate leaving the Valley in a day or two.

Now Mr. Emerson I do most cordially protest against your
going away so soon, and so also I am sure do all your instincts
and affinities. I trust that you will not "outweary their yearn-
ings." Do not thus drift away with the mob while the Spirits of
these rocks and waters hail you after long waiting as their kins-
man and persuade you to closer communion.

But now if fate or one of those mongrel and misshapen organizations called parties compel you to leave for the present, I
shall hope for some other fullness of time to come for you.

If you will call at Mr. Hutchings' mill I will give you as many
of Yosemite and high Sierra plants as you wish as specimens. I
invite you [to] join me in a months worship with Nature in the
high temples of the great Sierra crown beyond our holy Yosemite. It will cost you nothing save the time and very little of that
for you will be mostly in Eternity.

And now once more, in the name of Mounts Dana and
Gibbs[,] of the grand glacial hieroglyphics of Tuolumne Meadows and Bloody canyon, in the name of a hundred glacial lakes
of a hundred glacial daisy gentian meadows. In the name of a
hundred cascades that barbarous visitors never see. In the name
of the grand upper forests of *Picea amabilis* and *P. grandis*, and
in the name of all the spirit creatures of these rocks and of this
whole spiritual atmosphere. Do not leave us *now*.

> With most
> cordial regards
> I am yours
> in Nature,
>
> *John Muir*

The next morning, as they agreed, Thayer accompanied Emerson to Hutchings' mill to meet this John Muir. They mounted their horses— Emerson's a roan-and-white mustang and Thayer's a gray—and sauntered over, finding Muir alone, operating the mill. Thayer recognized Muir as the man who delivered the previous night's letter, which led Emerson to exclaim, "Why did you not make yourself known last evening? I should have been very glad to have seen you." Both men dismounted, and Muir ushered them into the mill. "He is a simple unaffected young fellow of real intelligence," wrote Thayer to Sophy, "a botanist mainly, who studied a year or two at Madison and then started for the south, 'zigzagging his way to the Gulf of Mexico' and got over to Cuba and then found this valley and has 'got entangled' here, in love with the mountains and the flowers, and doesn't know when he shall get away." Muir also told them of his days as a shepherd tending flocks of twenty-five hundred sheep and his monthlong rambles in the high country, and he "urged Mr. Emerson, with amusing zeal, to stay and go off with him on such a trip." As Muir later remembered it, "forgetting his age, plans, duties, ties of every sort, I proposed an immeasurable camping trip back in the heart of the mountains. He seemed anxious to go, but considerately mentioned his party. I said: 'Never mind. The mountains are calling; run away, and let plans and parties and dragging lowland duties all "gang tapsal-teerie." We'll go up a cañon singing your own song, "Good-by, proud world! I'm going home," in divine earnest. Up there lies a new heaven and a new earth; let us go to the show.'" At this bit of hyperbole, Emerson probably smiled and left it to Thayer to deflect the suggestion.

Despite the rebuff, Muir soon invited both men to his room and study, which "was a little rookery at one end of the saw mill." Muir described it as "not easy of access, being reached only by a series of sloping planks roughened by slats like a hen ladder." He called this room his "hang nest," well named as his sketch of it shows a rectangular structure projecting out from the west-end gable of the sawmill, high above the ground and seemingly unsupported from below. Apparently some thought the place unsafe, but "fortunately," Muir said with a wink, "only people I dislike are afraid to enter it." For those who did enter, however, the "hang nest" afforded views of Half Dome through a hole in one side of the roof and Yosemite Falls through a skylight on the other, as well as a magnificent view of the entire Valley through a window in the back wall.

Perhaps needless to say, the interior of the "hang nest" was cramped—Muir's bunk was suspended from the mill's protruding ridgepole and could be entered only by climbing the projections of a stout tree branch placed there for the purpose. Emerson and Thayer were thus forced to sit cross-legged on the floor. Yet the room was warm from the sun and smelled strongly of pinesap from the logs being cut below. Emerson, who shared a "cat-like love of garrets," must have felt right at home. Muir enthusiastically showed Emerson "hundreds of capital pencil sketches of the mountain peaks and the forest trees hereabouts, giving us all their botanical names and talking extremely well about them." He also brought out his entire collection of dried plants for inspection, discoursing about their properties and peculiarities, much to the delight of Emerson, who interrogated Muir closely. "All these treasures he poured out before Mr. Emerson and begged him to accept them," but Emerson demurred, although he did accept several stereographs of the valley from Muir. He also promised to bring others of the party to meet him before they left the valley.

That afternoon, good to his word, Emerson brought John Murray Forbes over to meet Muir, who reciprocated by visiting the party at Leidig's that night. The following day, Thayer and Holdrege made the pilgrimage to Hutchings' Mill for more conversation with Muir, soon to be joined by Emerson and Will Forbes. "We all like him exceedingly," wrote Thayer, and indeed, Muir exuded an infectious charisma that seemed to draw everyone to him like a magnet. When, for example, the English novelist, Thérèse Yelverton, Viscountess Avonmore (ca. 1833–81), had visited the valley the year before, she hired Muir as a guide. Within days, she was smitten and importuned him to run away with her to Asia as her personal secretary, but Muir beat a hasty retreat to the high country instead. Subsequently, as Yelverton was leaving the Valley, she managed to get lost and lose her horse during a snowstorm, and she had to be rescued the next day not by Muir but by Leidig. Nevertheless, when Yelverton published her experiences of the valley in the novel *Zanita: A Tale of Yo-Semite* (1872), she chose as her romantic hero not the hotelier but a wild-haired mountaineer named Kenmuir, whom she made to bear more than a passing resemblance to John Muir, right down to his physical appearance and loquacious sermonizing about nature—a portrayal Muir found both flattering and embarrassing at the same time. Although an extreme example, it is but one of both men and women falling hard for Muir's natural charm.

During their last day in Yosemite, Wednesday, May 10, most of the Emerson party stayed on the valley floor, taking it easy in preparation for the next day's long ride to the Mariposa Big Trees. Restless as usual, Thayer, Will Forbes, Holdrege, and Wilkie James all decided to strike out for Inspiration Point, a granite ledge up on the south canyon wall where one could get a wide-angled view of the valley. Despite rumors of snow, the four decided to risk it, as Thayer did not want to "miss that noble cliff, so meanly denominated 'Inspiration Point.'" Setting out about half past one in the afternoon, they followed a path on the south side of the swiftly flowing "sea-green" Merced River, which took them under Cathedral Rocks, "like a Norman Castle, vast and worthy of an almighty builder," and to the base of Bridalveil Fall, which again Thayer measured in units of Bunker Hill Monuments (three in this case). They were gratified to see that "a broad belt of rainbow lay right across it, seeming to pass into the substance of the fall, and wavering in the exquisite silver tissue of delicate vapor along its sides." The water as it fell seemed unsubstantial when blown about by the wind—"truly like a white veil," Thayer was forced to admit—but nevertheless coming down with "a great crash into the basin of rock below." From there, the four riders mounted a switchback trail for "a good stiff climb" to Inspiration Point. Here, they were "rewarded with superb views": "We looked up through the length of the valley, set like a jewel among these magnificent heights. A little grassy plain it seemed, excessively narrow, with a slender stream winding through it, and little trees dotted about. And yet we knew what trees these were, and recalled that we had paced one of them,—a pine that had fallen near the hotel,—and found it nearly two hundred and twenty feet long. We were up above the valley walls now, and looked along their tops, and saw the high country behind them, with its still ascending mountain peaks, and the swiftly falling valleys along which the waters ran that poured over into the gorge below." Of course, a literary allusion instantly came to Thayer: the whole magnificent scene reminded him of Bunyan's "Delectable Mountains." They returned to Leidig's late in the afternoon, well satisfied with the excursion.

LEAVING THE VALLEY

After six days on the valley floor, it was time for the party to depart back to San Francisco. Instead of leaving the way they came, the plan was to follow the Mariposa Route, which would take them south by thirty miles so as to take in the Mariposa Big Trees—all except Will Forbes and Wilkie, who, wishing to return to the city earlier, would take the shorter Coulterville Route out of the valley. On a whim, Emerson, who was much taken by John Muir, asked him to join their expedition to the Big Trees, to which Muir replied, "I'll go, Mr. Emerson, if you will promise to camp with me in the grove. I'll build a glorious camp-fire, and the great brown boles of the giant sequoias will be most impressively lighted up, and the night will be glorious." "At this," Muir recalled, Emerson "became enthusiastic like a boy, his sweet perennial smile became still deeper and sweeter, and he said, 'Yes, yes, we will camp out, camp out.'" With the promise made and Muir now in tow, the pack train left Leidig's Hotel a little before seven in the morning and wended its way along the Merced and then up the steep Mariposa Trail out of Yosemite Valley.

"The trail was quite as hard as the trail by which we came in," Thayer reported, but it was completely clear of snow, and the horses made good progress through "open pine groves and up and down hills and across small streams." Unlike the trek into the valley, the forest that day "was noble and full of sunshine." Thayer was amused by how Emerson engaged Muir during parts of the ride, speaking to him "like a father" and quizzing him on his literary tastes, which, as it turned out, favored the recently deceased American poet Alice Cary over Byron, indicating to Thayer that when it came to the area of literature, Muir was "not strong." Emerson, for his part, heartily recommended William Cullen Bryant, who with "a cold, clear eye . . . has a right to talk about trees and Nature." Muir, too, remembered that journey vividly: "We rode through the magnificent forests of the Merced basin, and I kept calling his attention to the sugar pines, quoting [Emerson's poem 'Woodnotes'], 'Come listen what the pine tree saith,' etc., pointing out the noblest as kings and high priests, the most eloquent and commanding preachers of all the mountain forests, stretching forth their century-old arms in benediction over the worshiping congregations crowded about them. He gazed in devout admiration, saying but little, while his fine smile faded away." Indeed, at certain points, Emerson almost seemed to be in a trance as he rode through the Sierra forest. John Murray Forbes noticed that "once, when riding down the steep side of a mountain," Emerson's "reins [were] hanging loose, the bit entirely out of the horse's mouth, without his being aware that this was an unusual method of riding Pegasus, so fixed was his gaze into space, and so unconscious was he, at the moment, of his surroundings."

Around noon, the party stopped to picnic under the pines, and after a pleasant lunch, the group idled for a while. Mrs. Russell took a nap on a bed of pine needles, while Thayer lounged on the ground and smoked. Emerson, also reclining on the ground with a cigar in hand, conversed with Mr. and Mrs. Forbes about some lines from Sir Walter Scott, which somehow led him to reminisce a bit about his school days at Harvard. Later, Sarah Forbes would remark with wonder, "How *can* Mr. Emerson be so agreeable all the time without getting tired!" "It was the *naïve* expression of what we all had felt," Thayer would write years later in *A Western Journey*. Casting back to that idyllic spring day, Thayer mused that "there was never a more agreeable travelling-companion; he was always accessible, cheerful, sympathetic, considerate, tolerant; and there was always that same respectful interest in those with whom he talked, even the humblest, which raised them in their own estimation." Putting a metaphysical spin on it, Thayer attributed Emerson's behavior to the fact that he "really *believed* in an immortal life, and had adjusted his conduct accordingly; so that, beautiful and grand as the natural objects were, among which our journey lay, they were matched by the sweet elevation of character and the spiritual charm of our gracious friend."

THE MARIPOSA BIG TREES

Tired but happy, the party arrived at Clark's Station a little before six. Their intention was to get rooms at Clark's Hotel for the night and then visit the sequoias, six or seven miles further on, the next morning. Muir, expecting Emerson to honor his promise to camp out that night, was much annoyed by this: hadn't Emerson's paean to the footloose natural-ist, "Woodnotes," celebrated the fact that "Where darkness found him he lay glad at night; There the red morning touched him with its light"? Many years later, Muir recalled that he "was surprised to see the party dismount [at Clark's]."

And when I asked if we were not going up into the grove to camp they said: "No; it would never do to lie out in the night air. Mr. Emerson might take cold; and you know, Mr. Muir, that would be a dreadful thing." In vain I urged, that only in homes and hotels were colds caught, that nobody ever was known to take cold camping in these woods, that there was not a single cough or sneeze in all the Sierra. Then I pictured the big climate-changing, inspiring fire I would make, praised the beauty and fragrance of sequoia flame, told how the great trees would stand about us transfigured in the purple light, while the stars looked down between the great domes; ending by urging them to come on and make an immortal Emerson night of it. But the house habit was not to be overcome, nor the strange dread of pure night air, though it is only cooled day air with a little dew in it. So the carpet dust and unknowable reeks were preferred.

"And to think of this being a Boston choice!" he added sourly. "Sad commentary on culture and the glorious transcendentalism." In a fit of pique, Muir almost rode off to camp among the Big Trees alone, "but since Emerson was so soon to vanish, I concluded to stop with them."

As it was, they may have indeed been more comfortable camping out in the grove, as Clark's Hotel, a "plain country tavern," "was already full up." A photo from the time shows the hotel to have been a long, single-story wood building, obviously built in several sections over the years and joined together by a single long porch covered by the projecting eaves of three different rooflines. The interior, as described by Thayer, was just as rudimentary, with a large common dormitory from which branched smaller rooms with curtains for doors. Thayer was horrified to learn that he had been assigned to share a bed with Emerson that night, which was unthinkable given Emerson's stature and age, so he elected to sleep on one of the cots in the dormitory along with Holdrege and Muir, a sacrifice not made in vain, since Emerson thanked him the next morning for the gift of such a good night's sleep. Once all were settled in and after a hearty meal served in the communal dining room, Emerson and Thayer repaired to chairs in front of one of the hotel's "great stone fireplaces," so large as to accommodate logs up the three feet long. In front of a roaring fire, a welcome indulgence because of the cool night air, the two smoked their customary cigars and chatted with Muir, who remembered that Emerson "hardly spoke a word all evening, yet it was a great pleasure simply to be near him, warming in the light of his face as at a fire." Soon other hotel guests, whom Emerson and Thayer just happened to know from Lynn, Massachusetts, joined them before the hearth, as did another transplanted New Englander, mine host Galen Clark (1814–1910).

Born on a farm in New Hampshire, Galen Clark had knocked about a bit as a young man, working as a farmhand in his native state, a chair maker and painter in Philadelphia and New York—and even a stint in the Missouri State Militia as a soldier fighting against Brigham Young during the Mormon War of 1838. Attracted by tales of California gold, Clark headed west in 1853, ending up in Mariposa County working as a miner and a surveyor. Four years later he settled on the south fork of the Merced River, building there what came to be called Clark's Station and his celebrated hotel. That same year, based on information related to him by the local Miwok Indians, Clark and his friend Milton Mann "discovered" the nearby Mariposa Big Trees, a substantial grove covering four square miles and consisting of some six hundred specimens of *Sequoiadendron giganteum*, including the massive "Grizzly Giant," the oldest and largest tree then known on the continent.

Partly due to Clark's promotional efforts, when Congress deeded Yosemite to the state of California in 1864, the Mariposa Big Trees were included in the grant as part of the park, and Clark was first made one of the park's commissioners. Two years later, he was named the park's resident "guardian." Clark was a savvy entrepreneur and had long recognized that his station, halfway between Yosemite and the Big Trees, was the ideal stopping point for visitors plying the Mariposa Route. He therefore supplemented his state wages by becoming hotelier, provisioner, and guide to the growing number of tourists venturing into the Sierra to see the Yosemite Grant. Indeed, with his wealth of knowledge about the mountains' flora and fauna, his great fund of Indian lore, not to mention his naturally gregarious personality, Galen Clark soon found himself a popular tourist attraction, exactly the kind of loquacious person Emerson loved to sit back and listen to while puffing his cigar. Emerson, in fact, may have already heard tales about Clark because two of Clark's brothers were Unitarian ministers in Massachusetts—either way, he was looking forward to the meeting. Emerson was not disappointed. Photos of Clark show him as something of a wild-haired mountain man, which must have reminded Emerson of the bear-fighting California hunter George Nidiver, immortalized in the poem prefacing his essay "Courage." The two men hit it off instantly, with Clark agreeing to personally guide Emerson's party to the big trees the next day, *"honoris causa."*

At eight the next morning, which was pleasantly sunny, Clark left his hotel in the charge of his Harvard-educated son, Alonzo, and led the Emerson party on horseback the six or seven miles to the Mariposa Grove. Muir, who had long been a friend and ally of Clark's, went along as well and rode by Emerson's side through most of the trip. This gave the two more time to debate the literary merits of Byron and Coleridge and for Emerson to indulge in more reminiscing about his time at Harvard, when he had encountered the likes of Richard Henry Dana Sr. and the Boston painter Washington Allston. He also pumped Muir on what he knew of Charles Warren Stoddard, a poet from San Francisco whose work Emerson admired. For his part, Thayer reported, Muir "talked of the trees; and we grew learned, and were able to tell a sugar pine from a yellow pine, and to name the silver fir, and the 'libocedrus,' which is almost our arbor-vitæ and second cousin to the great sequoia." Soon they entered into a mountain hollow, and Muir called out that he could see the sequoias. As had happened to Thomas Starr King before them, upon first encountering "California's 'vegetable Titans,'" it was hard for the group to grasp the true size of the trees. As Thayer put it, "They were 'big trees,' to be sure; and yet at first they seemed not so very big. We grew curious, and looked about among them for a while; and soon began to discover what company we were in."

As the party spread out through the upper grove, Thayer clambered up the side of a prostrate sequoia labeled with a tin sign "The Fallen Monarch." He then proceeded to pace off its length: 83 paces, or 249 feet. That, plus the trunk measuring 19 feet in diameter, began to give him a sense of just how big these trees really were, as did the fact that the grove was studded with pines and firs large enough to be considered giants in their own right if it hadn't been for the looming presence of the sequoias. Nearby, the Grizzly Giant gave Thayer the opportunity to measure with a rope the circumference of a living tree, which was an astonishing 91 feet. Clark called his attention to the Grizzly Giant's lowest branch, some one hundred feet above the ground, which itself was nearly six and half feet in diameter. For the fun of it, one of the guides instructed the party to park their thirteen horses nose to tail to form a ring around the base of the tree—at least six more horses were needed to complete it.

Despite their massiveness and seeming invulnerability, Thayer noticed the evidence of fire on many trees, whose thick, dry bark was often kindled by lightening strikes. In one case, the trunk of one downed tree had been burned, creating a "hollow tube" through which Thayer rode "without inconvenience," although his horse "hated to go into the black thing." In another case, fire had bit deeply enough into the base of one living tree that it had been hollowed out by axes to create a tunnel through which one could ride as through a barn door. And in one last instance, fire had burned off most of the bark on what had once been the grandest trees in the grove—the "Forest Giant"—yet its diameter still measured a respectable thirty feet. Of the living trees, however, Thayer was struck by their beauty and symmetry and was fascinated when Muir pointed out that the top of the sequoias formed a parabola like an umbrella and not the peaked shape of most evergreens. Thayer was particularly glad to see young sequoias thriving in the grove. "That is good!" he said to himself, "they are not, then, a mere decaying thing of the past."

During most of the tour of the grove, which Muir later described rather tetchily as being spent "mostly in ordinary tourist fashion, — looking at the biggest giants, measuring them with a tape line, riding through prostrate fire-bored trunks, etc.," Muir managed to steal some moments alone with Emerson, whom he found "sauntering about as if under a spell. As we walked through a fine group, he quoted, 'There were giants in those days,' recognizing the antiquity of the race." Later, Clark led the group to Wawona Point for a vista of the unbroken forest and the snowcapped mountains beyond, and then to a small shack, Galen's Hospice, where the party lunched and relaxed, which gave them "a chance to sit and *absorb* the trees a little." As their time in the grove drew to an end, Galen Clark tried "in vain to get Mr. Emerson's leave to name one of the giants for him, as was then the fashion." Emerson wouldn't hear of it, but he would be happy to bestow the name of a more worthy person, perhaps a Native American, since the tree species had been named after the Cherokee chief Sequoyah. At first Emerson proposed "Logan," most likely Logan the Orator, an eighteenth-century leader of the Haudenosaunee (more commonly known as the Iroquois Confederacy), but then he hit on another Native American more dear to New

Englanders' hearts: Samoset, the "first Indian ally of the Plymouth Colony." Emerson proudly recorded the event that day in his diary, noting that he "gave Mr. Clark directions to procure a tin plate, & have the inscription painted thereon in the usual form of the named trees; Samoset—12 May. 1871. & paid him its cost. The tree was a strong healthy one, girth 2½ feet from the ground, 50 feet [tall]." Taking some of the bark of the tree as a souvenir, Emerson remarked, "The greatest wonder is that we can see these trees and not wonder more. They seem so natural and grow used to it."

And then "the poor bit of measured time was soon spent," as Muir put it, and the group was due back at Clark's Station to catch the stages down out of the mountains. Muir, of course, protested their going so soon: "It is as if a photographer should remove his plate before the impression is fully made." He again implored them to spend at least one night camping out in the grove, of which, according to Thayer, "we all felt the temptation." "You are yourself a sequoia," Muir said to Emerson directly. "Stop and get acquainted with your big brethren." But their conveyances were waiting, and all mounted up to leave, except for Muir, who would indeed stay the night there, fortified by the leftovers from lunch. He would return to Yosemite Valley on foot. Years later, Muir would write of the episode that Emerson "was past his prime, and was now as a child in the hands of his affectionate but sadly civilized friends, who seemed as full of old-fashioned conformity as of bold intellectual independence": "It was the afternoon of the day and the afternoon of his life, and his course was now westward down all the mountains into the sunset. The party mounted and rode away in wondrous contentment, apparently, tracing the trail through ceanothus and dogwood bushes, around the bases of the big trees, up the slope of the sequoia basin, and over the divide. I followed to the edge of the grove. Emerson lingered in the rear of the train, and when he reached the top of the ridge, after all the rest of the party were over and out of sight, he turned his horse, took off his hat and waved me a last good-by. I felt lonely, so sure had I been that Emerson of all men would be the quickest to see the mountains and sing them." The group was also sad to leave Muir in the grove, because, as Thayer wrote Sophy, "he really enjoyed being with us and it was pleasant to see him. Of course, Mr. Emerson was his especial delight, but he enjoyed seeing everybody. He is a nice fellow and will be heard from yet." For his part, Muir stood "gazing awhile on the spot where he vanished" and then "sauntered back into the heart of the grove, made a bed of sequoia plumes and ferns by the side of a stream, gathered a store of firewood, and then walked about until sundown." Now that the grove was quiet, the birds came out and sang until nightfall, after which Muir built a great roaring fire and brooded over his encounter with Emerson. For the first time he felt loneliness in the forest, but this feeling soon passed: "I quickly took heart again,—the trees had not gone to Boston, nor the birds; and as I sat by the fire, Emerson was still with me in spirit, though I never again saw him in the flesh."

RETURN BY SLOW STAGES

Leaving the grove at 2:45 that afternoon, the party—at least those who cantered their horses—arrived at Clark's Station at 4:15 and began to pack while waiting for the stragglers to trickle in. The two stages left a half an hour later, bound for White and Hatch's Hotel down in the foothills twelve miles west. Two hours later, the stages pulled up in front of a simple one-story building with the typical covered porch, or piazza, along its front side. There to greet them was probably either Dexter White or James H. Hatch, his nephew, who ushered the party into a small dining room for supper before a warming fire. Here they met another hotel guest, the illustrious William J. Seward, Civil War general and son of Lincoln's secretary of state, who happened to be on his way up to Yosemite. After supper, both Emerson and Thayer wished to have their cigar, but Thayer didn't want Emerson to take a chill on the piazza, so he enquired of Mr. White whether there was a room they could use that would not disturb the others. The landlord was happy to oblige, leading the pair "to an obscure, low, rather large room, with a couple of beds, and the nearly burned-out remains of a wood-fire upon a large hearth. It was dim and cosy [sic], and we were very comfortable. 'Is this not,' said Mr. Emerson, slowly, and looking cautiously about, 'the conjugal bedroom?' It seemed not unlikely." Left with a single candle with which to light their cigars, both settled into chairs on opposite sides of the fire and luxuriated in their smoking.

As was usual in these situations, Thayer remained smilingly silent, allowing Emerson to talk and reminisce at his leisure. Emerson spoke of his early acquaintance with Wilkie's father, Henry James, and the "frank sudden way about him." Emerson used to visit James often at home back in the day, but lately the friendship had cooled, and he felt that James was having now "a rather heavy time and didn't see anybody much." It was at James's house that he had met the abolitionist William Tappan, who struck him on first impression as "a taciturn, handsome fellow—ready to *stab* you!" Emerson was surprised when Tappan showed up unannounced at his home in Concord to see Caroline Sturgis, who was living with his family at the time and with whom Emerson was deeply smitten. Tappan and Sturgis became very close and eventually married, and now Emerson never saw Tappan, much to his regret. Despite the melancholy nature of these memories, Thayer relished listening to Emerson speak: "It was like a poem, to hear him and to see him as he told the story in his musing, pausing way, in the dim light,—rather perhaps from what his face and his tones suggested, than from his words."

At this point, George Holdrege appeared, casually grousing that he had been assigned along with four others to a tiny room with limited ventilation and that Mr. Emerson would have to share an equally tiny room with Thayer. Again not wishing to discommode Emerson, Thayer suggested that he and Holdrege drag their beds onto the piazza and "sleep *al fresco*," to which Emerson protested loudly: it was one thing for Holdrege to sleep on the porch, but Thayer had a wife and children! Nevertheless, Thayer and Holdrege won out and had their beds set up under the shade of a large pine growing up through the piazza floor. There they "passed a perfectly comfortable night." The next day, Thayer wrote with amusement to Sophy that "Mr. Emerson eyed me gravely, and asked, with a sceptical[sic] look, about the night" and then complained to Mr. Forbes "that the party 'was dandling him all the way, and he should soon be only ready for a pap-spoon!'" This was not the first time on the trip he complained, albeit good humoredly, of being "managed": earlier in the trip he had written to a friend that "between my helplessness as a traveler and the formidable skill of my companions I am tamed down to an obedience which would edify, if it did not shock you."

Departing the next morning at 6:30, it took the party the entire day to get back to Roberts Ferry on the Tuolumne River. Now heading west, Thayer noted that while he "missed the great mountains and their snowy tops," he could now see across "the vast sea-like stretch of the San Joaquin

Valley, and far beyond, dimly, the Coast Range Mountains." Along the way, they passed through Mariposa, once the location of a thriving quartz mill operation run by John C. Frémont but now largely abandoned and littered with great piles of powdered rock. The area around Mariposa was even more unlovely still, greatly disfigured as it was by the ongoing large-scale placer mining, which had caused the topsoil to be washed away "like Wycliffe's ashes" into the rivers, leaving just "rocks, the only insoluble things, lying about." They next passed through the hamlet of Hornitos ("little ovens"), aptly named because, as they neared the valley floor, it became almost unbearably hot. Further on they made a stop at Snelling's Hotel for lunch, served by a "stout Scotch landlady." They rested the horses and relaxed for a couple of hours out of the sun.

From Snelling it was fourteen miles to the Tuolumne River and Roberts Ferry, where the party arrived "in unexpectedly good condition after sunset, having made (as these people reckon making) 57 or 58 miles" that day. Crossing the Tuolumne on the ferry, Thayer must have felt a sense of déjà vu, as they were again preceded by two great mule teams hauling wagons loaded with merchandise. The evening began to cool, and after supper, Thayer found himself again by Emerson's side in chairs smoking on the piazza, admiring the boundless sky, and gossiping about people they knew, especially the Concord poet William Ellery Channing, whose odd character, Emerson said laughing, was "a hopeless subject for Christian education" and made him a terrible father to his children. Nevertheless, Emerson had to admit that he was one of the few who admired Channing as a poet, albeit an undisciplined one who refused to revise his work. Soon, the cigars were finished and there was now a definite chill in air. It was after nine and time for bed, of which, happily, there were plenty.

In Thayer's estimation, "Roberts's, considered as a tavern, was a place to leave," so he must have been happy that the stages made an early start the next morning. As the party continued rolling across the plain of the great San Joaquin Valley, he saw again the same profusion of squirrels, jack rabbits, cottontails, and "shad-belly" owls in a landscape of "handsome, drooping oaks." After crossing the Stanislaus River, Thayer noted the occasional mirage that created the illusion of vast sheets of water in whose distorted reflections could be seen giant trees and giant men on horseback. "How would it be possible for a savage looking at these things *not* to believe in magicians and devils and giants!" he wondered.

Catching the train at Merced, the party reached the town of Stockton early that afternoon, an event noted by *Stockton Daily Independent*, which announced the next day that "a party of nine, including Ralph Waldo Emerson, one of the greatest of American authors and one of the most distinguished lecturers now living, arrived in this city yesterday direct from Yosemite Valley." The "distinguished visitors" quickly checked into the Stockton Grand Hotel, and after a leisurely lunch and smoke, Emerson and Thayer toured the town, off to see the prolific artesian well for which the town was famous. Along the way, the pair remarked with pleasure the number of plain white houses, each with their lush yards and gardens irrigated by their own windmills, which, "like butterflies, were fluttering on every side." The green of the town was a welcome and restful relief from the sere plains of the San Joaquin.

The next afternoon, the Emerson party arrived by train at the Oakland depot. All of the party except for Emerson boarded the ferry for San Francisco straight away, arriving at the Occidental Hotel by noon. Emerson, however, decided he had to pay a quick visit to the home of Professor Ezra and Jeanne Carr before returning, feeling duty-bound to thank Jeanne for her introduction to John Muir. Thick fog blanketed the city, however, and Emerson was soon lost among the unfamiliar streets. Only with difficulty did he find the Carrs' cottage, and when Jeanne Carr went to answer a knock at her back door, she found Emerson standing there, slightly confused but smiling, with a cloak tightly wrapped around his shivering frame. The two had not seen each other for years, so Jeanne ushered her old friend into the bright parlor, bid him to sit, and likely offered him a cup of warming tea. Jeanne had just returned from "a hard day's work in examining classes at the Girls' High School," but the mere presence of Emerson energized her: "How weariness fled and my delight was full," she wrote to Muir the next day, "you do not need to be told." Emerson proceeded to give her a full account of his trip to the valley, especially his pleasure in meeting Muir. Carr was ecstatic that the two hit it off, writing Muir that "if there is joy of angels to be had in the flesh, it is that of finding your soul 'confirmed in its faith through the soul of another.'" Indeed, she was overjoyed that yet again others saw in Muir what she had seen there first herself: "I laugh to think how they go up to the mountains, the beautiful ones, to find *you* in the confessional, the only soul I know whom the mountains fully own and bless."

As tired as he must have been, Emerson was apparently in no hurry to leave the Carrs' comfortable parlor and talked at length. Jeanne Carr hung on his every word: "I have laid up in my heart so much that he told me of his trip, never have I heard him so delightful in conversation, his silver speech flowed on and on and it was hard to remember engagements, as we were both compelled to do." It was late by the time Emerson finally did get up to leave, but by now the fog had lifted somewhat, and armed this time with the proper directions, he had little trouble finding the Oakland terminal to catch the evening ferry back to San Francisco and the Occidental Hotel.

Chapter 7

LAST DAYS IN CALIFORNIA

(MAY 15 TO MAY 21, 1871)

Still thou playest;—short vacation
Fate grants each to stand aside;
Now must thou be man and artist,—
'T is the turning of the tide.

—Ralph Waldo Emerson, "Holidays" (1842)

Despite the arduousness of the trip to Yosemite and back, the Emerson party's last days in San Francisco would not be idle ones. There was still much more to see in the city, and a trip down the San Francisco Peninsula had been planned. In fact, after dinner the night they returned from Yosemite, Emerson expressed a desire to take in a performance of "the theatre of the roughs,—the lowest thing in the city, the 'place,' he said, 'where the miners went.'" Ever since childhood, when his overprotective mother prevented him from mingling with the "rude boys" of his neighborhood, Emerson had been fascinated with the working-class demimonde that, much to his lasting regret, he had been barred from exploring as a youth. It is not clear whether Emerson had a particular theater in mind, but there were plenty to choose from. As Bancroft put it in his *Tourist's Guide*, "We hardly anticipate that the average tourist will care to be 'guided' into places under this heading, but the philosophic student of human nature, as well as the curious observer of social customs, cannot consider his knowledge of any city complete until he has personally seen and actually known, not only the highest, but the lowest amusements extensively patronized by its people." San Francisco was no different from other cities, having "its share of low haunts in which really modest, and sometimes meritorious performances blend with a much larger proportion of immodest, meretricious and disgraceful

FIGURE 12. The Bella Union Theatre and Portsmouth Plaza, photograph by G. R. Fardon, ca. 1855. —F869.S3.9 F138x:25—VAULT, The Bancroft Library, University of California, Berkeley.

ones." Given that Emerson specifically requested "the lowest thing in the city," it was apparently the latter kind of show he was seeking.

The city's "melodeons," as they were called, clustered around the so-called Barbary Coast, which ran along the waterfront from Pacific Street to Kearny Street. Its "theaters" were widely advertised by handbills called "dodgers" plastered everywhere on walls and fences. Bearing names such as The What Cheer, Gilbert's Melodeon, the New Idea, the Comique (pronounced "comi-cue"), and the Bella Union, these glorified saloons were, as one historian has put it, "randy progenitors of vaudeville," "presenting brash, eclectic revues of music, comedy, and dance." The dodger for the Bella Union, for example, promised a program of "Wonderful ECCENTRICITY," a euphemism that often meant blue jokes, raucous music, and bawdy dancing. Definitely not places for women visitors, Emerson managed to cajole Will Forbes and Thayer to go with him, but sadly for Emerson, the quintessential "philosophic student of human nature," whatever the melodeon was they chose to attend, it didn't satisfy. After paying the "two-bits" cover charge, settling into chairs with special built-in racks to hold their drinks, and buying cigars from a passing danseuse-cum-waitress the show turned out to be an anticlimax. According to Thayer, "All through the early hours of the evening the performance was flat and dreary," and since Emerson "was tired out," they all decided to leave early. Nevertheless, Emerson could at least say he'd visited both of San Francisco's more infamous locales— Chinatown and the Barbary Coast—even if they turned out to be a bit tamer than expected.

A TRIP DOWN THE PENINSULA

If the "theatre of the roughs" was an example of lowbrow popular culture in the Bay Area, then the next day's excursion down the peninsula would be an opportunity to experience the opposite end of the social spectrum: the exclusive world of the California elite. The peninsula is a thirty-mile stretch between San Francisco and the Santa Clara Valley, bounded on the west by the Coast Range and the bay on the east. Well watered and protected from the ocean fogs, covered with magnificent oaks and redwoods, and within easy driving distance of the city, the peninsula held some of the most desirable real estate in the region during the 1860s and 1870s. It was during this period that wealthy families rich from mining, banking, and mercantile pursuits bought up great tracts of land and built extensive estates, replete with mansions designed by famous eastern architects and outfitted with the most luxurious and costly furnishings that money could buy. Not a few boasted elaborate formal gardens noted for their roses, massive stables for both racehorses and workhorses, and fruit orchards stretching out as far as the eye could see. Although some of these estates were intended to be the hidden resorts of the rich, others were meant to serve as conspicuous advertisements of California's abundant wealth and were often open for visitors' inspection. Indeed, Bancroft's *Guide* includes a section on the peninsula, recommending especially a stop at William C. Ralston's Belmont, "whose country seat, in beauty of location, extent of accommodations, with variety and completeness of appointments, happily combines the elegance of a palace with the simplicity and comfort of a home." Some of the estates were large enough to generate local economies that quickly developed into towns, such as Ralston's Belmont, banker Darius Ogden Mills's Millbrae, and Atherton, named after the shipping magnate Faxon Dean Atherton (1815–77).

At the last minute Emerson decided to stay behind at the Occidental Hotel to put some finishing touches on his last talk at First Unitarian on Wednesday and to spend more time with Edith, who had since returned from the Barbers in San Rafael. In the meantime, the rest of the party boarded the train south to Atherton, invited guests of the town's namesake. Originally from Dedham, Massachusetts, Faxon Dean Atherton had shipped out in 1834 for Valparaiso, Chile, where he worked in a ship's chandlery before becoming a successful merchant plying the hide and tallow trade between Boston, Valparaiso, and Monterey. It was on one of these trips that he met fellow New Englander Thomas O. Larkin, who convinced Atherton to relocate to California with his Chilean wife, Dominga de Goñi, which he did in 1860, investing his fortune in 640 acres of prime land on the peninsula. Here he built his estate, Valparaiso Park, and raised seven children in a substantial house surrounded by expansive lawns and extensive gardens containing scores of imported flowers and ornamental trees. It is unknown how the Forbes became acquainted with the Athertons, but because Faxon Atherton had remained in close contact with New England—he was still a subscriber to the Boston *Advertiser* and had regularly corresponded with the likes of Daniel Webster and Louis Agassiz—it is likely that the two families had friends in common who arranged the visit. Thayer found Mr. Atherton "a quiet, perfectly unaffected, plain man, sensible, kind and good and a *gentleman*,—without any effort or pretension or any particular conformity to rule," but said little of his wife, who presented a voluble contrast to her husband. While Faxon was tall, handsome, taciturn, and retiring, "Mrs. Atherton was exactly five feet in height and weighed two hundred pounds," and it was either "her breadth and width that made her impressive, or her enormous Spanish dignity that diverted attention from her negligible inches," according to their daughter-in-law, the future best-selling novelist Gertrude Atherton. Somehow, this odd couple worked, and the party found the hospitality at Valparaiso Park simple, comfortable, and "homelike," albeit a tad unsophisticated according to Thayer, who noted in wry amusement that on a shelf in his room he found side by side a Catholic catechism and Emerson's *English Traits*.

What captivated the party most about Valparaiso Park was the seemingly effortless lushness of the grounds. Both Will Forbes and Thayer enthused about the "abundant magnificent roses" that filled the air with "sweet June odor" and were better than anything seen in Florida. Indeed, roses seemed to flourish everywhere: "Great heavy clusters of white roses," Thayer wrote Sophy, "hang over the piazza and bushes of every variety stand all about: some of them are very large (the 'Pauline Lanzizeur') nearly reaching the size of five inches in diameter to which Mr. A. says they sometimes grow; you cannot conceive a richer red; the eye almost *feels* the delight in seeing it." The secret behind all this abundance was Mr. Atherton's complicated system of irrigation, including a portable sprinkler system that Thayer found ingenious. Later, on a drive around the estate, Thayer took the opportunity to inspect Mr. Atherton's orchards, which again stunned him by their variety and fertility: "Here were great quantities of grape vines, cherries, and pears, peaches, nectarines, and apricots (what loads of these on the trees!), rows of almond trees (looking like the peach) and figs and English walnuts (resembling the ash) with fruit well advanced and olive trees in blossom. These fig and nut trees supply them fully and more; and the birds get their fill of figs besides: they ripen in July, August, and September. The fig trees were twenty feet high and they were loaded." Atherton's grounds also contained "little elms, a rare tree in these parts, acacias, some in full bloom and the blue gum or 'eucalyptus,'" a fast-growing tree newly introduced to California from Australia on the mistaken assumption that it would provide vast quantities of usable lumber—it would not, unfortunately, its wood being too soft and pulpy.

The next day, after what Thayer called a "model breakfast," the party took it easy, lounging in the California sunshine. "A warmer, sunnier, pleasanter sight than Mr. Atherton's piazza offered to one sitting in the sun this morning it would be hard to find," wrote Thayer, "what with the roses and the grass and the movable fountain that watered it all, now set up here and now there." They chatted amiably with Mr. Atherton about his irrigation schemes in the San Joaquin Valley, his high hopes for the eucalyptus, and his delight at fishing in the Charles River during his boyhood in Massachusetts. Rousing themselves, some of the group took a long drive in the company of Faxon Atherton and his son George, who took them see the country homes of Thomas Henry Selby, then mayor of San Francisco, and of the mining magnate William Eustace Barron, where they admired his deer park and trout pond and stopped to pick strawberries for an impromptu midmorning picnic.

After lunch at Valparaiso Park, the party was collected along with the Athertons by "a sort of English wagon like a domestic omnibus with four lively bay horses," which had been sent by William Ralston to "fetch them over" to his country house, Belmont. Ralston would not be there that day, but he maintained his house as a kind of public attraction, and visitors were always welcome to wander through it at will. Belmont was by far the most extravagant estate on the peninsula. Bought from the Italian nobleman Count Leonetto Cipriani in 1864, Ralston developed the 180-acre property to include formal gardens, orchards, barns and stables for sixty-six horses, a Turkish bathhouse, a bowling alley, and a freestanding gymnasium. The centerpiece, however, was a 55,000-square-foot Italianate mansion with an interior characterized as Steamboat Gothic and furnished to match: Chinese vases, lush oriental carpets, drapes from Paris, heavy mahogany furniture from England, walnut parquet floors, and oak doors with silver handles, not to mention busts on Carrara marble stands and paintings by Albert Bierstadt, Gilbert Munger, and Thomas Hill. The highlight of the mansion was an immense ballroom lined with mirrors like Versailles, where Ralston regularly hosted large, lavish balls with hundreds of guests in attendance. Thayer was impressed by this ostentatious display of new money, but not uncritical: "It is an extraordinary establishment," he wrote, "pleasantly situated and finished, and furnished with splendor,—not, however, without an occasional *lapse*." Indeed, given the size and extravagance of the place, he concluded that Ralston's "entertaining" was "plainly of the retail sort" and later repeated to Sophy the rumor that Bank of California assets had been used to fund Ralston's extravagant lifestyle. After a couple of hours "gaping about," as Thayer put it, the party left the Atherton family at the Belmont Station and caught the 4:30 p.m. train to San Francisco, arriving at the Occidental Hotel just in time for a late tea.

CARLETON WATKINS

Meanwhile, Emerson, back at the Occidental with Edith and hoping to polish his talk, probably wished he had gone on the excursion after all.

Edith wrote indignantly to Ellen that her father was positively "flooded with callers and bores" who would, as Emerson complained, "stay as long as if it was Massachusetts." When the *Examiner* had announced Emerson's original arrival in the city, it had expressed the hope that he would "be allowed to enjoy himself without the annoyances of flunkyism." But such was not to be. Particularly bad, according to Edith, was a "woman-suffrage committee who badgered him with one proposal and another until he was finally crushed into sitting for his photo for their Bazaar!" Emerson thus dutifully sat for a portrait at William Shew's New Photographic Establishment on Kearny Street (a compromise that the *Examiner* summed up rather cryptically as "the shadow for the substance, but the consolation comes at last"). In a satirical squib, the *Detroit Free Press* poked fun at Emerson's "Lack of Preparation" in his unwillingness to address the "Woman's Suffrage Convention," thus proving that even with nineteenth-century celebrities, no good deed went unpunished: "If Ralph had been asked a year before hand, or had been given the opportunity to rummage through the Mercantile Library for a fortnight, he would not thus rudely have declined the invitation of the ladies. Ralph loves the cause of woman suffrage, and as a lack of prepared speech kept him from public gaze, he did what he could to advance the cause and make himself familiar to private gaze by presenting the society with a number of photographs for sale. This is good of Ralph and keeps him before the community."

Not even mealtimes were exempt from these intrusions, as Edith noted: "A gentleman came and summoned him from the breakfast table and sat on him until he made promise of a lecture at Oakland—for charity Father understood—but he wouldn't take no for an answer and finally having extorted the promise—Father had to rise and send him away for he would not take the poor man's twice repeated hint—that his daughter was waiting at the breakfast table for him—They did give him $50 after all, but we were all indignant that he should be bothered." Everyone who approached Emerson had a story or request or claimed to be a distant relative, and polite as usual, he felt duty-bound to listen to each. At one point, Edith "found him going along the corridor with a hunted look—and close behind a little lady who wanted he should help her get a school [position] somewhere out of the city!" This was Sarah Clarke from Northampton, Massachusetts, whom Emerson knew from

FIGURE 13. *Ralph Waldo Emerson*, photograph by
William Shew, San Francisco, 1871. —Courtesy of
the Joel Myerson Collection of Nineteenth-Century
American Manuscripts, Images, and Ephemera,
University of South Carolina University Libraries,
Columbia.

reform meetings at the homes of Cyrus Bartol and John Turner Sargent.
Now destitute and finding herself stranded in San Francisco, Emerson
duly wrote a letter for her to the Reverend Stebbins to see if he could
get her a position so that she would not be forced to sell the last prized
possession—her piano.

At some point, probably at the urging of Edith, Emerson escaped the
clamoring mob at the hotel and strolled over to visit the photo studio
and gallery of Carleton Watkins (1829–1916), located near the hotel at

425 Montgomery Street. Watkins, who was then the most famous photographer of the West, had been born to Yankee parents in Upstate New York and migrated to California during the gold rush in the company of Collis P. Huntington, who would become one the "Big Four" of the Central Pacific Railroad. It was in California that Watkins took up photography, pioneering the use of the so-called mammoth-plate camera that produced 18- by 22-inch glass negatives for images of unparalleled clarity. In July 1861, Watkins made his first trip to the Yosemite Valley and the Big Trees, which resulted in an immensely popular series of photographs and stereographs that came to be widely circulated through the United States. Indeed, California senator John Conness was said to have showed Watkins's photographs to Abraham Lincoln as part of the lobbying effort to approve the Yosemite Grant in 1864. What's more, at a salon hosted by Jessie Benton Frémont, Watkins met Thomas Starr King, who in turn introduced Watkins to the works of Ralph Waldo Emerson, making him a lifelong devotee, especially of Emerson's *Nature*. And perhaps because Edward Emerson had brought a photograph of his father as a gift during his 1861 visit, King sent back with Edward two of Watkins's photographs of the Grizzly Giant for the Emerson home, including a note that read, "The artist, my friend Watkins, wandered in the Sierra wilds last year, with a thousand pounds of photographic luggage, crossing steeps seven thousand feet high, to report the Yo Semite cliffs & the neighboring wonders. These are the only photographic likenesses that have yet been taken of the great cedars in our State." Emerson wrote back, thanking King for the "two wonderful photographs of your big Sequoia, which are proud curiosities here to all eyes," adding, "They are entirely satisfactory to the beholder, and make the tree possible [i.e., credible]." It is entirely likely that Emerson's desire to see these trees in person dated from his first glimpse of Watkins's images, and it definitely would have been on Emerson's to-do list while in the city to visit Watkins's studio and acquire more of these magical images, especially since Mrs. Russell had asked him to pick out a photo for her.

When Emerson returned to the Occidental from the studio, he told Edith that he had managed to pick out a set for himself, but he fretted that he couldn't decide which would be best for Mrs. Russell. Edith proposed going back to the studio with him, as she and Will also wished to buy some Watkins works for their own home. Thus, while they were browsing in the gallery, looking at the pictures hanging on the walls and in the glass vitrines, a young female clerk approached and said, "Mr. Emerson, Mr. Watkins told me to ask you to choose 6 of the large photographs and accept them from him. He did not recognize you this afternoon and was much annoyed that he charged you anything for the small ones you bought." Edith related later that "Father was astounded— made her say it over again—seemed very much pleased—and said he would see Mr. W. tomorrow and forthwith I made a list of the few Will and I wanted. We returned rejoicing to the hotel—Father saying, 'There are advantages to being old.'" To this day, two Watkins photographs — *Cathedral Spires* and *Mt. Shasta*—still hang at Emerson's home.

Back again at the Occidental, Emerson and Edith encountered the party returning from their trip down the peninsula, so while Emerson and Edith dined and the others had late tea, the travelers recounted the details and pleasures of the excursion. Everyone agreed that the trip had been hugely enjoyable, although Will expressed disappointment that Edith had not been there to see the roses. In lieu of this, he produced from his pocket "two gorgeous specimens of Pauline Lanzizeur—a velvet rose—larger and a trifle darker than Giant of Battles." Soon, however, it was getting late and time for Emerson to head off for his last talk in the city. All but the elder Forbes and Mrs. Russell, now too tired to move, trooped out with him, bound again for First Unitarian.

"CHIVALRY" AND "HOSPITALITY"

"RALPH WALDO EMERSON—LAST LECTURE!" the *San Francisco Bulletin* ad blasted from its columns on the day before and the day of the lecture: "Subject: 'CHIVALRY.'" The same ad appeared in the other four daily papers, along with squibs touting the lecture, such as that in the *Daily Alta California*, which admonished its readers: "An opportunity to hear so eminent a thinker read his own writings is seldom afforded, and a large audience will no doubt bid him farewell." It has been said that the Reverend Stebbins worked hard to get this press coverage because he was worried about poor turnout. By all indications, however, the attendance was good, and even Julia King, the widow of Thomas Starr King, was in the audience, to whom Emerson eagerly repeated his now stock observation that Yosemite was "the only place that comes up to the brag about it and exceeds it!"

The lecture itself, such as it was, generated yet another mixed response. Edith was pleased with it and said she thought it went well, whereas Thayer was distinctly unimpressed with Emerson: "It was disappointing. He took some of the extracts that he read a winter or two ago in Boston, having little or no connection with 'Chivalry' especially and read them, with a brief introduction. It was a pity." In *A Western Journey*, Thayer excused the poor performance, claiming that Emerson "had extemporized from certain fragments,—having failed to find one of his best lectures that had been brought along, but lay hidden somewhere in his trunk."

Unfortunately, no copy of "Chivalry" has ever been published, but the précis of it in the *San Francisco Chronicle* indicates that, despite Thayer's assessment, the lecture did touch on the stated theme, although in a highly idiosyncratic way. Emerson began by stating that primitive societies gain civilization by two means: by generating it internally over a great time through sheer necessity or by coming into contact with more civilized peoples. The Goths and Huns, for example, were civilized by their conquest of the Roman Empire, but these northern tribes brought with them their native idealism. The result was a fusion out of which came the high culture of the Middle Ages, replete with its cult of chivalry, which, he claimed, played such a large role in the history of the Crusades. Emerson ended the lecture with a curious example of chivalry culled from Albert Crantz's *Saxon History* (1520), in which Edward III's queen decided to test the valor of a courtier by letting loose a lion in her garden. When the courtier encountered the lion, he quickly overwhelmed it with his superior manner and led it tamely back to its cage wearing the courtier's nightcap. It is impossible to say why Emerson thought this particular lecture was appropriate for this occasion, although one is tempted to find in it, if only obliquely, a sly commentary on the chaotic collision of cultures then under way in California and the need for more Anglo Saxons to tame it.

The newspapers next day were predictably divided about Emerson's performance. The *San Francisco Examiner* cuttingly stated, "This had been announced as the last of his lectures, and the impression produced on the audience at its conclusion was that it was well that it was so; for his expiring effort in San Francisco was tame and uninteresting, by no means sustaining his claims to the position which he is thought to occupy in the lecture room." The *Golden Era* agreed: "Ralph Waldo

Emerson's lectures have inspired little interest. Unless there is elo-
quence in delivery, men prefer to read for themselves than have authors
read for them." The *Bulletin*, on the other hand, reported that "Ralph
Waldo Emerson addressed a large, intelligent audience at the Unitarian Church, last evening, on the subject of *Chivalry*. Commencing at the
earliest period of civilization, the eminent scholar and profound thinker
gave learned, interesting and historical dissertations upon Chivalry in
its embryo state. . . . The lecture was listened to with marked attention,
and made a lasting impression upon those present." The *San Francisco
Chronicle*, for its part, after an uncharacteristically approving summary
of the talk, concluded by reporting: "The gentleman's remarks were
loudly applauded at their close."

The next day, Thursday, May 18, the Emerson party's final day in the
Bay Area, was a full one for all. Most of the group would join Mr. Forbes
for a visit to Millbrae, the country home of Darius Ogden Mills, who,
along with William Ralston, owned the Bank of California. Mrs. Forbes
and Mrs. Russell decided to stay behind at the hotel, while Will and
Edith took the opportunity do some shopping—jewelry at Chy Leung's
Chinese store, back to Watkins's studio for more stereographs, and then
last to a florist to order native California plants for shipment back to
their home in Milton. Meanwhile, Emerson himself felt he needed some
fresh air, so he joined Thayer, the Reverend Stebbins, and Henry Augustus Pierce, a wealthy San Francisco businessman and former American
minister to Hawaii, for a carriage ride down the peninsula as far as San
Bruno. Their drive took them "along the side of the hills overhanging
the bay—a warm, sunny shelf looking out upon a surface of water" that
reminded Thayer of Italy. Indeed, "Italians, in good earnest, were out
fishing with a seine" and others cultivated "little gardens where they
raise vegetables for the city market." They ended up at Thorpe's Tavern,
famous for its "delicate viands artistically served," and had a meal and
drinks outdoors in the tavern's rose garden.

On the way back, the party stopped at the lot slated for the new City
Hall, and Mr. Pierce pointed out the constant work that needed to be
done just to keep the lot clear of sand. "It was a good illustration of
the way the city work is done," Thayer later remarked, "the dumping
carts were shoveled full, the fine sand running, all the while, in slender but copious streams out through the bottom; the carts were walked

slowly away by the perfunctory Irishmen who drove them—looking like hour glasses ('forty minutes' was about the time of them, Mr. Pierce reckoned),—and there taken around behind the same sand hill and dumped again: what was left by gravity would come back by wind pretty soon. Perhaps it added to the spectacle to reflect that it was the votes of these same Irishmen that gave them the job." After this ludicrous but instructive sight, the four returned to the Occidental Hotel for tea and to give Emerson time to change for that night's talk in Oakland, which he would attend alone. Although he must have felt dragooned into the talk, at least it would give him another opportunity to see his friends and family across the Bay before he left for the East.

Reflecting the rivalry between San Francisco and its "Brooklyn," the pressure on Emerson to lecture in Oakland had been intense since he arrived. As early as April 27, the *Oakland Daily News* had run an extremely complimentary article on Emerson, citing him as "this distinguished metaphysician and philosopher" who "is eminently brave, and confident in his avowal of his own belief, declaring steadfastly, to us his own words 'that a popgun is a popgun, though the ancient and honorable of the earth affirm it to be the crack of doom.'" Indeed, "the Pacific Railroad, among the manifold advantages, present and prospective, which it bestows on California and the Pacific Coast, deserves our gratitude for importing to San Francisco, a live intelligence, in the shape of Ralph Waldo Emerson." The importance of all this fawning, of course, was simply to wind up the pitch: "We in Oakland have souls quite as big and as immortal as those of San Francisco—in fact, we flatter ourselves rather more so—and we entreat the great moral philosopher to come across the Bay, and see if we don't appreciate his ethics as much as the worthies of Geary street. He is too great a man to be monopolized by a church, and too eclectic to be bound by the horizon of any one creed." If he would only make the journey across the Bay, the great man would "find a willing audience in Oakland, prepared to the fullest extent to call a popgun a popgun, and a spade a spade, and to hail with hearty welcome one of the greatest American authors." It is not known whether this article actually influenced Emerson's decision to lecture there. Most likely it was the urgent, last-minute appeal to Emerson in the Occidental's dining room the day before that had sealed the deal, and almost before Emerson had finished eating his breakfast, the ads for his talk,

"Hospitality, and How to Make Homes Attractive," were running in the Oakland papers.

Originally prepared by Emerson for a private lecture series in 1868 at the Meionaon in Boston, "Hospitality" also has never been published, so its exact contents are unknown. The *San Francisco Bulletin* summarized it as dwelling "on the beauties of the country home, the gardens, the landscape, the river and all the treasures which set the rural life far above the dweller in cities. . . . The lecture was full of fine maxims, and graphic descriptions of the happy homes." The *Oakland Daily News* painted it as even more miscellaneous: "His vivid picture of country life and all he had purchased without paying for, in landscape, and sunrise, and river, and shady lanes, when he bought his farm in Massachusetts; his definition of walking as a fine art, and the natural qualifications required for it; his description of the right sort of companion in a country walk; his rare and impressive anecdotes; the wit that sparkled here and there in the midst of what seemed prosy; his remarks on books and friends and mental hospitality, and the deeper courtesies of heart of which social intercourse is the external form; his quotations, terse and pointed, from great observers past and present—all contributed to impress the audience with a sense of depths of thought, philosophic, and humane, beneath the surface of his speech." Ironically, as forgettable as this lecture may have been, Emerson did manage to utter one of his most iconic of apothegms that night in Oakland. Who hasn't heard, "If a man can write a better book, preach a better sermon, or make a better mouse-trap, than his neighbor, though he builds his house in the woods, the world will make a beaten path to his door"? Apparently this gem was embedded in "Hospitality," but because this late lecture was never published, this so Emersonian phrase would have been lost to history if it hadn't been for the fact that sixteen-year-old Sarah S. B. Yule was taking notes in the audience that night. Years later in 1898, she submitted the "mousetrap" maxim as her favorite quotation to a publication of the Oakland Unitarian Church, which subsequently led to its being picked nationally, destining it to become an Emersonian staple for generations of quote books.

According to the Oakland papers the next day, the lecture, whatever its content, had been a moderate success. The *Oakland Daily Transcript* reported that it "was well attended, and evidently gave the highest satisfaction to his audience," while the *Oakland Daily News* noted that "a

large and cultivated audience [had] assembled in College Hall last evening to hear the famous representative of modern thought, Ralph Waldo
Emerson." The *Daily News* reporter evidently shared the great sense of
anticipation of the audience that night: "As he entered the room, and
quietly sat down on the bench beside Professor Durant, every eye was
turned upon him. Those who had never seen him before, must have felt
instinctively 'that is Emerson.' He reminded us forcibly in feature of
John Henry Newman, and is very like him both in the condensation
of his style and the hesitancy of his manner. This latter peculiarity is
almost tantalizing to those who caught a great idea from him and long
to be led by his ultimate results." The lecture itself, though, was somewhat anticlimactic: "But the lecturer set us a thinking and often left us to
scramble out the best we could. It was a rather desultory chat, a friendly
gossip about men, places, nature, and 'things' than a lecture," leaving the
reporter with the impression that Emerson lacked "the ways and means
of the conventional lecturer."

After the lecture, Emerson unwound by paying several calls in Oakland: first to his cousin Ralph Emerson and his wife and children, then
again to visit the Carrs—perhaps to discuss more his adventures in
Yosemite with Muir—and then finally to the home of Walt Whitman's
friend, the war correspondent and Civil War historian William Swinton,
who at that time was a professor of English at the University of California. There, Emerson was introduced to his namesake, Swinton's son
Ralph Waldo Swinton, and encountered an old friend from Cambridge
and London, the southern lawyer Samuel C. Prioleau. These pleasant
duties accomplished, Emerson, according to his own notes, "returned
at 11 o'c P.M. by rail & boat to St. F.," and soon after Thayer found him
happily eating a late dinner in the Occidental's dining room. Edith had
already done his packing, so Emerson went straight to bed in anticipation of tomorrow's early start.

DEPARTURES

After feverish early morning shopping, the settling up of bills, and tip-
ping Captain Cragin, the hotel manager, and Walter, the hotel maître d',
the party left the Occidental Hotel for the last time and boarded the 7:30
Oakland Ferry, arriving an hour later at the Central Pacific terminal.

As it turned out, the Huron Palace Car would not be available for the return trip until the following Monday. However, because Mr. Forbes and Will were keen to fish in Lake Tahoe—"silver trout," remarked Emerson, "were the magnet in the mind of our commanders"—the party was to take the regular cars to Truckee City and stay at the lake until the Huron arrived. Edith, who wished to get her father away from all the favor seekers and curious, carefully hid from him the fact of the Pullman's unavailability because she was afraid he might insist on staying in the city and, even though their departure had been announced in the papers, remain subject to the "vultures." Edith swore everyone to silence, although Thayer prayed that a "little bird" would whisper the secret to him. Not much interested in fishing, Thayer had decided to stay behind for a few days for business; he would have loved to have Emerson for company. Nevertheless, he kept mum and Emerson departed.

Although Thayer was a bit blue to be left behind, he kept himself busy for the next three days. He ran last-minute errands and picked up packages for Mr. Forbes, Alice, Edith, and even Mrs. Russell, who found that she'd left her boots behind and telegraphed back to get them. Thayer also had to settle some outstanding bills for Mr. Forbes and for Alice, who was being dunned for four dollars by a chiropodist, Dr. Popper, "the corn doctor" (after paying this bill, Thayer couldn't help but notice all the signs featuring giant feet in the city). In between his own business calls, Thayer managed, too, to sit for a photographic portrait by I. W. Taber (yet another New Bedford man), but he was less than thrilled by the results: "I would rather have given five dollars *not* to have them taken. It took away all my peace of mind for the day to see some of the negatives. . . . I am not joking when I say that the painfully inefficient and vacuous, feeble face that looked at me from some of the negatives has haunted me all day." Nevertheless, he found one that was the least objectionable and sent it back as a present for Sophy. Finally, mindful of how little cash he had left in his pocket, Thayer totted up the expenses of the trip and was somewhat taken aback that all told, the trip cost him close to a thousand dollars.

It wasn't all chores and bills, though. Thayer also went to the theater, dined with friends at the Union Club, made calls, and passed an afternoon at San Francisco's amusement park, Woodward's Gardens. Here, he spent most of his time watching the grizzly bears, tigers, monkeys, and kangaroos, speculating on whom among his acquaintances each looked the most like. Finally, though, Thayer felt the itch to move on, especially because he, too, was starting to attract favor seekers, so he left San Francisco on Sunday morning, bound for Sacramento, where he wished to discuss a legal matter with a lawyer there and visit his Harvard classmate Henry Brown, a local minister. On Monday, he would catch the Huron as it passed through.

LAKE TAHOE

Meanwhile, the rest of the party had enjoyed a quiet respite in the Sierra before the long push home. Leaving Oakland, the train carried them through fields of blazing poppies and mustard that stretched seemingly endlessly toward the brown foothills and blue, snow-capped mountains far away. At Sacramento, Edith managed to buy small boxes of fresh strawberries and cherries and nuts and cakes, and although they had already eaten at Lathrop, they all gorged themselves nevertheless. At four, the train entered the Sierra, and the observation car was attached so everyone could experience again the thrill of Cape Horn and admire the high mountain peaks and sheer canyon walls, some of which, Edith noticed, were covered with carpets of ceanothus. Emerson, for his part, felt that "the forest has lost much of its pretension by our acquaintance with grander woods, but the country is everywhere rich in trees & endless flowers, & New England starved in comparison." Dinner was held at the mountain station of Alta, after which time, given the growing darkness, the seats were made up as couches in case anyone wished to sleep before they reached Truckee City at 11:00 p.m. There they would stay the night in a hotel.

The next morning, after a hearty breakfast of mountain trout, everyone climbed into two carriages, which carried them on an "excellent soft road" the twelve miles to Lake Tahoe—all except Mr. Forbes, who, of course, insisted going on horseback. Despite some stubborn snowpack, spring flowers were making their appearance—"great mats of trailing cyanothus" and the elusive snow plant, with its "scarlet cone like a great strawberry." Golden moss hung from the boughs of the great pines and firs, which grew parklike, allowing for the occasional glimpse of the mountains and then Lake Tahoe itself. The road then bent down to the rocky lakeshore, crossed the Nevada border, and brought the travelers to a simple inn constructed so close to the edge of the vast blue lake that one could hear the lapping of the waves from the dining room window. Recently built, the inn had been made ready for habitation only the previous Tuesday, but all found it comfortable, and undoubtedly John Murray Forbes found the adjacent hot springs bathhouse a welcome relief after hours in the saddle. The prime location of this new inn must have reminded Emerson of a joke he made the year before concerning an inn on Nantasket Beach: that the shrewd innkeeper, "by buying a few acres well-chosen of the sea-shore, which cost no more than land elsewhere, & building a good house, he shifts upon nature the whole duty of filling the house with guests," for which he doesn't have to pay a dime.

In the afternoon, after another meal of grilled trout, Will and Holdrege rowed Alice and Edith out onto the lake, where they all admired the changing shades of the ice-cold water, from "Prussian-blue thick" to a delicate ultramarine, depending on how it was struck by wind and sun. Emerson spent his time strolling the black sand beach and wandering through the pines of the forest, perhaps admiring the antics of the squirrels. In his essay "Art," he had written, improbably, that "a squirrel leaping from bough to bough, and making the wood but one wide tree for his pleasure, fills the eye not less than a lion,—is beautiful, self-sufficing, and stands then and there for nature." The day ended with Edith and her father sitting on the piazza watching "the sunset light on the snowy mountains—the opal tints and clear yellow sky in the southern horizon." Emerson was pleased to see "the minute new moon, and when that had set the evening star was so bright it made a path of light across the water, and the dashing water against the rocks made the last perfecting charm." Thus, on this quiet porch perched high in the Sierra Nevada on the edge of this gently lapping mountain lake, did Ralph Waldo Emerson spend his last evening in the West.

Chapter 8
EMERSON AFTER CALIFORNIA

I am ready to die out of nature, and be born again into this new yet unapproachable America I have found in the West.

—Ralph Waldo Emerson, "Experience" (1844)

The record of the Emerson party's return trip becomes disappointingly sketchy after they left Lake Tahoe. In *A Western Journey*, Thayer summarily disposes of the entire journey back by writing, "There was no longer occasion to write letters, and I have no notes of this part of the journey." We do have a bit more from the jottings in Emerson's and Edith's respective pocket diaries. On Monday, they returned from Lake Tahoe to Truckee City in time for a brief walk to Donner Lake, famed as the scene of the Donner Party ordeal in the winter of 1846–47, and then boarded the Huron for Ogden, Utah, at eleven that night. Two days later, May 25, somewhere on the plains of Wyoming, Ralph Waldo Emerson celebrated his sixty-eighth birthday. We can imagine the returning travelers marked the occasion by making good use of the champagne and other fresh provisions with which John Murray Forbes had undoubtedly restocked the Huron before leaving the West Coast. The next day, they passed through Omaha and back across the Missouri River, and at three the next morning the Huron, with Mr. and Mrs. Forbes and Alice still aboard, was switched off for Ottumwa, Iowa. The rest of the party continued in a regular Pullman sleeper to Burlington, which was George Holdrege's hometown. Wilkie James would get off here also to catch a train north to Milwaukee, Wisconsin, where he hoped to get a position on the Chicago, Milwaukee, and St. Paul Railroad.

At this point, Emerson's cares were returning to him and he was exceedingly anxious to return to Concord to get back to business. Edith, however, suggested that they stop for a day at Niagara Falls so that she could see it "in Summer Dress." At first, Emerson resisted, saying that "Niagara was just on the edge of my field—I can see it anytime," but Edith insisted, arguing that Emerson would be home in plenty of time for his appointments. And so, reaching Niagara at noon on May 28, Emerson, Edith, and Mrs. Russell bid good-bye to Will and Annie Anthony and checked into the Cataract House. They spent that afternoon and the morning of the next day viewing the falls from both the American and Canadian sides, as well as taking a drive to Goat Island. In the end, Emerson was glad they had made the stop: "Niagara," he wrote in his pocket diary, "was never so great to my eyes as today."

Of course, there was an ulterior motive behind Edith's delaying their arrival back in Concord. Edward was still at Bush convalescing from the chicken pox and the house continued under quarantine. Even so, when Emerson arrived in Concord on the afternoon of May 30, much to his frustration he found himself still barred from home. As he wrote later to Thomas Carlyle, "My long journey to California ended in many distractions on my return home. I found Varioloid in my house (which my son had ignorantly brought home from his Medical Hospital,) & I was not permitted to enter it for many days, & could only talk with wife, son & daughter from the yard." Emerson had been warned in letters from Ellen that the house would be under quarantine until June 3, but he had hoped that it would be lifted sooner. In any case, instead of a joyful return to hearth and family, Emerson was forced to lodge at the Old Manse, a guest of Elizabeth Ripley.

It took several days before Edward was strong enough to be moved, after which he went to stay with the Forbes in Milton for the rest of his convalescence. Unfortunately for Emerson, both Lidian and Ellen decided that they, too, needed to get out of the house and promptly decamped with Edward, leaving Emerson behind at Concord. Unwilling to let her husband stay alone at Bush, Lidian locked Emerson's bedroom door and hid the key, thus forcing him to continue taking his meals and sleeping at the Old Manse, although during the day he could still work in his study at home. Soon, however, Emerson grew too restless with this routine, and Ellen, knowing that she and Lidian were to return by June 14, revealed that his keys were in the third drawer of his cabinet, after which he moved back in on June 9. Eventually, with everybody back in place, Emerson's beloved world reconstituted itself, gradually returning to normal. Emerson began to poke away at the troublesome book for the

English publisher Hotten, and more agreeably, he continued to polish up the manuscript for his poetry anthology, *Parnassus*.

EMERSON'S IMPRESSIONS OF CALIFORNIA

Shortly after Emerson's return east, the *San Francisco Chronicle* ran a rather snarky squib noting the fact that "Ralph Waldo Emerson, who has arrived at his home in Concord, Mass., from his California trip, expresses much satisfaction with his journey, but thinks everything connected with the western country is magnified except for the Yosemite Valley. RALPH didn't find his own reputation magnified much out West; perhaps that accounts for the sour milk in the EMERSONIAN cocoanut." Although Emerson in an unguarded moment may have given such an assessment to reporters on the return trip, his overall impression of California was for the most part positive. Even before leaving California, Emerson had written to Lidian and Ellen about the endless sunshine and fertility of the state, not to mention its promise of future prosperity once it had matured beyond its spendthrift frontier stage and Yankees predominated: "[California's] immense prospective advantages, which only now begin to be opened to men's eyes by the new railroad, are its nearness to Asia and South America; and *that* with a port such as Constantinople, plainly a new centre like London, with immense advantages over *that*, is here. There is an awe and terror lying over this new garden, all empty as yet of any adequate people, yet with this assured future in American hands; unequalled in climate and production. Chicago and St. Louis are toys to it in its assured felicity." And when on his way home he stopped briefly at the offices of his publisher, James T. Fields, Emerson was also full of enthusiasm for the state, citing the splendors of not only Yosemite—and chiding those tourists too soft to make the trip—but also the Golden Gate, so called "not because of its gold, but because of the lovely golden flowers which at this season cover the whole face of the country down to the edge of the great sea." "We must not visit San Francisco too young," he told Fields, "or we shall never wish to come away." This was a variation of a similar remark he made in the earlier letter to Lidian from Calistoga, which indicates he meant it in earnest.

Emerson's most extended remarks about his trip to California came in the same June 30 letter to Thomas Carlyle in which he had complained about the inconvenience of the quarantine. This letter was a response to

Carlyle's June 4 letter congratulating him on his "magnificent adventure ... climbing the backbone of America [and] looking into the Pacific Ocean." In reply, Emerson wrote,

> I had crowded & closed my Cambridge lectures in haste, & went to the land of Flowers invited by John M. Forbes one of my most valued friends, father of my daughter Edith's husband. With him & his family & one or two chosen guests, the trip was made under the best conditions of safety, comfort & company, I measuring for the first time one entire line of the Country. . . . On the plains we saw multitudes of antelopes, hares, gophers—even elks, & one pair of wolves on the plains; the grizzly bear only in a cage. We crossed one region of the Buffalo, but only saw one captive. We found Indians at every railroad station—the squaws & papooses begging, and the "bucks" as they wickedly call them, lounging.

And as for California itself, he again unreservedly sang its praises:

> California surprises with a geography, climate, vegetation, beasts, birds, fishes even, unlike ours; the land immense: the Pacific Sea; Steam brings the near neighborhood of Asia; and South America at your feet; the mountains reaching the altitude of Mont Blanc; the State in its 600 miles of latitude producing all our Northern fruits, & also the fig, orange & banana. But the climate chiefly surprised me. The Almanac said April; but the day said June;—& day after day for six weeks uninterrupted sunshine. November & December are the rainy months. The whole Country was colored with flowers and all of them unknown to us except in greenhouses. Every bird that I know at home is represented here, but in gayer plumes.

Carlyle wrote back, thanking Emerson for his "letter from the Far West," which he found "charmingly vivid and free"—"one seemed to attend you personally, and see with one's own eyes the notabilia, human and other, of those huge regions, in your swift flight through them to and from." Still, for Carlyle, there was "something huge, painful, and almost appalling . . . in that wild Western World of yours." Like Emerson, he too hoped that "all-wise Providence" had used the gold bait to draw "English Populations" to the West, so that out the "hideous stew of Anarchy" would eventually arise a civilization that still reads "Shakespeare and the English Bible." For all of California's beauty, Emerson and Carlyle were on the same page in this regard: the state still lacked a sufficient population of solid, middle-class Anglo Saxons—read "Yankees" for Emerson—to make it a true paradise.

Something of the same issue came up when the Emersons hosted Bret Harte (1836–1902) for dinner in Concord later that October. Harte was at that time California's most famous writer. He had made a name for himself with tales of the gold rush such as "The Luck of the Roaring Camp," which featured romanticized depictions of miners, gamblers, and prostitutes with hearts of gold. Having managed to place a story in the *Atlantic Monthly* alongside essays by Emerson and Thoreau, Harte had come east in 1871 to capitalize on his growing fame. There he met Emerson at a Boston dinner party in February, and Emerson's long fascination with frontier and western humor probably led to the later invitation to Concord. According to Emerson's journal entry, the visit got off to a contentious start. In his essay "Civilization" in *Society and Solitude*, Emerson had insisted on the importance of the moral element in the transformation of a frontier society from primitive to civilized, noting as a homey illustration how quickly pianos appear even in log cabins. Harte disagreed: "Do you know that, on the contrary, it is vice that brings them in? It is the gamblers who bring in the music to California. It is the prostitute who brings in the New York fashions of dress there, and so throughout." Emerson responded that he drew "from Pilgrim experience, and knew on good grounds the resistless culture that religion effects." Harte, though, stuck to his guns: California was just fine with the rough civilizers it had and would find its way to its own kind of society. Despite this disagreement, the two seemed to like each other, and both enjoyed talking about their experiences in California.

The following month, Harte was invited back, and he and Emerson sat in the parlor before the fire discussing such diverse aspects of the state as the prevalence of artesian wells—Emerson talked of the one he had seen in Stockton, while Harte championed San Jose's—as well as the reputations of new western poets, such as Joaquin Miller and Charles Warren Stoddard (Harte liked the latter but had little use for the former). At dinner, Edith monopolized Harte, perhaps sharing their mutual California experiences, but it was Lidian who again brought up the issue of who were true civilizers of the West, challenging the veracity of Harte's stories of self-sacrificing miners and soft-hearted prostitutes: "Mr Harte," she said pointedly, "I wanted to ask you if you really have witnessed the instances of disinterested feeling, which you describe, in rough people, or rather you know that such have been by personal experience?" His noncommittal reply raised suspicions in both Lidian and Ellen, that despite his attractive personality, Harte "created his tales out of the whole cloth." It is not recorded what Emerson thought of this exchange, but he clearly had his doubts as well. Although Emerson had every confidence that the "World Soul" could eventually bring good out of evil in California, he apparently returned from his trip disturbed by the chaotic state of its culture and convinced that the swift progress of civilization out west would ultimately depend on high-minded Yankee and other Anglo-Saxon settlers, not the ethnically diverse and feckless population of rowdies and roughnecks that Harte celebrated. California may indeed become the "new garden," but it would need the right kind of Adams and Eves to make it so.

ECHOES OF JOHN MUIR

There was already at least one person in California who fulfilled Emerson's conception of the ideal immigrant, even if he wasn't a Yankee. Emerson had been immensely impressed by John Muir in Yosemite, and in a list of his personal heroes entitled "My Men" jotted down in his journal shortly after returning, Emerson included Muir's name along with those of Thomas Carlyle, Louis Agassiz, John Murray Forbes, and several others. Muir, for his part, told a friend soon after meeting Emerson that "I wanted to steal him —to kid[nap him] from civilization," for "how naturally he would have taken his place among the pure and happy ghosts of the upper mountains." Encouraged by their meeting, Muir soon began what amounted to an epistolary campaign to lure Emerson back to the Yosemite, starting with a long, plaintive letter that set the ecstatic tone of those to follow.

> YOSEMITE
> *July 6th [1871]*
>
> Dear Emerson,
> You are in the calm of home & perhaps will be glad to hear this small echo from our Mariposa trees. Here is Samoset with whom you are acquainted & with whom I spent a night & day. He is noble in form & behaviour as any Sequoia friend that I

have—less proper—less orthodox than his two companions but has more dignity—more freedom, wh' he manifests by the curving & thrusting of every limb. . . .

I remember that some of your party remarked the silence of our woods & the absence of birds. Well, ere you were half way down the hill a gush of the richest forest song that ever tingled human soul came in grand confidence from the whole grove choir of trees, birds, & flies. When you went away I walked to the top of the ridge commanding a view of the arterial grooves of the Fresnoe, to calm, & when I returned to the grove near Samoset I was welcomed by five or six birds. . . . The Grizzly giant was full of birds, & as I was about to start for Clarks while I lingered among farewell impressions at the base of the last Sequoia a bird came down to one of the lowest branches near my head & uttered loud & clear a bosomful of the most startling worded song that I ever felt. From first to last all of Nature seemed to hear the call of another King David & joined in one grand rejoicing. There was the sweetest wavings & hushings of trees[,] hummings of insect wings[,] open jointed warblings of birds & the rocks too pulsed to the general joy, & every crystal & individual dust.

In a few days I start for the high Sierra East of Yosemite & I would willingly walk all the way to your Concord if so I could have you for a companion—the Indians & hot plains would be nothing. . . .

. . . I have just finished a first reading of your Society & Solitude. The poems I have heard several times. I have been very deeply interested with them & am far from being done with them. Excepting the woodnotes wh' Mrs Carr read me & the Burly bumble bee I have not seen any of your poems before.

Since I cannot have yourself I want your photograph.

Ever Yours,
John Muir

This letter, for all its urgency, did not elicit an immediate answer from Emerson, so on January 10 of the following year, Muir sent another, this time with a gift of the cones of the incense cedar, whose fragrance was spicy and intoxicating. With this letter and its fragrant gift, Emerson was finally induced to reply:

CONCORD,
5 February, 1872

My Dear Muir,
Here lie your significant cedar flowers on my table, and in
another letter; and I will procrastinate no longer. That singular
disease of deferring, which kills all my designs, has left a pair of
books brought home to send to you months and months ago, still
covering their inches on my cabinet, and the letter and letters
which should have accompanied to utter my thanks and lively
remembrance, are either unwritten or lost, so I will send this
peccavi, as a sign of remorse.

I have been far from unthankful—I have everywhere testified
to my friends, who should also be yours, my happiness in finding
you, the right man in the right place in your mountain tabernacle, and have expected when your guardian angel would pronounce that your probation and sequestration in the solitudes
and snows had reached their term, and you were to bring your
ripe fruits so rare and precious into waiting society.

I trust you have also had, ere this, your own signals from
the upper powers. I know that society in the lump, admired at a
distance, shrinks and dissolves, when approached, into imprac-
ticable or uninteresting individuals, but always with a reserve
of a few unspoiled good men, who really give it its halo in the
distance. And there are drawbacks also to Solitude, who is a
sublime mistress, but an intolerable wife. So I pray you to bring
to an early close your absolute contracts with any yet unvisited
glaciers or volcanoes, roll up your drawings, herbariums and
poems, and come to the Atlantic Coast. Here in Cambridge Dr.
Gray is at home, and Agassiz will doubtless be, after a month
or two, returned from Terra del Fuego—perhaps through San
Francisco—Or you can come with him. At all events, on your
arrival, which I assume as certain, you must find your way to
this village, and my house. And when you are tired of our dwarf
surroundings, I will show you better people.

With kindest regards
Yours,

R. W. Emerson

[P.S.] I send two volumes of collected essays by book-post.

Heartened by this response, Muir renewed his plea for Emerson to return to the Sierra in another letter even more baroque in its rhetoric than his first:

YOSEMITE VALLEY
March 18th 72

Dear Emerson,
Come to our mountain fountains, come to Yosemite. Last year you left against law, & I turn to you now in your town & up the valley to Tissiack to see if there be no misunderstanding betwixt you. There are no apologies in Nature else you would owe her one. You cannot be content with last year's baptism. 'Twas only a sprinkle, come be immersed. Your hitherward affinities are not half satisfied. I can't understand the laws that control you to Concord. You are called of the Sierra—an atom elect. Strange you come not to your magnets. If you will come about June & stay until October I will have a hut & horse ready for you. You will see not only Yosemite so-called but a hundred others besides & all their compassing Sierra. Yosemite is only one of many & we will dwell with the whole Merced brotherhood, & we will know how they were made, & how they are now changing from glory to glory. You will lose no time, nothing but civilized sins. Think of the soul lavings & bathings you will get. Think of the glow of your after life. You have been able to look past the fogs of culture to the fountain loves & lives beyond. Here those fountains are bare & unmingled. Here are the shores of all our eternities. How blessed 'twill be after all your hard toils to rest hushed & soothed on those plain spirit shores. [...]

Most cordially yrs,

John Muir

In rapid succession Muir followed this up with two more letters, one (March 26, 1872) containing a magnificent description of an earthquake in Yosemite (although how this would be an enticement to return is not clear) and another (April 3, 1872) ostensibly to acknowledge receipt of Emerson's books but concluding with almost an incantation, again praying for Emerson's return:

Dear Soul, Holy Mountain Spirits compel me to say you another Come. You will not be deaved with theories, nor aimed nor dragged about. You will drift like a winged seed transparent to every light. The mountains will melt that you may drink them. They will thin to sky that you may breathe them. Fountain beauty will go among your tissues as light goes in glass. You will home in holy light. Holy light will home in you.

Unhappily, these letters elicited no replies from Emerson, and a disappointed Muir would not again renew his plea for his return. And yet, despite receiving but one letter from Emerson, Muir treasured it, and though dismissing Emerson's summons to come east, he clearly was extremely flattered by the offer. In a letter to Jeanne Carr shortly after receiving Emerson's missive, Muir made much of the invitation, although he was quick to assert that he was to be as individualistic in his chosen path as was his idol:

I had a letter from Emerson. He judges me and my loose drifting voyages as kindly as yourself. The compliments of you two are enough to spoil one, but I fancy that he, like you, considers that I am so mountain-tanned and storm-beaten I may bear it. I owe all of my best friends to you. A prophecy in this letter of Emerson's recalled one of yours sent me when growing at the bottom of a mossy maple hollow in the Canada woods—that I would one day be with you, Doctor, and Priest in Yosemite. Emerson prophesies in similar dialect that I will one day go to him and "better men" in New England, or something to that effect. I feel like objecting in popular slang that I can't see it. I shall indeed go gladly to the "Atlantic Coast" as he prophesies, but only to see him and the Glacier ghosts of the North. [President] Runkle [of M.I.T.] wants to make a teacher of me, but I have been too long wild, too befogged and befogged to burn well in their patent, high heated, educational furnaces.

It would have been interesting indeed if Muir had followed Emerson back east—how different his career might have been. According to Muir, while they were together in Yosemite, Emerson had spoken glowingly of Thoreau, and perhaps as bait, he asked Muir if he "knew anyone in Cal this side of the continent[,] any young genius likely to be able to edit [Thoreau's] unpublished MS notebooks, etc.—that he must be scholarly acquainted with the Classics—as well as with wild nature etc." But Muir would not be tempted, and Thoreau was an unknown quantity to him then, so he stayed in California. Just as Emerson's failure to return to Yosemite was a great disappointment for Muir, Muir's reluctance to journey east and become the next Thoreau must likewise have been a great disappointment for Emerson.

By 1874, Muir was based in Oakland, furiously writing. His series of periodical articles, later published as *Studies in the Sierra*, launched his writing career, which would bring him national fame and international renown. Muir's final letter to Emerson (May 9, 1874) was simply to alert him to these publications and made no further claims on him. During the rest of 1870s, Muir traveled widely, including to Alaska, before marrying Louisa Strentzel in 1880 and settling down to a decade as a successful rancher and fruit farmer in Martinez, California. Once financially secure, Muir turned his hand to full-time nature writing in the 1890s, after which he turned out some three hundred articles, many for national magazines such as *Century*, as well as ten books, including *Our National Parks* (1901) and *The Yosemite* (1912).

Muir's writing went hand in hand with his continued advocacy for the preservation of the country's wilderness areas, and both activities were instrumental in the conversion of Yosemite into a national park in 1890 and the creation of many new national parks in the coming years. Out of his boyish enthusiasm for Yosemite, Muir evolved into a remarkably savvy lobbyist for preservation, institutionalizing his vision as the first president of the Sierra Club and carefully cultivating important relationships with the rich and powerful, such as E. H. Harriman of the Union Pacific Railroad and President Theodore Roosevelt. His advocacy for wilderness, however, was always an uphill battle. Muir often found that the nature mysticism he shared so easily with Emerson was a hard sell to the vast majority of Americans who would rather exploit the natural world for profit than revere it for its sacred beauty. Nevertheless, Muir has since come to be seen as the father of American environmentalism, as well as the indispensable bridge between Emerson's Transcendentalism and the environmental writers of the twentieth and twenty-first centuries.

Interestingly, Muir's attitude toward Emerson would always remain a touch ambivalent, perhaps due to some "anxiety of influence" on Muir's part. Muir carefully read the two volumes of essays that Emerson sent him (*Nature* and *Essays, First Series*), but he did not hesitate to write vehement disagreements with certain points in the margins. What's more, Muir, who never tired of telling the story of his meeting with Emerson in Yosemite, made much of the fact that Emerson failed to camp out with him in the Mariposa Grove. In his fullest account of their meeting in *Our National Parks* (1901), he specifically highlighted this event, attributing Emerson's reluctance to "rough it" not only to his age and the overprotectiveness of his friends but also by implication to a certain effeteness in Transcendentalism that contrasted poorly with his own nature mysticism. Through his many retellings, Muir's ambivalence was picked up by his friends, such as Theodore Roosevelt, who said to Muir that "I always grudged Emerson's not having gone into camp with you. You would have made him perfectly comfortable and he ought to have had the experience." Muir's later biographers and academic commentators have also read into this incident a deeper conflict between Emerson's monistic idealism and Muir's pantheism. Perhaps, but what is clear is that Muir's subsequent career as an environmental advocate and nature writer would not have been possible without Emerson's Transcendentalism, a fact that Muir himself, for all his ambivalence, recognized. There was a reason why Muir christened "a grand *wide-winged* mountain" in the Sierra for Emerson, kept Emerson's photograph on his mantelpiece, and always had Emerson's collected works within easy reach on his bookshelf. As he said himself, he had never found anyone "half warm enough until Emerson came."

EMERSON'S FINAL YEARS

As his friends and family had hoped, the trip to California filled Emerson with new energy. His son Edward believed that "the excursion greatly refreshed him and very probably prolonged his life." Emerson thus fell back into his old routines of social calls and Harvard duties, and he also began lecturing again, including accepting an invitation to participate in the Star Lecture course in Chicago that fall. After the great Chicago fire destroyed the city in October 1871, Emerson thought he would be released from this obligation, but that was not to be; in fact, he was informed that he was expected to arrive even earlier than he had thought, which, much to his disappointment, necessitated his missing Thanksgiving with the Forbes and the Thayers. He made the best of it, however, and even added lectures in Quincy and Springfield, Illinois, and Dubuque, Iowa. It was not a happy experience, though. Audiences were not enthusiastic, and the local newspapers thought his performances were "stiff and awkward," which served to dampen Emerson's spirits, so recently buoyed in California. Nevertheless, and much to his daughter Ellen's exasperation, Emerson continued to overextend himself with more and more speaking engagements, including one in Baltimore, where he again read "Homes and Hospitality." Walt Whitman, who happened to be in the audience at some of these lectures, found them repetitious of old ideas and "quite attenuated," like a pot of tea on its "*third or fourth* infusion." Emerson moreover was now finding it increasingly difficult to keep his place in his text and not become confused during his talks. After a particularly poor performance at Boston's Mechanics' Hall in April 1872, in which he read the same page twice without noticing, Ellen insisted that she always accompany him from then on to give him prompts and to keep lectures on track.

At this point, disaster struck. Around 5:30 a.m. of July 24, 1872, Emerson awoke to see flames in his bedroom. A defective chimney flue had apparently ignited the house. He leapt out of bed, alerted Lidian, and, oblivious to the rain, ran to the front yard yelling, "Fire!" Within minutes, the Concord Fire Department was on the scene and set to work. All the occupants of Bush escaped unharmed, and the quick action of friends and neighbors meant that most of the family's furniture and clothing, not to mention the contents of Emerson's library, including books and manuscripts, were hauled into the yard and saved. The house itself, though, was almost a total loss. Louisa May Alcott, who with her sister Anna took charge of safeguarding the Emersons' property, wrote that Ralph Waldo "looked pathetically funny that morning wandering about in his night gown, pants, old coat & no hose. His dear bald head lightly covered with his best hat, & an old pair of rubbers wobbling on his Platonic feet." The burning of Bush House, which had been Emerson's home since 1835, disturbed him profoundly. One of Emerson's biographers has even suggested that he suffered a mild stroke that morning, which then affected his physical health, causing his hair and teeth to fall out and hastening his mental deterioration.

And yet, as Emerson himself had preached, all calamities had their compensations. Almost immediately, the family was overwhelmed by substantial gifts of money from friends and admirers, which meant that the underinsured Bush could be speedily rebuilt. There was also more than enough money for Emerson to take an extended holiday while this occurred, and Ellen decided that a long journey to Europe and the Mediterranean was in order—perhaps it would have the same effect as California. Thus, from October 23, 1872, to May 27, 1873, the pair traveled extensively in England, Europe, and Egypt (where he happened to meet a very young Theodore Roosevelt rowing on the Nile). Emerson enjoyed parts of the trip, especially seeing longtime friends like Carlyle (as he suspected, for the last time), but for the most part he found the trip a trial, especially when he was forced into social events that exposed his mental confusion. He was also tremendously homesick. Happily, though, in his absence Bush House was restored to what it had been (if not better), and when Emerson and Ellen returned, all of Concord turned out to take them in procession to their rebuilt home. Emerson was confused by all the hoopla but immensely grateful when he entered his restored study and saw that all its furniture, pictures, books, and papers were back in their usual places.

Despite the festive homecoming, it was clear that Emerson's failing mind had become much, much worse since the fire. In addition to the fact that he no longer had the wherewithal to write anything of any length, he was finding the details of day-to-day living increasingly bewildering too. Will Forbes and Thayer continued to manage Emerson's finances, which included renegotiating book contracts and demanding back royalties from delinquent publishers. The Emerson children—Ellen, Edith, and Edward—took over the duties of editing those works still owed for publication, including the Hotten volume, which Edith completed with the help of the man who would become became Emerson's literary executor, James Elliot Cabot. The book, *Letters and Social Aims* (1876), was the last to be published in Emerson's lifetime, and it contained versions of four of the lectures Emerson gave in California: "Immortality," "Society in America" (published as "Social Aims"), "Resources," and "Character" (published as "Greatness"). Ironically, the volume's heavily edited essays were praised by one critic for their "slightly increased love of structure, and a dawning taste for a beginning, a middle, and an end."

Despite the care and attention lavished on Emerson, his family and friends could not stop the steady erosion of his memory and his increasing aphasia. Ellen dated his aphasia to as far back as 1867, and Thayer had remarked on their trip to California that Emerson's speech had become slower and more deliberate. At first, Emerson's lapses could be amusing. In 1872, Ellen wrote to her sister: "You ought to hear how funny Father is now. He forgets names of people and things, and the exercise of his favorite metonymy is on these occasions so witty that I wish it could be recorded. . . . I never tell him what he is trying for, that I may prolong the entertainment." John Muir, for example, became "that bearded young man in California," or the word "umbrella" became a riddle: "I can't tell its name, but I can tell its history. Strangers take it away." Eventually, Emerson's loss of words became profound, such that he could communicate with his family only with difficulty, and with others, even old friends, he dared not even try. In the presence of company, he retreated into a sphinxlike silence that was often misunderstood. After he dined at Henry James Sr.'s home in April 1874, for example, the usually perceptive William James wrote his brother Henry that "Emerson looks in magnificent health, but the refined idiocy of his manner seems as if it must be an affectation." Sadly, it was not. Three years later, Emerson attended the seventieth birthday party for the poet John Greenleaf Whittier, at which Mark Twain gave a humorous speech in which he poked fun at Emerson. Seeing Emerson sitting in stony silence, Twain was sure he had offended him and later wrote a letter apologizing for his performance. He never responded, but Ellen sent a letter to Twain's wife, telling her that her husband had nothing to worry about: "To my father it is as if [the speech] had never been; never quite heard, never quite understood it, and he forgets easily and entirely."

More modern commentators have tried at this distance to diagnose Emerson's exact mental condition, from Broca's aphasia to Alzheimer's disease, and anecdotes from his last years have been cited in several books as examples of how one can deal positively with dementia. However, this modern perception may result from friends' overly rosy accounts of Emerson's last years. Walt Whitman, for example, observed that "the senile Emerson is the old Emerson in all that goes to make Emerson notable: this shadow is a part of his—a necessary feature of his nearly rounded life: it gives him statuesqueness—throws him, so it seems to me, impressively as a definite figure in a background of mist." William Dean

Howells, on the other hand, sought to protect Emerson's reputation by playing up his seeming cheerfulness in the face of his decline:

> He was . . . beginning to forget, to achieve an identity indepen-
> dent of the memory which constitutes the unsevered conscious-
> ness of other men. This gift of purely spiritual continuity evinced
> itself publicly as well as privately, and it was the singular pleasure
> of hearing him lecture, to see him lose his place in his manuscript,
> turn the leaves over with inaudible sighs, and then go smiling on.
> Once I remember how, when some pages fell to the floor and were
> picked up for him and put before him, he patiently waited the result
> with an unconcern as great as that of any in his audience. He was,
> in fact, the least anxious of those present, for by that time it had
> come about that the old popular . . . doubt of him had turned into a
> love and reverence so deep and true that his listeners all cared more
> than he to have the distractions of the accident end in his triumph.

And yet, the private correspondence of his children reveals that Emerson was subject to the same kinds of obsessive behavior, impatience, and depression as other sufferers of dementia. In his 1870 essay "Old Age," Emerson had hoped that his spiritual achievements would result in satisfaction and patient serenity in his last years, but this depended on the continued acuteness of his mind, especially his memory, the failure of which was a bitter blow to his equanimity. There were good days, of course, and he still enjoyed the presence of his friends, such as Bronson Alcott, his grandchildren, the quiet hours in his study, and his walks in nature. And even in his very last years, Ellen allowed him to read a lecture in public on occasion, although these events were carefully managed (ironically, one lecture oft repeated was "Memory"). His last public appearance was reportedly at the Concord School of Philosophy in July 1881, where, among friends, he could feel comfortable. After this, there was only silence, and all that was left for the public was Emerson's benign, sometimes dreamy, smiling face that many interpreted as angelic.

THE DEATH AND AFTERLIFE OF RALPH WALDO EMERSON

As early as 1849, an anonymous reporter for the *Boston Post* speculated on Emerson's eventual death: "We wonder if he will ever die like other men? It seems to us he will find some way of slipping out of the world and shutting the door behind him before anyone knows he is going. We cannot believe he will be *translated*, for this would be too gross a method of exit. He is more likely to be evaporated some sunshiny day, or to be exhaled like a perfume. He will certainly not be seen to go—he will only *vanish*." In a sense, this is exactly what happened. By 1882, the decay of Emerson's mind was almost complete. Ellen feared that total loss of language was only a matter of time. On March 26, 1882, Ellen took Emerson to the funeral service for Henry Wadsworth Longfellow at Mount Auburn Cemetery. Emerson had long known Longfellow, but staring into the casket that day, he couldn't remember who it was. "Where are we?" he asked Ellen, "And who is the sleeper?" From then on, Emerson's major activity of the day was to take a long walk, which Ellen and Lidian allowed him to do, as neighbors knew to send him home if he became befuddled.

It was on one of these walks that Emerson was caught in a rainstorm and thoroughly soaked. A cold resulted, developing into pneumonia, but typical of dementia sufferers, Emerson would not be managed. According to his son Edward, "He did not know how to be sick and desired to be dressed and sit in his study, and as we had found that any attempt to regulate his actions lately was very annoying to him, and he could not be made to understand the reasons for our doing so in his condition, I determined that it would not be worth while to trouble and restrain him." Finally, on April 22, he remained in bed, where he managed to quip that if this was to be his end, he would rather have "fallen down cellar." His condition worsened, and as the family gathered, he tried his best to say his good-byes. Emerson died on the evening of the April 27. Three days later, borne by pallbearers who included Will Forbes and Thayer, he was buried in Concord at Sleepy Hollow Cemetery on Author's Ridge near the graves of Hawthorne and Thoreau. Once when Edward had asked his father what he thought the afterlife might hold, Emerson said he didn't know, but "I think we may be sure that, whatever comes after death, no one will be disappointed." Given all the tribulations of his last years, it is not hard to believe that, for all his belief in the immortality of the soul, he would have found even utter oblivion satisfactory.

In the wake of his death, news of which was carried in major newspapers throughout the country, Emerson soon achieved apotheosis as the Sage of Concord, a kind of culture hero whose reputation was simplified and sentimentalized into what a contemporary critic called the "Emersonian Cult." Anything that had made his thought controversial

or inconsistent—or Emerson himself seem less than morally perfect—
was suppressed and forgotten. Part of the process of sanctification had
already begun in the last years of his life when his aphasia was interpreted as the rarefication of a personality on the verge of ultimate spiritual transformation. Once dead, however, the process accelerated to an
extraordinary degree, promoted by the publication over the next two
years of no fewer than five hundred books and articles, including four
major biographies by George Willis Cooke, Alexander Ireland, Moncure
Conway, and Oliver Wendell Holmes Sr. This output tended to fix Emerson in the public mind as an American secular saint of the Victorian
age, a bland perception that persists to this day.

Of course, all this outpouring of ink included James Bradley Thayer's
A Western Journey with Mr. Emerson, published in 1884. While it, too,
sanded off many of the rough edges of its subject, the book nevertheless
had the advantage of presenting Emerson as a real person enjoying the
very real pleasures of overland travel with friends. Thayer was proud of
his publication, even if it was little more than, as he said in his preface,
"wreccum maris" or flotsam and jetsam. He had copies sent to family
and friends, including Lidian and Ellen Emerson, the Forbes family, as
well as to Mrs. Russell, Horatio Stebbins, Moncure Conway, and James
Elliot Cabot. All were delighted with the volume, returning thank-you
letters that extolled its fidelity to Emerson's language and personality. In
addition, he had the publisher send the book out for review, and Thayer
employed a clipping service to collect those that came in. Most reviewers
enjoyed the book's anecdotes and lauded the author's efforts in recording
some of Emerson's more pithy remarks. Others praised it for illustrating
Emerson's homely Yankee habits and humane manners, so at odds with
his reputation as an "abstract seer, dwelling in the atmosphere of pure
thought." Indeed, given Emerson's equanimity as a traveler, one review
went so far as to recommend that the book "be generally distributed to
American tourists as an illustration of the possibility of adapting oneself
to circumstances and preserving a desirable balance by meeting the inevitable increase of fatigue by a corresponding increase of good spirits and
generous tolerance." Even the usually cantankerous *San Francisco Chronicle* took notice of the book and published a favorable review. And yet,
not all were so positive, with one dismissing the volume as merely adding
"a few stones to the increasing cairn of Emersoniana" and another stating
that the book's only major revelations were that Emerson smoked cigars

and ate pie for breakfast. Whatever the reviews, *A Western Journey with Mr. Emerson* was unlikely to become a best seller. It quickly faded into obscurity as a minor footnote in the ever-expanding Emerson bibliography, and the trip to California was soon largely forgotten.

But not by everyone. For some, such as Horatio Stebbins, Charles Murdock, Galen Clark, and Jeanne Carr, not to mention those lesser known in his audiences, such as Sarah S. B. Yule of "mousetrap" fame, Emerson's visit to California was a high point in their lives, long to be remembered. John Muir himself finally made the pilgrimage to Concord in 1888. Standing by Emerson's grave beneath a pine tree on Author's Ridge at Sleepy Hollow, Muir cast his mind back to their meeting in Yosemite seventeen years before and imagined that, although now "gone to higher Sierras," Emerson "was again waving his hand in friendly recognition." Indeed, a residual memory of Emerson's presence in California lasted into the twentieth century. The year 1903 was the centennial of Emerson's birth, and many communities and organizations across the country geared up to celebrate it. These included many Unitarian churches, which by this time had thoroughly claimed Emerson as one of their own. In San Francisco, the Reverend Bradford Leavitt, the minister who inherited the pulpit of First Unitarian from Horatio Stebbins, thought it especially appropriate that his church—the one in which Emerson had once spoken and his friend Thomas Starr King had preached—should host just such a celebration. He sent out invitations to speak to several local notables, such as David Starr Jordan, president of Stanford University, who jumped at the chance, and John Muir, who was forced to decline because he was to be traveling overseas (he responded kindly, though, saying that he would be there in spirit among the "Emerson lovers" and wished the celebration "every Emersonian blessing").

Even without Muir, the May 17 event was a great success. First Unitarian was packed to standing room only, and the audience cheerfully sat through both a full church service and three ponderous papers by Leavitt ("Emerson and Religion"); Professor H. C. Stephens of the University of California ("The Influence of Emerson on Modern English Literature, Especially on Kipling"); and Jordan ("Emerson's Conception of Fate as Compared with That of Darwin"). The newspapers the next day made little of the content of these lectures but much of the fact that they were delivered from the very pulpit Emerson himself had lectured from thirty-two years before.

FIGURE 14. *Ralph Waldo Emerson Tree in the Muir Woods*, photograph by Alexander J. "Zan" Stark, ca. 1937. —Courtesy of the Zan Postcard Negatives Collection, Anne T. Kent California Room, Marin County Free Library, San Rafael, CA.

Notably, this event was not the only celebration of the legacy of Emerson in and around the Bay Area. On May 18, the Unitarian Club of California met in the rooms of San Francisco's Merchants' Club to read even more scholarly papers on Emerson's legacy, while the Unitarian churches of both Oakland and Berkeley held special services to commemorate his life and work the following week. This was capped off on the actual day of Emerson's birth, May 25, 1903, when a group of "literary folk," including Jack London and George Sterling, converged on Redwood Canyon (now Muir Woods National Monument) outside San Rafael. After a "pleasant luncheon," the newspaper editor F. Bailey Millard rose and read letters from Edward Emerson and John Muir, both of whom gave their blessings on the day's festivities, after which a number of other dignitaries spoke at length. Finally, the speeches over, the ceremony culminated with the unveiling of a brass plaque affixed to the trunk of one of the largest sequoias of the grove. It bore a simple inscription: "1803—Ralph Waldo Emerson—1903." Thus, even if the Sage of Concord himself had rejected a like honor so many years ago, California was not to be denied its Emerson Big Tree.

THE LATER LIVES OF THE CALIFORNIA FELLOWSHIP

And what became of the rest of California fellowship? On their return from California, John Murray and Sarah Hathaway Forbes resumed their lives of privilege at their mansion at Milton and their palatial summerhouse on Naushon Island. Shortly after returning, they gifted Emerson with a picture as a souvenir of their trip that he greatly appreciated. "Not contented with taking such a heavy load as an old pedant three or four thousand miles and back again, to California, and home," he wrote Mrs. Forbes, "you have insisted on decorating his wall with this grand reminder of the Western Paradise." "I have always had a good opinion of my species," he added, "but I own that it mends with my age."

John Murray Forbes returned to the management of his far-flung businesses, refreshed for the challenges ahead, which would be many. His western railroad interests continued to consume much of his energies, as he was confronted with a serve economic depression in 1873, increasingly sharp competition from financiers such as Jay Gould, and a crippling railroad strike in 1877. Worn out, Forbes finally decided to retire, at least from the railroads, in 1881. By this time, the CB&Q spanned four western states and ran 2,294 miles of track, earning over $21 million in revenue that year alone.

Mr. and Mrs. Forbes would always retain a lively interest in California, traveling there again several times over the years, even acquiring a ranch and citrus grove in Montecito, near Santa Barbara, which they christened Mt. Saint George. It was here that Mrs. Forbes met Henry Chapman Ford, a noted painter and advocate for the preservation of the California missions. Perhaps first inspired by their 1871 visit to Mission Dolores in San Francisco, the Forbes decided to bolster Ford's cause and commissioned a series of eighteen now-iconic paintings of the missions in 1882, which currently reside in Harvard's Fogg Museum. Mrs. Forbes also corresponded for a time with John Muir, he providing her with seeds and bulbs from California, and she relaying news of her husband and of Emerson, of whom she offered some candidly shrewd assessments: "There is much in Mr. Emerson's writings to admire, yet in him I always feel the want of the genial sympathy with human everyday life—if he was musical perhaps he would have a touch of Robbie Burns, which united with his purity of thought would be fine—but each has his own individuality, and each must work that out for himself as best he may." In any case, she concluded, "He is getting old now and I fancy will not go beyond his earlier efforts in what he does, but he is always kind and gentle." Mrs. Forbes also encouraged Muir's efforts on behalf of the national parks, although not without including a bit of her own class conservatism mixed with Emersonian themes: "Of late we hear much of the beauty and grandeur of the geysers of the Yellowstone river, and that our government is going to secure the finest part of it. I wish it might do so of all the finest of our scenery, for we are not a sufficiently poetical people to revere such beauty and wonder as we ought. But food and clothing for families must be provided, and the doing that develops much that is manly and fine in character, and self reliant. We must wait a while for the highest and finest culture—when I am in the south and when I think of parts of the West I saw, it seems a quite herculean task to bring our whole country out of the barbaric." Both the Forbes would continue to live in Milton until their deaths, he in 1898 and she two years later.

Of the two daughters, Sarah and Alice, less is known. Alice H. Forbes married the Boston businessman Edward Montague Cary in 1875, and Sarah, the wealthy English sherry importer William Hastings Hughes in 1887 (Hughes's sister, Jane Elizabeth Hughes, was the cofounder of the British Red Cross). Sarah eventually developed into a talented editor, and beginning in 1891, she worked intensively with her father to produce *Letters and Recollections of John Murray Forbes* (two volumes, 1899) and

Reminiscences of John Murray Forbes (three volumes, 1902). Both of the Forbes daughters continued to live in their Milton mansions, wedding gifts from their father, until their deaths in 1917.

Arriving back from California, Edith and Will Forbes also easily resumed their routines in Milton. Will returned to work in his father's company, J. M. Forbes & Company, where he became an expert in the handling of the company's far-flung investments, especially railroads (no sentimentalist, Forbes thought the Pullman system of leasing its cars was a "fungus growth" on the industry to "be worked out sooner or later"). Edith gave birth to a son on August 27, 1871, who was named John Murray Forbes after his grandfather but nicknamed Don. In all, the Forbes would have seven children, six boys and a girl, although Don would die young of appendicitis in 1888.

Today, Will Forbes is best remembered not for his service to the railroads but for the part he played in bringing telephone service to the nation. In 1879, Forbes became an investor in, and then the president of, the National Bell Telephone Company. Over the next eight years, Forbes would help build the company into a fabulously successful near monopoly, the precursor of the American Telephone and Telegraph Company (AT&T). Will Forbes not only oversaw the development of telephone technology but also fought off rival corporations such as Western Union and adroitly lobbied state and national governments to forestall regulation of Bell Telephone's reach. Worn out by these labors, Forbes semiretired in 1887 and devoted the last years of his life to his family and to his hobbies: horse breeding, yachting, and traveling, including several trips to Europe and an 1890 expedition to Honduras. In 1897, Will Forbes's health began to decline. Edith believed that he had never fully recovered from his experience as a prisoner of war, but the immediate cause was tuberculosis of the throat, from which he succumbed, surrounded by his family at his Naushon house, on October 11, 1897. Edith continued living at Milton and summering at Naushon. Perhaps stimulated by her work on her father's poetry collection, *Parnassus*, Edith would go on to edit two volumes of children's literature: *The Children's Year-Book: Selections for Every Day in the Year* (1893) and *Favourites of a Nursery of Seventy Years Ago* (1916). She died in Milton in 1929.

James Bradley Thayer returned to his wife Sophy and their four children in Milton and resumed his successful Boston law practice. By this point, Harvard had taken notice of Thayer, and the following year, in light of literary criticism he had published in the 1860s, offered him a professorship of English. The law, however, was Thayer's first love, so he declined, only to be offered an even better position at Harvard—the Royall Professorship of Law—in 1874. Here he stayed for the rest of his career, instrumental in helping to modernize the Harvard law curriculum. Thayer was a charismatic teacher noted for both kindness and rigor; as one of his colleagues put it, "He was infinitely patient with the poorly-gifted, but he did not let the limits of their comprehension define the boundaries of the work of his courses." He also authored several influential papers and casebooks; the importance of his concept of judicial restraint was later acknowledged in the rulings of Supreme Court justices Louis D. Brandeis, Oliver Wendell Holmes Jr., and Felix Frankfurter. Perhaps as a direct result of his trip west, Thayer consulted in drafting the constitutions of three western states (the Dakotas and Washington), and true to his prejudices, he became a vociferous advocate for the iniquitous Dawes Act of 1887, legislation designed to convert Native American lands into private property in an effort to force assimilation and destroy Native culture. It was resistance to the Dawes Act by the Lakota, who had adopted the Ghost Dance to this end, that led to the Wounded Knee Massacre of 1890.

In addition to his legal work, Thayer kept to his literary pursuits, continuing to contribute articles to newspapers and magazines. He spent countless hours editing the letters of his good friend the philosopher Chauncey Wright, whose work would have a profound impact on the philosophical pragmatism of C. S. Peirce and William James. An active Unitarian, Thayer also addressed the American Unitarian Association on the seventy-fifth anniversary of its founding in 1900. He spoke, of course, on "Emerson and Religion." A year later, shortly after his seventieth birthday, Thayer's strength began to fail due to heart trouble, and on February 24, 1902, after a leisurely dinner with Sophy at their Cambridge home, he got up to leave the table, lost consciousness, and died of heart failure. The end was sudden and unexpected, but it appears that Thayer was sanguine in the face of death. Shortly before he died, a friend had asked him what he thought the afterlife would be like, and—channeling Emerson—he replied, "I don't know the what or the how, but I believe that somehow it will be all right."

Of the two young men on the expedition, the later lives of Wilkie James and George Holdrege followed two strikingly different trajectories. In fall 1871, Wilkie moved permanently to Milwaukee, Wisconsin, to take a position on the Chicago, Milwaukee, and St. Paul Railroad. It was there in 1873 that he married Caroline Cary, daughter of a moderately wealthy local businessman, Joseph Cary. Although the James family did not approve of the match, "Carrie" was a dutiful and supportive wife, and together they had two children. The year following his marriage, Wilkie left the railroad to go into manufacturing, but the economic recession of the early 1870s, not to mention Wilkie's complete lack of business sense, eventually drove him into bankruptcy in 1877. Moreover, his health had begun to deteriorate—heart and kidney problems—and his war wounds contributed to crippling rheumatism. From then on, Wilkie remained largely an invalid, living on his wife's wealth and the occasional infusions of cash from his brother, Henry James Jr. The situation was not improved when, following the death of his father on December 12, 1882, Wilkie learned that he had been cut out of the will, apparently because of the money still owed from the earlier Florida plantation debacle. After much foot dragging by William James, who thought Wilkie feckless, Henry did manage to arrange for Wilkie to get an equal share of the estate, but by August 1883, he was confined to his bed and died on November 15, 1883, at the age of thirty-eight. Despite his haplessness, however, Wilkie always remained a lovable character, well indicated by the fact that every Milwaukee paper carried his obituary. The *Milwaukee Sentinel* noted, "He possessed rare conversational powers, and was eminently social in his nature. He was a delightful companion, genial, unpretending, genuine. Everybody that knew him loved him, and his death will cause unaffected sorrow through the wide circle of his friends. He was genuine and kindly, and without guile." Henry Jr. later observed of his brother that "he was touchingly young to have such big things, and difficult and trying things, happen to him, and I see how he bore the mark of them for good and for harm (to his poor overstrained and injured physical man) ever afterwards." Despite his naturally buoyant personality, the war, Henry Jr. believed, had doomed him to a life of frustration and failure.

George Holdrege, on the other hand, knew only success. After his return from California, Holdrege continued to work for the Burlington and Missouri River Railroad, a subsidiary of the Chicago, Burlington

& Quincy (CB&Q). He advanced rapidly, rising from assistant paymaster to general manager of the Omaha office in 1882. The year after the California trip, he journeyed east to marry his betrothed, Emily Cabot Atkinson. The story goes that shortly after the wedding, he ran into John Murray Forbes, who asked him what he was doing in Boston. "I've just come from being married," Holdrege replied, to which Forbes cried, "To hell with matrimony, young man, get back out west and build me more railroads!" Sadly, this marriage was short lived, as Emily died in childbirth the following year. Holdrege then threw himself into his work, and after five years he married again, to Frances Rogers Kimball of Omaha. The match was perhaps as much for business as for love, since Frances was the daughter of the supervisor of a rival railroad. Whatever the reason for the "merger," as the Omaha newspapers called it, the marriage was a success, and together they had three daughters.

For the next forty-two years until retirement in 1920, Holdrege worked diligently for the interests of the CB&Q and his boss, Charles Elliott Perkins, whom he yearly hosted on grand tours to survey the railroad's progress west. These tours always included President Perkins's two favorite pastimes: hunting and poker. Perhaps inspired by his experience on the Pullman Palace Car to California back in 1871, Holdrege always made sure that he had "the finest private car of any official of the line, and his chef, Henry, was renowned as the best cook in the company." In addition to his railroad work, Holdrege invested widely in Nebraska land, which he later developed as town sites—the town of Holdrege, in Phelps County, bears his name to this day. Such land speculation, coupled with his high position in the CB&Q, brought him great wealth and political influence throughout the region. By the time he died of a heart attack at his Omaha home on September 16, 1926, his biographer could accurately cite him as "one of the West's most illustrious sons, and the man who supervised more miles of railroad construction than any other individual in American history."

Of Mrs. Russell's subsequent history, we know little. We can guess that she returned to her comfortable home in West Roxbury and resumed her place as matriarch of the Russell clan. Because her son Henry Sturgis Russell had married Mary Hathaway Forbes, we can also posit that she maintained close friendships with the Forbes family and probably summered with them on Naushon Island. Mrs. Russell spent the remaining years of her life devoted equally to family and to a variety of reform movements, especially women's suffrage. She died on August 13, 1888, and the following year, her life and work were eulogized by none other than Julia Ward Howe at the annual Women's Suffrage Convention in Boston.

And finally, of Mrs. Russell's cousin, Annie Anthony, we know a little bit more, but not much. In February 1872, Anthony finally consented to be engaged to George Garrison, the son of William Lloyd Garrison, but the wedding was postponed several times because her betrothed could not keep a job and frequently fell into depression. Finally, George Garrison secured work as a bookkeeper, for which his father paid surety, and he and Annie were married on October 1, 1873. After honeymooning with Annie's relatives in Ohio, the couple went to live with Annie's parents in Boston. Despite George being prone to depression, the marriage was a happy one by all accounts, and together the couple had three children. George died in 1904, after which Annie moved back to Cincinnati to be with her family, presumably living in that city until her death in 1922.

TERMINUS

Despite the obscurity into which Emerson's 1871 trip to California fell after the failure of Thayer's book, it nevertheless forms a meaningful episode in Emerson's long life and an illuminating event in the history of California and the West. Emerson and his party were encouraged to have found that the Yankee diaspora had indeed strongly taken root there and that New Englanders were sedulously pursuing their self-appointed roles as educators and institution builders as they were wont to do wherever they found themselves. What's more, they were gratified to find that Yankee ideals—not least Emerson's own brand of Transcendentalism—had also found fertile soil in California in the minds of such people as Thomas Starr King and John Muir. However, the Yankee ethos of materialism was, if anything, worse in the West than in the East, and just as bad was the cult of celebrity that made people like Ralph Waldo Emerson public property. Of course, looking at the trip through twenty-first-century eyes, other things stand out: the largely unacknowledged historical complexity of the West and the barely acknowledged human diversity of the region that was either deprecated when noticed, such as with the American Indians, the Chinese, and Irish, or totally invisible, such as with the African Americans who undoubtedly served them as porters on the train.

What's more, from our vantage point we can also see that by coming to California so soon after the completion of the transcontinental railroad in 1869, Emerson and his party were traveling in a unique and all-too-brief period, just at the beginning of mass tourism in the West. A few years earlier and the lack of infrastructure would have made such a trip difficult, if not impossible, even for the well-heeled nabobs that they were; a few years later, the presence of large numbers of other tourists would have made their experiences of such places as Salt Lake City and Yosemite totally different. One scholar of western tourism notes that as early as the 1880s, travelogues took on a certain snarkiness in regard to other tourists in an effort to persuade readers that the writer's experience was somehow more authentic. No such self-consciousness is to be found in Thayer's writings, pointing perhaps to a fundamentally different—and now irretrievable—experience of the West.

As for the meaning of the trip for Emerson, it is, of course, difficult to ascertain with any precision, because most of what we know is refracted through Thayer's somewhat worshipful eyes and Emerson's few letters. Nevertheless, Emerson's willingness to go, his demeanor on the trip, and what little he did say about it all suggest that his California days did have a profound impact on him. In 1866, Emerson had startled his son Edward by reading to him a new poem entitled "Terminus," in which "the god of bounds / Who sets to seas a shore" announced to Emerson that "It was time to be old / To take in sail" and "No farther shoot / Thy broad ambitious branches, and thy root." Evidently, even at this early date, Emerson felt that his "ebbing veins, / Inconstant heat and nerveless reins" were telling him to "trim [himself] to the storm of time." And yet, despite this *momento mori*, Emerson never did heed the god of bounds or "reef" his sail in his last years, as his journey to the far edge of the continent and his other later journeys, both physical and imaginative, attest. I would like to think that, after the debacle at Harvard, California allowed Emerson to reconnect with something fundamentally buoyant in his psyche, something more resilient than mere optimism, an element of his character that allowed him to confront with some dignity and aplomb the coming "storm of time." By 1871, Emerson may have considered himself too old an Adam to inhabit the "Western Paradise" that was California, but he was not too old to be reenergized by the experience and the vision of it.

NOTES

ABBREVIATIONS

ECW   Ralph Waldo Emerson, *Complete Works*, 12 vols. (Boston: Riverside Press, 1900).

EEFP Edith Emerson Forbes and William Hathaway Forbes Papers and Additions, 1827–1969, Cartons 2, 7, and 24, Massachusetts Historical Society, Boston, MA.

ETEL Ellen Tucker Emerson Letters (Transcribed), 1850–1920, Vault A45, Emerson, Unit 5, box 1, folder 9, Concord Free Public Library, Concord, MA.

JBTP James Bradley Thayer Papers, 1831–1902 (Law-MMS-093), series V, box 16, folders 2, 3, and 5, Historical and Special Collections, Harvard Law School Library, Cambridge, MA.

JMP   John Muir Papers, Holt-Atherton Special Collections and Archives, University of the Pacific Library (scholarlycommons.pacific.edu/jmc/). © 1984 Muir-Hanna Trust.

TAWJ James Bradley Thayer, *A Western Journey with Mr. Emerson* (Boston: Little, Brown, 1884).

PREFACE

x *"Always take notes on the spot":* J. B. Thayer to Sophia Thayer, Yosemite, May 10, 1871, folder 3, JBTP; compare TAWJ, 83.

three letters a week: Ellen Emerson to Ralph Waldo Emerson, April 28, 1871, ETEL.

xi *Travelogues about the American West:* Charles Nordhoff, *California: For Health, Pleasure and Residence* (New York: Harper & Brothers, 1872); Richard Francis Burton, *The City of the Saints and across the Rocky Mountains to California* (London: Longman, Green, Longman and Roberts, 1861); and Mark Twain, *Roughing It* (Hartford, CT: American Publishing, 1872). See also Anne Farrar Hyde, *An American Vision: Far Western Landscape and National Culture, 1820–1920* (New

York: New York University Press, 1990), and Jeanne Olson, "Writing the Wild West: Travel Narratives of the Late Nineteenth Century Tourist" (PhD diss., Arizona State University, 1996).

Thayer had to pay for the publication: Receipt from Little, Brown and Co. to J. B. Thayer, January 17, 1885; A. Perrin to J. B. Thayer, April 21, 1885; A. Perrin to J. B. Thayer, July 9, 1885; Receipt from Little, Brown and Co. to J. B. Thayer, January 11, 1886; Copyright Transfer to J. B. Thayer, January 20, 1886; Library of Congress Record of Copyright Assignment, February 2, 1886; all in folder 5, JBTP.

"almost too slight a performance" and subsequent quotes: TAWJ, 5–7.

INTRODUCTION

1 *"I hope the ruin of no young man's soul"*: Charles Eliot Norton, ed., *The Correspondence of Thomas Carlyle and Ralph Waldo Emerson, 1834–1872: Supplementary Letters* (Boston: Ticknor, 1886), 78.

old age was "not disgraceful" and subsequent quote: ECW, 7:302.

Emerson, a graduate of Harvard: John McAleer, *Ralph Waldo Emerson: Days of Encounter* (Boston: Little, Brown, 1984), 52–64, 79–87, 101–41, 156–69, 200–216, 370–83.

2 *"blowing clover and the falling rain"*: ECW, 1:109.

Emerson's brand of Transcendentalism: Ralph L. Rusk, *The Life of Ralph Waldo Emerson* (New York: Charles Scribner's Sons, 1949), 240–43; Gay Wilson Allen, *Waldo Emerson* (New York: Viking Press, 1981), 268–82; McAleer, *Ralph Waldo Emerson*, 164–67; Robert D. Richardson, *Emerson: The Mind on Fire* (Berkeley: University of California Press, 1996), 224–34.

"a transparent eye-ball" and subsequent quotes: ECW, 1:11, 17.

"the courtly muses of Europe" and subsequent quote: ECW, 1:75, 95–96. For "The American Scholar," see also Rusk, *Life of Ralph Waldo Emerson*, 262–66; Allen, *Waldo Emerson*, 297–303; McAleer, *Ralph Waldo Emerson*, 234–39; and Richardson, *Emerson*, 262–65.

3 *"noxious exaggeration"* and subsequent quote: ECW, 1: 109. For the "Divinity School Address," see also Rusk, *Life of Ralph Waldo Emerson*, 266–74; Allen, *Waldo Emerson*, 319–24; McAleer, *Ralph Waldo Emerson*, 245–70; and Richardson, *Emerson*, 286–92.

"the latest form of infidelity": Rusk, *Life of Ralph Waldo Emerson*, 271.

Some of his essays . . . and his poems: "Self-Reliance," ECW, 2:41–76; "The Over-Soul," ECW, 2:211–36; "Woodnotes," ECW, 9:55–69; "Hamatreya," ECW, 9:44–46.

"Patriarch of American letters": Philip F. Gura, *American Transcendentalism: A History* (New York: Hill and Wang, 2007), 270.

Cambridge alma mater: Allen, *Waldo Emerson*, 640; McAleer, *Ralph Waldo Emerson*, 590; Ronald A. Bosco, "Historical Introduction," in *The Collected Works of Ralph Waldo Emerson*, ed. Ronald A. Bosco, Glen M. Johnson, and Joel Myerson, vol 8., *Letters and Social Aims* (Cambridge, MA: Harvard University Press, 2010), lxx–lxxi.

4 *a course titled the Natural History of the Intellect:* Allen, *Waldo Emerson*, 645–46; David M. Robinson, *Emerson and the Conduct of Life: Pragmatism and Ethical Purpose in the Later Work* (Cambridge: Cambridge University Press, 1993), 181–95;

Lawrence Buell, *Emerson* (Cambridge, MA: Belknap Press of Harvard University Press, 2003), 206–38; Bosco, "Historical Introduction," lxxi–lxxxi.

The task of preparing the Harvard course: McAleer, *Ralph Waldo Emerson*, 591–94; Bosco, "Historical Introduction," lxxxi–lxxxiii, xcviii–ci.

"anecdotes of the intellect": ECW, 12:15.

he wrote to Carlyle: Norton, *Correspondence: Supplementary Letters*, 78.

Natural History of the Intellect: ECW, 12:7–53.

5 *tantalizing offer:* Edward Waldo Emerson and Waldo Emerson Forbes, eds., *Journals of Ralph Waldo Emerson, with Annotations*, 10 vols. (Boston: Houghton Mifflin, 1914), 10:351–52.

"My dear Friend": Sarah Forbes Hughes, ed., *Letters and Recollections of John Murray Forbes*, 2 vols. (Boston: Houghton Mifflin, 1899), 2:175–76.

Lidian was apparently not quite so enthusiastic: Dolores Bird Carpenter, ed., *The Selected Letters of Lidian Jackson Emerson* (Columbia: University of Missouri Press, 1987), 272.

son Edward and elder daughter, Ellen: Bosco, "Historical Introduction," cii.

"carry me off to California": Norton, *Correspondence: Supplementary Letters*, 79.

6 *one scholar even claims:* Kris Fresonke, *West of Emerson: The Design of Manifest Destiny* (Berkeley: University of California Press, 2003), 90–91.

works by explorers: Richardson, *Emerson*, 508.

"manifest destiny": ECW, 1:297, 8:86.

"good World-soul understands us well" and subsequent quotes: Emerson and Forbes, *Journals of Ralph Waldo Emerson*, 8:7–8.

"a rush and a scramble" and subsequent quotes: ECW, 6:201.

7 *"'T is tubs thrown to amuse the whale":* a common phrase in Emerson's day, meaning to create a diversion; according to William Pulleyn's *Etymological Companion* (London: Thomas Tegg, 1828), "The Greenland vessels, and indeed the South Sea vessels, are sometimes (especially after stormy weather) so surrounded with whales, that the situation of the crew becomes dangerous. When this is the case, it is usual to throw out a [wash]tub in order to divert their attention; when the marine monsters amuse themselves in tossing this singular sort of a plaything into the air, to and fro, as children do a shuttlecock. Their attention being drawn, every sail is hoisted, and the vessel pursues its course to its destination. Hence came the saying, 'Throwing a Tub to the Whale!'" (325).

"whole creation": ECW, 6:160.

special trip to the Boston Athenaeum: Bosco, "Historical Introduction," cii.

"sublime and friendly Destiny": ECW, 1:297.

Edward, who had made the overland trip: Rusk, *Life of Ralph Waldo Emerson*, 415, 417; Walter Kenneth Cameron, ed., *Young Reporter of Concord: A Checklist of F. B. Sanborn's Letters to Benjamin Smith Lyman, 1853–1867, with Extracts Emphasizing Life and Literary Events in the World of Emerson, Thoreau and Alcott* (Hartford, CT: Transcendental Books, 1978), 37; Allen, *Waldo Emerson*, 617; Linda Allardt and David W. Hill, eds., *The Journals and Miscellaneous Notebooks of Ralph Waldo Emerson*, vol. 15, *1860–1866* (Cambridge, MA: Harvard University Press, 1982), 256; Eleanor M. Tilton, ed., *The Letters of Ralph Waldo Emerson*, 10 vols. (New York: Columbia University Press, 1994), 9:75, 77, 80–81; Carpenter, *Letters of Lidian Jackson Emerson*, 141.

"make war on the Mormons": Tilton, *Letters of Ralph Waldo Emerson*, 9:96.

8 *"jaw-teeth of the Sierra"*: T. S. King to R. W. Emerson, September 9, 1862, MS Am 1280, box 16, Houghton Library, Harvard University, Cambridge, MA. Perhaps Emerson was thinking of his son Edward when he wrote in his essay "Greatness": "Young men think that the manly character requires that they should go to California, or to India, or into the army. When they have learned that the parlor and the college and the counting-room demand as much courage as the sea or the camp, they will be willing to consult their own strength and education in their choice of place" (ECW, 8:247–48). Remarkably, just as Abel Adams paid for Edward's trip to California, he also paid for his education at Harvard, this as recompense for once giving bad financial advice to this father (Emerson and Forbes, *Journals of Ralph Waldo Emerson*, 10:431–32).

"he needs not go to see the Yosemite": T. S. King to R. W. Emerson, September 9, 1862, MS Am 1280, box 16, Houghton Library, Harvard University, Cambridge, MA.

John Murray Forbes confided: Carpenter, *Letters of Lidian Jackson Emerson*, 142.

"The timeliness of this invention": Emerson and Forbes, *Journals of Ralph Waldo Emerson*, 8:7.

9 *"An unlooked for consequence"*: ECW, 1:292.

first American steam engine: Larry Tye, *Rising from the Rails: Pullman Porters and the Making of the Black Middle Class* (New York: Picador, 2004), 6; Amy G. Richter, *Home on the Rails: Women, the Railroad, and the Rise of Public Domesticity* (Chapel Hill: University of North Carolina Press, 2005), 13.

early literary tourists: Horace Greeley, *An Overland Journey from New York to San Francisco in the Summer of 1859* (New York: C. M. Saxton, Barker, 1860); Bayard Taylor, *At Home and Abroad: A Sketch-Book of Life, Scenery, and Men, Second Series* (New York: G. P. Putnam, 1862); Charles Nordhoff, *California: For Health, Pleasure and Residence* (New York: Harper & Brothers, 1872).

tourism would grow to become a major industry: Kevin Starr, *Americans and the California Dream, 1850–1915* (New York: Oxford University Press, 1973), 175; John F. Sears, *Sacred Places: American Tourist Attractions in the Nineteenth Century* (Oxford: Oxford University Press, 1989), 123; Anne Farrar Hyde, *An American Vision: Far Western Landscape and National Culture, 1820–1920* (New York: New York University Press, 1990), 53–115; Earl Pomeroy, *In Search of the Golden West: The Tourist in Western America* (Lincoln: University of Nebraska Press, 2010); Jen A. Huntley, *The Making of Yosemite: James Mason Hutchings and the Origin of America's Most Popular Park* (Lawrence: University Press of Kansas, 2014), 109, 130, 140–41; Tyler Green, *Carleton Watkins: Making the West American* (Berkeley: University of California Press, 2018), 279, 288, 289, 298.

10 *New Englanders*: ECW, 1:309.

"Anglo-Saxon race": Ralph Waldo Emerson, "The Genius and National Character of the Anglo-Saxon Race," in *The Later Lectures of Ralph Waldo Emerson, 1843–1871*, ed. Ronald A. Bosco and Joel Myerson, 2 vols. (Athens: University of Georgia Press, 2010), 1:7. That Emerson expressed his ethnocentrism on occasion in frankly racist terms is not in doubt, but how to understand his racism is still debated; for different opinions, see Buell, *Emerson*, 258–70; Susan Castillo, "'The Best of Nations'? Race and Imperial Destinies in Emerson's 'English Traits,'" *Yearbook of English Studies* 34 (2004): 100–111; Nell Irvin Painter, "Ralph Waldo Emerson's Saxons," *Journal of American History* 95, no. 4 (March 2009): 977–85; and Daniel

Koch, *Ralph Waldo Emerson in Europe: Class, Race and Revolution in the Making of an American Thinker* (London: Bloomsbury, 2020).

"universal Yankee Nation": *American Agriculturalist* (New York), February 1849, 58–59.

New Englanders never formed more than 10 percent: Richard L. Power, "A Crusade to Extend Yankee Culture, 1820–1865," *New England Quarterly* 12 (December 1940): 647; Stewart H. Holbrook, *The Yankee Exodus: An Account of Migration from New England* (Seattle: University of Washington Press, 1950), 165.

Richard Henry Dana: McAleer, *Ralph Waldo Emerson*, 69–70; Glena Matthews, *The Golden State in the Civil War: Thomas Starr King, the Republican Party, and the Birth of Modern California* (Cambridge: Cambridge University Press, 2012), 73.

Thomas O. Larkin: Holbrook, *Yankee Exodus*, 146–49.

Gold, of course, the irresistible instrument: Holbrook, 149–60.

11 *Yankee culture*: Matthews, *Golden State*, 73–74, 131–54; Sandra Sizer Frankiel, *California's Spiritual Frontiers: Religious Alternatives in Anglo-Protestantism, 1850–1910* (Berkeley: University of California Press, 1988), xi–xii, 18–31.

"a choice collection": Taylor, *At Home and Abroad*, 137; for more on Bayard Taylor, see Larzer Ziff, *Return Passages: Great American Travel Writing, 1780–1910* (New Haven, CT: Yale University Press, 2000), 118–69.

"new civilization": *Overland Monthly*, August 1869, 191.

"the literary pioneer" and subsequent quote: *Oakland Daily News*, May 27, 1871.

12 *Forbeses' traveling party*: There had long been some confusion about the composition of the traveling party (for example, see the arrival notice in *Daily Alta California*, April 21, 1871), but John Murray Forbes himself settles the issue in his memoirs. See Sarah Forbes Hughes, ed., *Reminiscences of John Murray Forbes*, 3 vols. (Boston: George H. Ellis, 1902), 3:278; see also "Excursion Party," *Salt Lake Herald-Republican*, April 4, 1871, which also gets the group's composition right.

"New England's best": Ralph L. Rusk, ed., *The Letters of Ralph Waldo Emerson*, 10 vols. (New York: Columbia University Press, 1939), 6:152.

close to the Forbes family: Carlos Baker, *Emerson among the Eccentrics: A Group Portrait* (New York: Penguin, 1997), 404–9.

"an American to be proud of" and subsequent quotes: Emerson and Forbes, *Jounals of Ralph Waldo Emerson*, 10:72–73.

13 *invited the Emerson clan*: Emerson and Forbes, 10:393–94.

"Prospero's Island": Eleanor M. Tilton, ed., *The Letters of Ralph Waldo Emerson*, 10 vols. (New York: Columbia University Press, 1991), 8:623.

It was probably on Naushon: Baker, *Emerson among the Eccentrics*, 415–16, 445–47, 50–51; Eleanor M. Tilton, ed., *The Letters of Ralph Waldo Emerson*, 10 vols. (New York: Columbia University Press, 1990), 7:77–78; Tilton, *Letters of Ralph Waldo Emerson*, 9:132.

"never have any hope of Edith Emerson now": Baker, *Emerson among the Eccentrics*, 447; see also Arthur S. Pier, *Forbes: Telephone Pioneer* (New York: Dodd, Mead, 1953), 11–17.

"I am rejoiced" and subsequent quote: Rusk, *Letters of Ralph Waldo Emerson*, 5:410.

14 *marriage between Will and Edith*: Rusk, *Life of Ralph Waldo Emerson*, 431; Pier, *Forbes*, 7–8, 11–17, 45–46; Baker, *Emerson among the Eccentrics*, 455, 458–59.

"the Day of Judgement": Edith E. W. Gregg, ed., *The Letters of Ellen Tucker Emerson*, 2 vols. (Kent, OH: Kent State University Press, 1982), 1:346.
"several agreeable circumstances": Gregg, *Letters of Ellen Tucker Emerson*, 1:353.
advantages to the marriage: Pier, *Forbes*, 70–77.

15 *Garth Wilkinson James*: Jane Maher, *Biography of Broken Fortunes: Wilkie and Bob, Brothers of William, Henry, and Alice James* (Hamden, CT; Archon Books, 1986), 1–20; Baker, *Emerson among the Eccentrics*, 436.
"adipose and affectionate Wilkie": Edward Waldo Emerson, *The Early Years of the Saturday Club, 1855–1870* (Boston: Houghton Mifflin, 1918), 328.
Wilkie as "incomparable" and subsequent quote: Julian Hawthorne, *The Memoirs of Julian Hawthorne*, ed. Edith Garrigues Hawthorne (New York: Macmillan, 1938), 121.
"the happiest, queerest boy" and subsequent quotes: Gregg, *Letters of Ellen Tucker Emerson*, 1:297.
Wilkie's halcyon days ended abruptly: Maher, *Biography of Broken Fortunes*, 23–26, 35–56.

16 *Annie Keene Anthony*: Hughes, *Reminiscences of John Murray Forbes*, 3:171, 209.
John Gould Anthony: Harriet Hyman Alonso, *Growing Up Abolitionist: The Story of the Garrison Children* (Amherst: University of Massachusetts Press, 2002), 220, 237–38, 245, 331.
"genial and sunny" and subsequent quote: Alonso, *Growing Up Abolitionist*, 246.
Sarah Parkman Shaw Russell: Lindsay Swift, *Brook Farm: Its Members, Scholars, and Visitors* (New York: Macmillan, 1900), 205–6; Hughes, *Reminiscences of John Murray Forbes*, 1:109, 2:238–39; "Henry Sturgis Russell," in *Biographical History of Massachusetts*, ed. Samuel Atkins Eliot, ed., 10 vols. (Boston: Boston Biographical Society, 1916), 6:n.p.; Joseph Slater, ed., *The Correspondence of Emerson and Carlyle* (New York: Columbia University Press, 1964), 582; Bronson Alcott, *Notes on Conversations* (Vancouver, BC: Fairleigh Dickinson University Press, 2007), 272; Paul Teed, *A Revolutionary Conscience: Theodore Parker and Antebellum America* (Lanham, MD: University Press of America, 2012), 31–32.

17 *"her manner was direct"*: George William Curtis, *From the Easy Chair* (New York: Harper and Brothers, 1891), 162.
James Bradley Thayer: James Parker Hall, "James Bradley Thayer," in *Great American Lawyers*, ed. William Draper Lewis (Philadelphia: James C. Winston, 1907), 8:345–52.

19 *did hear Emerson speak*: S. Lothrop Thorndike, "Tribute to James Bradley Thayer," *Proceedings of the Massachusetts Historical Society* 16 (March 1902): 16; David J. Langum, "James Bradley Thayer (1831–1902)," in *American National Biography*, ed. John A. Garraty and Mark C. Carnes (Oxford: Oxford University Press, 1999): 490–91.
"elicited hisses, shouts, and catcalls" and subsequent quote: James Elliot Cabot, ed., *The Works of Ralph Waldo Emerson: With a General Index and a Memoir* (New York: Houghton, Mifflin, 1887), 14:586.
liminality of travel: Jeanne Olson, "Writing the Wild West: Travel Narratives of the Late Nineteenth Century Tourist" (PhD diss., Arizona State University, 1996), 33–53.

CHAPTER 1: FROM EAST TO FAR WEST

20 *On Tuesday, April 11, 1871:* Edith Emerson Forbes line-a-day diary, April 11, 1871, EEFP; Ronald A. Bosco and Glen M. Johnson, eds., *The Journals and Miscellaneous Notebooks of Ralph Waldo Emerson*, vol. 16, *1866–1882* (Cambridge, MA: Harvard University Press, 1982), 408.

"but his son thinks" **and subsequent quotes:** Oliver Wendell Holmes Sr., *Ralph Waldo Emerson* (Boston: Houghton Mifflin, 1884), 359–61.

His voice: Ronald A. Bosco and Joel Myerson, eds., *Emerson in His Own Time* (Iowa City: University of Iowa Press, 2003), 201.

purple satchel: TAWJ, 14.

21 *Already waiting for Emerson:* Edith Emerson Forbes line-a-day diary, April 11, 1871, EEFP; Ellen Emerson to Edith [deL. D.], April 12, 1871, ETEL.

"young Vandals in Concord" **and subsequent quote:** Ellen Emerson to Edith [deL. D.], April 12, 1871, ETEL; see also Ellen Emerson to Sally, April 5, 1871, and Ellen Emerson to Father, April 12, 1871, both in ETEL.

Thayer bid a heartfelt farewell: J. B. Thayer to Sophia Thayer, Chicago, April 13, 1871, folder 2, JBTP; TAWJ, 9–10.

Wagner sleeping car: Henry T. Williams, *The Pacific Tourist: William's Illustrated Guide to the Pacific R. R. and California and Pleasure Resorts across the Continent* (New York: Henry T. Williams, 1876), 12.

"night was a jolty one" **and subsequent quotes:** J. B. Thayer to Sophia Thayer, Chicago, April 13, 1871, folder 2, JBTP.

"a fresher and more cheerful object" **and subsequent quotes:** J. B. Thayer to Sophia Thayer, Chicago, April 13, 1871, folder 2, JBTP. For Congress Hall, see Edith Emerson Forbes line-a-day diary, April 12, 1871, EEFP.

22 *Niagara Falls Suspension Bridge:* J. B. Thayer to Sophia Thayer, Chicago, April 13, 1871, folder 2, JBTP; TAWJ, 10; Bosco and Johnson, *Journals and Miscellaneous Notebooks*, 408.

favorite metaphor: see, for example, ECW, 8:11–12.

"We took a carriage" **and subsequent quote:** Holmes, *Ralph Waldo Emerson*, 263.

Emerson nearly died: Gay Wilson Allen, *Waldo Emerson* (New York: Viking Press, 1981), 620; Bosco and Myerson, *Emerson in His Own Time*, 205.

"travelling is a fool's paradise": ECW, 2:69–70.

the Lyceum: John McAleer, *Ralph Waldo Emerson: Days of Encounter* (Boston: Little, Brown, 1984), 98–99, 486; Lawrence Buell, *Emerson* (Cambridge, MA: Belknap Press of Harvard University Press, 2003), 22–31; Robert A. Gross, "Talk of the Town," *American Scholar* 84, no. 3 (Summer 2015): 31–43.

23 *"associations for mutual instruction":* quoted in Gross, "Talk of the Town," 34.

24 *"Plato" from the "Yankee Athens":* Bosco and Myerson, *Emerson in His Own Time*, 70.

Emerson traveled far and wide: Allen, *Waldo Emerson*, 534–38.

Mammoth Caves: ECW, 6:243–44; Ronald A. Bosco and Joel Myerson, eds., *The Later Lectures of Ralph Waldo Emerson, 1843–1871*, 2 vols. (Athens: University of Georgia Press, 2010), 2:350.

Iowa, Wisconsin, and Minnesota: Hubert H. Hoeltje, "Ralph Waldo Emerson in Iowa," *Iowa Journal* 25 (April 1927): 236–76; Hubert H. Hoeltje, "Ralph Waldo Emerson in Minnesota," *Minnesota History* 2, no. 2 (June 1930): 145–59; C. E. Schorer,

"Emerson and the Wisconsin Lyceum," *American Literature* 24, no. 4 (January 1953): 462–75.

"celebrated metaphysician": Hoeltje, "Ralph Waldo Emerson in Iowa," 238.

"Everything went smoothly" and subsequent quotes: J. B. Thayer to Sophia Thayer, Chicago, April 13, 1871, folder 2, JBTP.

25 *"low degree of the sublime"*: ECW, 1:47–50.

Parnassus: TAWJ, 14–15.

"was a destructive *and not an affirmative poem"* and subsequent quotes: J. B. Thayer to Sophia Thayer, Chicago, April 13, 1871, folder 2, JBTP; compare TAWJ, 15–16. For *Lyrical Ballads,* see William Wordsworth, *Poems including "Lyrical Ballads"* (London: Longman, Hurst, Rees, Orme, and Brown, 1815), xxxiv.

26 *"seemed a very timid person"* and subsequent quotes: J. B. Thayer to Sophia Thayer, Yosemite, May 8, 1871, folder 3, JBTP.

"at the furious tearing pace": J. B. Thayer to Sophia Thayer, Chicago, April 13, 1871, folder 2, JBTP.

"Athens marble": "Sherman House IV," Chicagology, chicagology.com/?s=sherman+house, accessed May 28, 2021.

27 *"Arrived here"* and subsequent quote: Charles Eliot Norton, ed., *The Correspondence of Thomas Carlyle and Ralph Waldo Emerson, 1834–1872: Supplementary Letters* (Boston: Ticknor, 1886), 79–80; see also Bosco and Johnson, *Journals and Miscellaneous Notebooks,* 408.

"Oh! to think he was here" and subsequent quote: Ellen Emerson to Ralph Waldo Emerson, April 12, 1871, ETEL.

"write soon": J. B. Thayer to Sophia Thayer, Chicago, April 13, 1871, folder 2, JBTP. As was the usual practice when celebrities came to town, Emerson's presence was noted in the paper: see the *Chicago Evening Mail,* April 13, 1871.

"a man of forty odd": J. B. Thayer to Sophia Thayer, En Route, April 14, 1871, folder 2, JBTP.

"raised an entire city block": John F. Stover, "George Mortimer Pullman (03 March 1831–19 October 1897)," in *American National Biography,* ed. John A. Garraty and Mark C. Carnes (Oxford: Oxford University Press, 1999), 937; see also Liston Edgington Leyendecker, *Palace Car Prince: A Biography of George Mortimer Pullman* (Niwot: University of Colorado Press, 1992), 33.

Growing rich: Joseph Husband, *The Story of the Pullman Car* (Chicago: A. C. McClurg, 1917), 48–57; Leyendecker, *Palace Car Prince,* 71–108.

28 *"spotters"*: Larry Tye, *Rising from the Rails: Pullman Porters and the Making of the Black Middle Class* (New York: Picador, 2004), 102–5.

maximum cleanliness: Husband, *Story of the Pullman Car,* 152–54.

Standing together: TAWJ, 10.

devout Universalist: Leyendecker, *Palace Car Prince,* 14–24. For the Calvinistic elements of Universalism, see Ann Lee Bressler, *The Universalist Movement in America, 1770–1880* (New York: Oxford University Press, 2001), 14–15, 26, 35, 72–73, 143–44.

29 *Pullman City:* Leyendecker, 163–77, 215–37, 239–41.

"abstract philosophy" and subsequent quote: Swing, quoted in Mrs. Duane Doty, *The Town of Pullman* (Pullman, IL: T. P. Struhsacker, 1893), 36–37.

"bear rolling over and over" and subsequent quotes: J. B. Thayer to Sophia Thayer, En Route, April 14, 1871, folder 2, JBTP; compare TAWJ, 10–11.

30 *last car of the train:* TAWJ, 62.
31 *"well economized"* and subsequent quote: J. B. Thayer to Sophia Thayer, En Route, April 14, 1871, folder 2, JBTP; see also Charles Nordhoff, *California: For Health, Pleasure and Residence* (New York: Harper & Brothers, 1872), 23–30, and Anne Farrar Hyde, *An American Vision: Far Western Landscape and National Culture, 1820–1920* (New York: New York University Press, 1990), 115–20.
Pullman had defended the elaborate furnishings: Amy G. Richter, *Home on the Rails: Women, the Railroad, and the Rise of Public Domesticity* (Chapel Hill: University of North Carolina Press, 2005), 71–74.
"I have always held": Pullman, quoted in Doty, *The Town of Pullman,* 23.
a full complement of staff: J. B. Thayer to Sophia Thayer, San Francisco April 23, 1871, folder 2, JBTP.
the others were Black: see Tye, *Rising from the Rails.*
32 *Mary Moody Emerson:* ECW, 10:307–33.
"soup, your choice of roast beef" and subsequent quotes: J. B. Thayer to Sophia Thayer, En Route, April 14, 1871, folder 2, JBTP.
33 *purple satchel:* J. B. Thayer to Sophia Thayer, En Route, April 14, 1871, folder 2, JBTP; TAWJ, 16–17.
"He goes up and down": ECW, 4:116.
"was like Linnaeus" and subsequent quotes: J. B. Thayer to Sophia Thayer, En Route, April 14, 1871, folder 2, JBTP; compare TAWJ, 16–18.
Burlington: J. B. Thayer to Sophia Thayer, En Route, April 14, 1871, folder 2, JBTP; TAWJ, 11.
34 *John Worthington Ames: Harvard College Record of Class of 1892: Secretary Report No. V* (Boston: The Fort Hill Press, 1912), 15.
Margaret ("Maggie") Plumley Ames: Gary Scharnhorst, *Julian Hawthorne: The Life of a Prodigal Son* (Urbana: University of Illinois Press, 2014), 30.
"'heart quite palpitated'" and subsequent quotes: J. B. Thayer to Sophia Thayer, En Route, April 14, 1871, folder 2, JBTP.
the Apple Trees: Edith Perkins Cunningham, ed., *Letters and Journal of Edith Forbes Perkins, 1908–1925* (Boston: Riverside Press, 1931), 1:xv–xxii; 2:62, 100, 4:222–23, 231–32; Hoeltje, "Ralph Waldo Emerson in Iowa," 260–62.
Also present at the Apple Trees: J. B. Thayer to Sophia Thayer, En Route, April 14, 1871, folder 2, JBTP.
George Ward Holdrege: Thomas M. Davis, "Lines West!—The Story of George W. Holdrege (Part 1)," *Nebraska History* 31 (1950): 27–46.
classmate of Edward Emerson: Ralph L. Rusk, ed., *The Letters of Ralph Waldo Emerson,* 10 vols. (New York: Columbia University Press, 1939), 6:159.
"he had a long thin face" and subsequent quotes: Davis, "Lines West!," 29.
35 *"dear little woman"* and subsequent quote: J. B. Thayer to Sophia Thayer, En Route, April 14, 1871, folder 2, JBTP.
"passed through the towns" and subsequent quotes: J. B. Thayer to Sophia Thayer, Council Bluffs, April 16, 1871, folder 2, JBTP.
"Have you been cutting off their heads" and subsequent quote: Davis, "Lines West!," 44.
"camping out": J. B. Thayer to Sophia Thayer, Council Bluffs, April 16, 1871, folder 2, JBTP; compare TAWJ, 18.

Council Bluffs: George A. Crofutt, *Great Trans-Continental Tourist's Guide* (New York, 1871), 10.

36 *"She was a thoughtful person"* and subsequent quotes: TAWJ, 19–20; compare J. B. Thayer to Sophia Thayer, En Route, April 17, 1871, folder 2, JBTP. See also Frederick B. Tolles, "Emerson and Quakerism," *American Literature* 10, no. 2 (May 1838): 142–65.
"superb view" and subsequent quote: J. B. Thayer to Sophia Thayer, En Route, April 17, 1871, folder 2, JBTP.
"stretching away towards the town" and subsequent quotes: TAWJ, 21.

37 *Omaha:* Crofutt, *Great Trans-Continental Tourist's Guide,* 19–22; J. B. Thayer to Sophia Thayer, Council Bluffs, April 16, 1871, and J. B. Thayer to Sophia Thayer, En Route, April 17, 1871, folder 2, JBTP; TAWJ, 11–12, 20–21.
"vast West": ECW, 1:180.
"sold on the cars": Nordhoff, *California,* 37.

37–38 *"Now as you are about to leave the busy hum"*: Crofutt, *Great Trans-Continental Tourist's Guide,* 25. By the 1870s, there were some twenty-five different guidebooks available for the West: see, for example, Hyde, *An American Vision,* 120–46, and Lloyd E. Hudman, "Tourism and the American West," *Journal of the West* 33, no. 3 (July 1994): 69. A copy of *Bancroft's Tourist Guide* can be found in Emerson's library as preserved at the Concord Free Public Library, although it is not known when Emerson acquired it (concordlibrary.org/special-collections/fin_aids/Emerson-Books, accessed May 28, 2021).

38 *"The woman stopped"* and subsequent quote: J. B. Thayer to Sophia Thayer, En Route, April 17, 1871, folder 2, JBTP.
"this poor, flat, worn-out common": TAWJ, 22.
take potshots at the massive herds: Hyde, *An American Vision,* 132.

39 *Unlike the eastern roads:* Williams, *Pacific Tourist,* 9; Nordhoff, *California,* 23–30.
"our life in the cars" and subsequent quotes: J. B. Thayer to Sophia Thayer, En Route, April 18, 1871, folder 2, JBTP.
"grew accustomed" and subsequent quote: TAWJ, 18–19.
James Camden Hotten: Simon Eliot, "Hotten: Rotten: Forgotten? An Apologia for a General Publisher," *Book History* 3 (2000): 61–93; Robert D. Habich, *Building Their Own Waldos: Emerson's First Biographers and the Politics of Life-Writing in the Gilded Age* (Iowa City: University of Iowa Press, 2011), 47–50; David Bradshaw and Rachel Potter, eds., *Prudes on the Prowl: Fiction and Obscenity in England, 1850 to the Present Day* (New York: Oxford University Press, 2013), 20.

40 *"No, he never read"*: J. B. Thayer to Sophia Thayer, En Route, April 17, 1871, folder 2, JBTP; compare TAWJ, 22–24.
"Nowadays, one must finish off a story well" and subsequent quotes: TAWJ, 25–26; compare J. B. Thayer to Sophia Thayer, En Route, April 18, 1871, folder 2, JBTP.

41 *Edward Emerson's friend:* Ellen Emerson to Ralph Waldo Emerson, May 10, 1871, ETEL.
Agoston Haraszthy: Brian McGinty, *Strong Wine: The Life and Legend of Agoston Haraszthy* (Stanford, CA: Stanford University Press, 1998).
"the largest vineyard in the world": McGinty, *Strong Wine,* 2.
Cheyenne: J. B. Thayer to Sophia Thayer, En Route, April 17, 1871, and J. B. Thayer to Sophia Thayer, En Route, April 18, 1871, folder 2, JBTP.
"the back-bone of the American Continent" and subsequent quote: Crofutt, *Great Trans-Continental Tourist's Guide,* 42, 60.

"towers into the highest mountains": ECW, 1:233–34.

"The Cross of Snow": James M. Cox, "Longfellow and His 'Cross of Snow,'" *PMLA* 75, no. 1 (March 1960): 97–100; Linda C. Hults, "Pilgrim's Progress in the West: Moran's 'The Mountain of the Holy Cross,'" *American Art* 5, nos. 1–2 (Winter–Spring 1991): 68–85.

42 *prairie dogs:* J. B. Thayer to Sophia Thayer, En Route, April 18, 1871, folder 2, JBTP.

"Yes, yes; a hundred and forty": TAWJ, 48; compare J. B. Thayer to Sophia Thayer, San Francisco, April 22, 1871, folder 2, JBTP.

St. Augustine: Rusk, *Letters of Ralph Waldo Emerson,* 1:192, 6:152–53; McAleer, *Ralph Waldo Emerson,* 89.

Sherman: Crofutt, *Great Trans-Continental Tourist's Guide,* 60.

"tree or a shrub" **and subsequent quotes:** J. B. Thayer to Sophia Thayer, En Route, April 18, 1871, folder 2, JBTP.

CHAPTER 2: SALT LAKE CITY

43 *"troublesome, unwholesome dust"* **and subsequent quotes:** J. B. Thayer to Sophia Thayer, En Route, April 18, 1871, folder 2, JBTP.

Church Butte: George A. Crofutt, *Great Trans-Continental Tourist's Guide* (New York, 1871), 82–83, 86.

Evanston: Crofutt, *Great Trans-Continental Tourist's Guide,* 89; J. B. Thayer to Sophia Thayer, Salt Lake City, April 19, 1871, folder 2, JBTP.

"inexpressible beauty" **and subsequent quotes:** TAWJ, 26–27; compare J. B. Thayer to Sophia Thayer, Salt Lake City, April 19, 1871, folder 2, JBTP; Ronald A. Bosco and Glen M. Johnson, eds., *The Journals and Miscellaneous Notebooks of Ralph Waldo Emerson,* vol. 16, *1866–1882* (Cambridge, MA: Harvard University Press, 1982), 408. For Echo, Weber, Devil's Gate, and other geographical features, see Crofutt, *Great Trans-Continental Tourist's Guide,* 90–98.

44 *Salt Lake City:* Thomas G. Alexander and James B. Allen, *Mormons and Gentiles: A History of Salt Lake City* (Boulder, CO: Pruett, 1984), 17–123; C. Mark Hamilton, *Nineteenth-Century Mormon Architecture and City Planning* (New York: Oxford University Press, 1995), 24–28.

45 *"principal material"* **and subsequent quote:** Crofutt, *Great Trans-Continental Tourist's Guide,* 99–100.

"There is an air of strain" **and subsequent quote:** Charles Nordhoff, *California: For Health, Pleasure and Residence* (New York: Harper & Brothers, 1872), 42.

Muslims of America: Richard Francis Burton, *The City of the Saints and across the Rocky Mountains to California* (London: Longman, Green, Longman and Roberts, 1861), for example, 240, 295, 359–60, 462.

"Trans-Continental Railroad has brought": William Wilson Ross, quoted in David Walker, *Railroading Religion: Mormons, Tourists, and the Corporate Spirit of the West* (Chapel Hill: University of North Carolina Press, 2019), 197.

46 *The Wildcat: Salt Lake Herald Republican,* April 18, 1871.

"queer as we drove up": J. B. Thayer to Sophia Thayer, Ogden, April 19, 1871, folder 2, JBTP; compare TAWJ, 27–28.

47 *"he was going to build a big 'fun hall'":* quoted in Walker, *Railroading Religion,* 158.

Salt Lake Theatre: J. B. Thayer to Sophia Thayer, Ogden, April 19, 1871, folder 2, JBTP; Horace G. Whitney, *The Drama of Utah: The Story of the Salt Lake Theatre*

(Salt Lake City: Deseret News, 1915); Walker, *Railroading Religion*, 157–60, 163–64.

"as if playing at a ball": J. B. Thayer to Sophia Thayer, Ogden, April 19, 1871, folder 2, JBTP.

New York Burglars: Charles Foster, *New York Burglars; or, a Wedding by Moonlight*, in Library of Congress Copyright Office, *Dramatic Compositions Copyrighted in the United States, 1870 to 1916* (Washington, D.C.: Government Printing Office, 1918), 1:1629; "Charles Foster Obituary," *New York Dramatic Mirror*, August 24, 1895. See also ads for the play in the *Deseret Evening News*, April 17, 1871, and *Salt Lake Herald*, April 18, 1871, as well as squibs in the *Salt Lake Herald*, April 16, 1871 and April 17, 1871.

"genteely dressed villain": *Brooklyn Daily Eagle*, December 6, 1871, which contains a full description of the play. For a brief discussion of nineteenth-century American melodrama as a genre, see Jeffrey D. Mason, *Melodrama and the Myth of America* (Indianapolis: Indiana University Press, 1993), 16–19.

48 *"a real bowery boy performance"* and subsequent quote: J. B. Thayer to Sophia Thayer, Ogden, April 19, 1871, folder 2, JBTP; compare TAWJ, 28–29.

"Everything that is popular": ECW, 1:211.

"rude warm blood": ECW, 4:156.

theater party returned to the Huron: J. B. Thayer to Sophia Thayer, Ogden, April 19, 1871, folder 2, JBTP.

"impressions of the west" and subsequent quote: Sarah Forbes Hughes, ed., *Letters and Recollections of John Murray Forbes*, 2 vols. (Boston: Houghton Mifflin, 1899), 1:8–9.

"Excursion Party": *Salt Lake Herald-Republican*, April 19, 1871.

49 *"shallow slosh"* and subsequent quote: TAWJ, 30–31; compare J. B. Thayer to Sophia Thayer, Ogden, April 19, 1871, folder 2, JBTP.

"burnt brick" chimney: J. B. Thayer to Sophia Thayer, Ogden, April 19, 1871, folder 2, JBTP; compare TAWJ, 30–31.

plural marriage: Danel W. Bachman and Ronald K. Esplin, "Plural Marriage," in *Encyclopedia of Mormonism*, ed. Daniel H. Ludlow (New York: Macmillan, 1992), 3:1091–95; J. Spencer Fluhman, *"A Peculiar People": Anti-Mormonism and the Making of Religion in Nineteenth-Century America* (Chapel Hill: University of North Carolina Press, 2012), 97–110, 117–25.

a quarter of all Mormon households: Bachman and Esplin, "Plural Marriage," 3: 1095.

"fine, lady-like women" and subsequent quotes: TAWJ, 30–31; compare J. B. Thayer to Sophia Thayer, Ogden, April 19, 1871, folder 2, JBTP.

50 *"lust of the flesh"* and subsequent quotes: J. B. Thayer to Sophia Thayer, Ogden, April 19, 1871, folder 2, JBTP.

"a sober quiet way": J. B. Thayer to Sophia Thayer, En Route, April 20, 1871 [2], folder 2, JBTP.

"seemed serious and well-meaning" and subsequent quote: TAWJ, 32–33.

Crofutt's New Map of Salt Lake City: for an example of the map, see www.geographicus.com/P/AntiqueMap/saltlakecity-crofutt-1871, accessed May 28, 2021.

tourist itinerary: Crofutt, *Great Trans-Continental Tourist's Guide*, 102–4; see also Hamilton, *Nineteenth-Century Mormon Architecture*, 33–46, and Walker, *Railroading Religion*, 119, 167–70.

51 *hot springs:* Edith Emerson Forbes line-a-day diary, Wednesday, April 19, 1871, EEFP; J. B. Thayer to Sophia Thayer, En Route, April 18, 1871, and J. B. Thayer to Sophia Thayer, Ogden, April 19, 1871, folder 2, JBTP.

Born in Vermont: Crofutt, *Great Trans-Continental Tourist's Guide*, 102–4; John G. Turner, *Brigham Young: Pioneer Prophet* (Cambridge, MA: Belknap Press of Harvard University Press, 2012), 7–174.

From his arrival in Salt Lake: Crofutt, *Great Trans-Continental Tourist's Guide*, 97–102, 104; Turner, *Brigham Young*, 175–413; Walker, *Railroading Religion*, 67–68, 77–78, 80–82.

52 *Young was first president and prophet:* Hamilton, *Nineteenth-Century Mormon Architecture*, 33–46; Turner, *Brigham Young*.

"to indorse or condemn any man" and subsequent quote: Crofutt, *Great Trans-Continental Tourist's Guide*, 102–4.

Temple Square: Hamilton, *Nineteenth-Century Mormon Architecture*, 112–14; Walker, *Railroading Religion*, 167–70.

53 *"too valuable a means":* quoted in Walker, *Railroading Religion*, 169.

"subacid": J. B. Thayer to Sophia Thayer, En Route, April 20, 1871 [2], folder 2, JBTP.

"thin, pallid man": TAWJ, 36.

"a handsome well furnished room": Bayard Taylor, "A Glimpse of the Mormons," extracts reprinted in *Latter-Day Saints' Millennial Star*, July 26, 1870, 466–68.

"nothing could be stronger": Sarah Forbes Hughes, ed., *Reminiscences of John Murray Forbes*, 3 vols. (Boston: George H. Ellis, 1902), 3:280.

54 *"a man of not over medium height"* and subsequent quotes: TAWJ, 33–34; compare J. B. Thayer to Sophia Thayer, Ogden, April 19, 1871, folder 2, JBTP.

Emerson who instigated the meeting: Hughes, *Reminiscences of John Murray Forbes*, 3:280–81; Bosco and Johnson, *Journals and Miscellaneous Notebooks*, 408.

preached against just such characterizations: Brigham Young, "The One-Man Power," in *Journal of Discourses by President Brigham Young, His Two Counselors, and the Twelve Apostles* (Liverpool, UK: Albert Carrington, 1872), 14:91–98; TAWJ, 36–37.

"it's easy to talk about that!": TAWJ, 34–35.

"was smoothed over" and subsequent quote: J. B. Thayer to Sophia Thayer, En Route, April 20, 1871 [1], folder 2, JBTP.

seagulls: *Latter-Day Saints' Millennial Star*, December 13, 1870, 788.

"Answers to Questions": TAWJ, 35–36; compare J. B. Thayer to Sophia Thayer, En Route, April 20, 1871 [1], folder 2, JBTP.

55 *Tabernacle:* Crofutt, *Great Trans-Continental Tourist's Guide*, 100; Bosco and Johnson, *Journals and Miscellaneous Notebooks*, 408; Hamilton, *Nineteenth-Century Mormon Architecture*, 53–60; Walker, *Railroading Religion*, 152–57.

"ordinary tones" and subsequent quotes: J. B. Thayer to Sophia Thayer, En Route, April 20, 1871 [2], folder 2, JBTP.

Deseret Museum: James E. Talmage, "The Deseret Museum," *Deseret Museum Bulletin*, n.s., 1 (August 16, 1911): 3–10.

56 *"a scalp"* and subsequent quote: Henry T. Williams, *The Pacific Tourist: William's Illustrated Guide to the Pacific R. R. and California and Pleasure Resorts across the Continent* (New York: Henry T. Williams, 1876), 136.

"Tell the boys" and subsequent quote: J. B. Thayer to Sophia Thayer, En Route, April 20, 1871 [2], folder 2, JBTP.

Dwyer's bookstore: J. B. Thayer to Sophia Thayer, Salt Lake City, April 19, 1871, folder 2, JBTP; Edith Emerson Forbes line-a-day diary, Wednesday, April 19, 1871, EEFP.

"that served as bureau of information": Chris Rigby, "Ada Dwyer: Bright Lights and Lilacs," *Utah Historical Quarterly* 43, no. 1 (Winter 1975): 42.

Ada Dwyer Russell: Rigby, "Ada Dwyer," 43–51; D. Michael Quinn, *Same-Sex Dynamics among Nineteenth-Century Americans: A Mormon Example* (Urbana: University of Illinois Press, 2001), 172–73, 367–68.

57 **Answers to Questions:** J. B. Thayer to Sophia Thayer, En Route, April 20, 1871 [2], folder 2, JBTP; George A. Smith, *The Rise, Progress and Travels of the Church of Jesus Christ of Latter-Day Saints Being a Series of Answers to Questions* (Salt Lake City, UT: Deseret News Office, 1869).

"Forty eight hours" and subsequent quotes: TAWJ, 38–39; compare J. B. Thayer to Sophia Thayer, Ogden, April 19, 1871, folder 2, JBTP. See also Edith Emerson Forbes line-a-day diary, Wednesday, April 19, 1871, EEFP; Bosco and Johnson, *Journals and Miscellaneous Notebooks,* 408.

"exceedingly interested in it" and subsequent quote: J. B. Thayer to Sophia Thayer, En Route, April 20, 1871 [2], folder 2, JBTP.

58 *"a strange discourse":* TAWJ, 36–37.

"impress the imaginations": J. B. Thayer to Sophia Thayer, Ogden, April 19, 1871, folder 2, JBTP.

"was a good deal interested": TAWJ, 37.

"after-clap of Puritanism" and subsequent quote: TAWJ, 39–40; compare J. B. Thayer to Sophia Thayer, Ogden, April 19, 1871, folder 2, JBTP.

"On our way out": Charles Eliot Norton, ed., *The Correspondence of Thomas Carlyle and Ralph Waldo Emerson, 1834–1872,* 2 vols. (Boston: Ticknor, 1886), 2:380–81.

59 *"did not seem to appreciate"* and subsequent quote: Oliver Wendell Holmes Sr., *Ralph Waldo Emerson* (Boston: Houghton Mifflin, 1884), 264.

King Follett Discourse: Joseph Fielding Smith, *Teachings of the Prophet Joseph Smith* (Salt Lake City, UT: Deseret Book Company, 1938), 342–62.

"union of man and God": ECW, 2:232.

"infinitude of the private man": Edward Waldo Emerson and Waldo Emerson Forbes, eds., *Journals of Ralph Waldo Emerson, with Annotations,* 10 vols. (Boston: Houghton Mifflin, 1911), 5:380.

"Every spirit builds itself a house" and subsequent quote: ECW, 1:66–67. For an extended discussion of this comparison, see Benjamin E. Park, "'Build, Therefore, Your Own World': Ralph Waldo Emerson, Joseph Smith, and American Antebellum Thought," *Journal of Mormon History* 36, no. 1 (Winter 2010): 41–72; for a dissenting opinion, see Turner, *Brigham Young,* 161–62.

60 *"Orion looks in"* and subsequent quote: J. B. Thayer to Sophia Thayer, Ogden, April 19, 1871, folder 2, JBTP. During his last trip to the West in 1890, John Murray Forbes stopped in again at Salt Lake City and "went over part of the same ground Mrs. Russell and Mr. Emerson had done with us. The Mormons still live there, but are out of power," since "our friend Brigham Young no longer presided there" (Sarah Forbes Hughes, ed., *Letters (Supplementary) of John Murray Forbes* [Boston: George H. Ellis, 1905], 3:244–45).

"the Great American Desert": Crofutt, *Great Trans-Continental Tourist's Guide,* 117–18, 124. Although Crofutt's *Guide* labeled the Nevada Desert as "the" Great American

Desert, this designation was actually quite elastic, having once been located as far east as the Great Plains: see Roger L. Welsch, "The Myth of the Great American Desert," *Nebraska History* 52 (1971): 255–65; Anne Farrar Hyde, *An American Vision: Far Western Landscape and National Culture, 1820–1920* (New York: New York University Press, 1990), 133; and Earl Pomeroy, *In Search of the Golden West: The Tourist in Western America* (Lincoln: University Nebraska Press, 2010), 31.

"*a desolate, barren country*" and subsequent quote: TAWJ, 40.

"*rough blocks*" and subsequent quote: J. B. Thayer to Sophia Thayer, En Route, April 20, 1871 [1], folder 2, JBTP.

61 *Humboldt River:* Crofutt, *Great Trans-Continental Tourist's Guide*, 122–24, 133–34.

"*broken into columns*" and subsequent quotes: J. B. Thayer to Sophia Thayer, En Route, April 20, 1871 [1], folder 2, JBTP.

"*The whole sum*": Crofutt, *Great Trans-Continental Tourist's Guide*, 144–45.

"*of the Bible and Asia*": TAWJ, 42; compare J. B. Thayer to Sophia Thayer, En Route, April 20, 1871 [2], folder 2, JBTP.

Bible-steeped Americans: Richard V. Francaviglia, *Believing in Place: A Spiritual Geography of the Great Basin* (Reno: University of Nevada Press, 2003), 134–45, 214–15.

The Guide *identified them as Shoshones or Paiutes:* Crofutt, *Great Trans-Continental Tourist's Guide*, 136; see also Hyde, *An American Vision*, 71–77, 140–42.

racism typical of tourists of the time: Pomeroy, *Golden West*, 38–39, 68–69.

"*short and dirty creatures*" and subsequent quotes: TAWJ, 40–41.

"*ugly and wild in their look*": J. B. Thayer to Sophia Thayer, En Route, April 20, 1871 [2], folder 2, JBTP.

"*was like horsehair*": TAWJ, 41.

62 "*smooth and full cheeks*": J. B. Thayer to Sophia Thayer, En Route, April 20, 1871 [2], folder 2, JBTP.

"*nice little fat innocent, happy little chaps*" and subsequent quotes: J. B. Thayer to Sophia Thayer, En Route, April 20, 1871 [2], folder 2, JBTP.

revitalization movement: Michael Hittman, *Wovoka and the Ghost Dance* (Lincoln: University of Nebraska Press, 1997); Ned Blackhawk, *Violence over the Land: Indians and Empires in the Early American West* (Cambridge, MA: Harvard University Press, 2006), 267–80; Rani-Henrik Andersson, *The Lakota Ghost Dance of 1890* (Lincoln: University of Nebraska Press, 2009).

west of Argenta: J. B. Thayer to Sophia Thayer, En Route, April 20, 1871 [2], folder 2, JBTP.

63 "*a flag station*": Crofutt, *Great Trans-Continental Tourist's Guide*, 138–46.

"*were troubled by the alkali dust*": TAWJ, 42–43.

CHAPTER 3: EMERSON IN CALIFORNIA

64 *Summit Station:* George A. Crofutt, *Great Trans-Continental Tourist's Guide* (New York, 1871), 162–64; Charles Nordhoff, *California: For Health, Pleasure and Residence* (New York: Harper & Brothers, 1872), 31.

"*it was good for New England eyes*": TAWJ, 43; compare J. B. Thayer to Sophia Thayer, San Francisco, April 23, 1871, folder 2, JBTP.

65 "*turned him off rather roughly*" and subsequent quotes: J. B. Thayer to Sophia Thayer, San Francisco, April 23, 1871, folder 2, JBTP.

Emigrant Gap: Crofutt, *Great Trans-Continental Tourist's Guide,* 165, 168–69; Edith Emerson Forbes line-a-day diary, April 21, 1871, EEFP; Ronald A. Bosco and Glen M. Johnson, eds., *The Journals and Miscellaneous Notebooks of Ralph Waldo Emerson,* vol. 16, *1866–1882* (Cambridge, MA: Harvard University Press, 1982), 408. *"much like an open horse car"* and subsequent quote: J. B. Thayer to Sophia Thayer, San Francisco, April 23, 1871, folder 2, JBTP.

66 *"The train is carried":* TAWJ, 43–44.

"one quite gives up": J. B. Thayer to Sophia Thayer, San Francisco, April 23, 1871, folder 2, JBTP.

"Mr. Emerson's own lines": TAWJ, 44–45.

Colfax: Crofutt, *Great Trans-Continental Tourist's Guide,* 169–71.

"there was a general falling back" and subsequent quotes: TAWJ, 45; compare J. B. Thayer to Sophia Thayer, San Francisco, April 23, 1871, folder 2, JBTP.

"In this refulgent summer": ECW, 1:101.

"mere utterance of delight" and subsequent quote: TAWJ, 45.

"lupine, larkspur, buttercups" and subsequent quotes: J. B. Thayer to Sophia Thayer, San Francisco, April 23, 1871, folder 2, JBTP.

67 *Sacramento:* Crofutt, *Great Trans-Continental Tourist's Guide,* 176–79, 191, 195–96, 200–202.

"all was greenness and beauty" and subsequent quote: J. B. Thayer to Sophia Thayer, San Francisco, April 23, 1871, folder 2, JBTP; compare TAWJ, 46.

final tips: Henry T. Williams, *The Pacific Tourist: William's Illustrated Guide to the Pacific R. R. and California and Pleasure Resorts across the Continent* (New York: Henry T. Williams, 1876), 10.

San Francisco in 1871: Doris Muscatine, *Old San Francisco: The Biography of a City from Early Days to the Earthquake* (New York: G. P. Putnam's Sons, 1975), 17–101; Tom Cole, *A Short History of San Francisco* (Berkeley, CA: Heyday, 2014), 41–59.

"an actual metropolis": quoted in Cole, *A Short History of San Francisco,* 42.

"Villainy flourished" and subsequent quote: A. L. Bancroft, ed., *Bancroft's Tourist's Guide* (San Francisco: A. L. Bancroft, 1871), 99.

"progress of San Francisco": Royce, quoted in Cole, *History of San Francisco,* 41.

68 *San Francisco had become calmer:* Muscatine, *Old San Francisco,* 105–41; Cole, *History of San Francisco,* 61–81.

William Ralston: David Lavender, *Nothing Seemed Impossible: William G. Ralston and Early San Francisco* (Palo Alto, CA: American West, 1975).

Charles Warren Stoddard: Eleanor M. Tilton, ed., *The Letters of Ralph Waldo Emerson,* 10 vols. (New York: Columbia University Press, 1994), 9:288; Ben Tarnoff, *The Bohemians: Mark Twain and the San Francisco Writers Who Reinvented American Literature* (New York: Penguin, 2014), 123.

69 *"Verily the Occidental Hotel"* and subsequent quote: Twain, quoted in Nigey Lennon, *The Sagebrush Bohemian: Mark Twain in California* (New York: Paragon House, 1990), 39–40.

"four hundred and twelve" and subsequent quote: Bancroft, *Bancroft's Tourist Guide,* 118–19.

"great grizzly bear!" and subsequent quote: J. B. Thayer to Sophia Thayer, San Francisco, April 30, 1871, folder 3, JBTP.

70 *Captain Oliver Eldridge:* J. B. Thayer to Sophia Thayer, San Francisco, April 21, 1871,

folder 2, JBTP; "Master Mariner of Note Goes to His Final Rest," *San Francisco Call*, December 18, 1902.

Pacific Mail Steamship Company: *San Francisco Bulletin*, April 21, 1871.

"raving thirst for news" and subsequent quotes: J. B. Thayer to Sophia Thayer, San Francisco, April 21, 1871, folder 2, JBTP.

"superb night" and subsequent quotes: J. B. Thayer to Sophia Thayer, San Francisco, April 22, 1871, folder 2, JBTP; compare TAWJ, 46–47.

71 *fraught relationship with Unitarianism:* David Robinson, *The Unitarians and Universalists* (Westport, CT: Greenwood Press, 1985), 25–38, 75–86.

Not all Transcendentalist ministers: Robinson, *Unitarians and Universalists*, 87–122.

72 *Born to a father:* Charles William Wendte, *Thomas Starr King, Patriot and Preacher* (Boston: Beacon Press, 1921), 5–68; Glena Matthews, *The Golden State in the Civil War: Thomas Starr King, the Republican Party, and the Birth of Modern California* (Cambridge: Cambridge University Press, 2012), 42–63.

Emerson himself envied King: Gay Wilson Allen, *Waldo Emerson* (New York: Viking Press, 1981), 596.

After eleven successful years at Hollis Street: Arnold Crompton, *Apostle of Liberty: Starr King in California* (Boston: Beacon Press, 1950); Arnold Crompton, *Unitarianism on the Pacific Coast: The First Sixty Years* (Boston: Beacon Press, 1957), 9–42; Matthews, *Golden State*, 73–83, 88–93, 159–70, 231–35.

73 *"the Apostle of Liberty"* and subsequent quote: Crompton, *Apostle of Liberty*, 32.

transmitter of Transcendentalist spirituality: Sandra Sizer Frankiel, *California's Spiritual Frontiers: Religious Alternatives in Anglo-Protestantism, 1850–1910* (Berkeley: University of California Press, 1988), 1–31; Sheri M. Prud'homme, "Gleam of the Infinite Majesty: The Interplay of Manifest Destiny and Ecotheology in Thomas Starr King's Construction of Yosemite as Sacred Text" (PhD diss., University of California, Berkeley, 2016), 75–79; Tyler Green, *Carleton Watkins: Making the West American* (Berkeley: University of California Press, 2018), 59–62.

Henry Ward Beecher: Thomas Starr King, *A Vacation among the Sierra: Yosemite in 1860*, ed. John Adam Hussey (San Francisco: Book Club of California, 1962), xxv.

"Substance and Show": Thomas Starr King, *Substance and Show, and Other Lectures* (Boston: Houghton, Mifflin, 1890), 1–33.

"quite eloquent with compliment and joy": Wendte, *Thomas Starr King*, 61.

The two corresponded: T. S. King to R. W. Emerson, November 13, 1852, June 27, 1855, December 17, 1856, December 22, 1856, September 9, 1862, MS Am 1280, box 16, Houghton Library, Harvard University, Cambridge, MA.

"salvation & future": Ralph L. Rusk, ed., *The Letters of Ralph Waldo Emerson*, 10 vols. (New York: Columbia University Press, 1939), 5:297.

That King had drunk deeply at the well of Emerson: Frankiel, *California's Spiritual Frontiers*, 21–31; Matthews, *Golden State*, 131–44.

74 *"Infinite Spirit"* and subsequent quote: Thomas Starr King, "Spiritual Christianity," in *The Pitts-Street Chapel Lectures* (Boston: John P. Jewett, 1858), 337, 356.

"the glory of sympathy" and subsequent quote: Thomas Starr King, *Christianity and Humanity: A Series of Sermons* (Boston: J. R. Osgood, 1878), 289, 323.

Horatio Stebbins: Horatio Stebbins, *Thirty-One Years of California* (San Francisco, CA: Channing Auxiliary of the First Unitarian Church of San Francisco, 1895); Charles A. Murdock, *A Backward Glance at Eighty: Recollections and Comment*

(San Francisco: Paul Elder, 1921), 189–95, 217–19; Charles A. Murdock, *Horatio Stebbins: His Ministry and Personality* (Boston: Houghton, Mifflin, 1921); Henry C. Meserve, "The First Unitarian Society of San Francisco, 1850–1950," *Proceedings of the Unitarian Historical Society* 9 (1951): 32–34; Alan Seaburg, "Horatio Stebbins," in *American National Biography*, ed. John A. Garraty and Mark C. Carnes (Oxford: Oxford University Press, 1999), 599–600.

"a regular brick": quoted in Murdock, *Horatio Stebbins*, 54. John Muir would later characterize Stebbins as "a dear young soul, though an old man" (John Muir, *Letters to a Friend: Written to Ezra S. Carr, 1866–1879* [Boston, MA: Houghton Mifflin Company, 1915], 147).

75 *"Dr. Stebbins once met"*: Murdock, *Horatio Stebbins*, 3.

liberal Christian: Murdock, *Backward Glance*, 245; Crompton, *Unitarianism on the Pacific Coast*, 55–56.

"tremendously impressive": Murdock, *Horatio Stebbins*, 47.

"freedom of the pulpit": Seaburg, "Horatio Stebbins," 600.

sightseeing: Edith Emerson Forbes line-a-day diary, Saturday, April 22, 1871, EEFP; TAWJ, 46–47; Bosco and Johnson, *Journals and Miscellaneous Notebooks*, 408.

"beach wagon": J. B. Thayer to Sophia Thayer, San Francisco, April 22, 1871, folder 2, JBTP.

"China-men" and subsequent quote: Rusk, *Letters of Ralph Waldo Emerson*, 6:160.

76 *"filled from side to side"*: Bancroft, *Bancroft's Tourist's Guide*, 145–46.

"blue and yellow lupine" and subsequent quote: TAWJ, 47.

"reviving sight" and subsequent quote: J. B. Thayer to Sophia Thayer, San Francisco, April 22, 1871, folder 2, JBTP.

77 *Cliff House:* Bancroft, *Bancroft's Tourist's Guide*, 145–46; Muscatine, *Old San Francisco*, 232–33.

"Smooth and shiny": J. B. Thayer to Sophia Thayer, San Francisco, April 22, 1871, folder 2, JBTP; compare TAWJ, 47–48.

"Pretty soon" and subsequent quote: Rusk, *Letters of Ralph Waldo Emerson*, 6:159–61.

78 *Mission Dolores:* Bancroft, *Bancroft's Tourist's Guide*, 165–66, 179–80; Muscatine, *Old San Francisco*, 23–24, 25, 31–33, 259–61; Cole, *History of San Francisco*, 10–12.

Helen Hunt Jackson: Earl Pomeroy, *In Search of the Golden West: The Tourist in Western America* (Lincoln: University Nebraska Press, 2010), 37–38; Kate Phillips, *Helen Hunt Jackson: A Literary Life* (Berkeley: University of California Press, 2003), 73, 89, 124–27; James J. Rawls, "The California Mission as Symbol and Myth," *California History* 71, no. 3 (Fall 1992): 342–61.

"quaint, covered with tiles" and subsequent quotes: J. B. Thayer to Sophia Thayer, San Francisco, April 22, 1871, folder 2, JBTP.

"He is greatly interested": J. B. Thayer to Sophia Thayer, San Francisco, April 30, 1871, folder 3, JBTP.

The next day, April 23: Edith Emerson Forbes line-a-day diary, Sunday, April 23, 1871, EEFP.

79 *"young sprout"* and subsequent quote: J. B. Thayer to Sophia Thayer, San Francisco, April 23, 1871, folder 2, JBTP.

At 5:30, they all dressed for dinner: J. B. Thayer to Sophia Thayer, San Francisco, April 23, 1871, folder 2, JBTP; Bosco and Johnson, *Journals and Miscellaneous Notebooks*, 408.

First Unitarian: Crompton, *Unitarianism on the Pacific Coast*, 41–42; Robert A. Monzingo, *Thomas Starr King: Eminent Californian, Civil War Statesman, Unitarian Minister* (Pacific Grove, CA: Boxwood Press, 1991), 226.

The church was filled to capacity: J. B. Thayer to Sophia Thayer, San Francisco, April 25, 1871, folder 2, JBTP; compare TAWJ, 49.

80 *"luminous expression":* Charles J. Woodbury, quoted in Ronald A. Bosco and Joel Myerson, eds., *Emerson in His Own Time* (Iowa City: University of Iowa Press, 2003), 174; see also 205 and 227 for Emerson's pulpit style.

"never loud" and subsequent quotes: Oliver Wendell Holmes Sr., *Ralph Waldo Emerson* (Boston: Houghton Mifflin, 1884), 363–64.

"Immortality" and subsequent quotes: ECW, 8:261–85; for the composition history of "Immortality," see Glen M. Johnson, "Emerson's Essay 'Immortality': The Problem of Authorship," *American Literature* 56, no. 3 (October 1984): 313–30.

81 *"the most original, profound":* San Francisco Chronicle, April 24 and 25, 1871; William Hawley Davis, "Emerson the Lecturer in California," *California Historical Society Quarterly* 20, no. 1 (March 1941): 3–4.

"An Intellectual Treat" and subsequent quote: *Daily Alta California*, April 24, 1871.

"was greatly entertained" and subsequent quotes: J. B. Thayer to Sophia Thayer, San Francisco, April 25, 1871, folder 2, JBTP; compare TAWJ, 49. They weren't the only ones who found the *Alta's* overblown language funny: see also the *San Francisco Bulletin*, April 24, 1871, but especially the *Oakland Daily News*, April 26, 1871, which reported on its front page that "we know Mr. Emerson to be mentally a very big man, but we had scarcely considered him big enough to patronize the Deity in so condescending a fashion. We trust the Great First Cause will not be rendered vain by the philosopher's approval and will accept the 'elegant tribute' to its 'creative genius' with becoming humility."

82 *not lacking in entertainment:* Davis, "Emerson the Lecturer," 2–3.

"Without being as erudite": San Francisco Chronicle, April 28, 1871; see also "Emerson and Gough, Plato and Punch—Two Celebrities Contrasted," *San Francisco Bulletin*, June 14, 1871.

Dwight L. Moody: San Francisco Bulletin, April 8, 1871.

laissez-faire attitude toward religion: see Laurie F. Maffly-Kipp, *Religion and Society in Frontier California* (New Haven, CT: Yale University Press, 1994).

"the great comic pantomime": Davis, "Emerson the Lecturer," 2.

"Skatorial Queen": Frank Preston Stearns, *Sketches from Concord and Appledore* (New York: G. P. Putnam's Sons, 1895), 14.

Pavilion Rink at Woodward's Gardens: Bancroft, *Bancroft's Tourist's Guide*, 130–40.

Sacramento Daily Union: Sacramento Daily Union, April 15, 1871; Lyle W. Dorsett, *A Passion for Souls: The Life of D. L. Moody* (Chicago: Moody Press, 1997).

"a basque of blue velvet": Sacramento Daily Union, February 16, 1867; see also the *San Francisco Chronicle*, April 19 and 29, 1871.

83 *"meant to see her yet":* J. B. Thayer to Sophia Thayer, San Francisco, April 30, 1871, folder 3, JBTP; compare TAWJ, 51.

"We live among surfaces": ECW, 3:54.

CHAPTER 4: TOURING SAN FRANCISCO AND THE BAY AREA

84 *"was really* hot*"* and subsequent quotes: J. B. Thayer to Sophia Thayer, San Francisco, April 25, 1871, folder 2, JBTP; compare TAWJ, 49.

John Codman Ropes: John Codman Ropes, *A Memoir of John Codman Ropes* (Boston: privately printed, 1901); Ronald A. Bosco and Glen M. Johnson, eds., *The Journals and Miscellaneous Notebooks of Ralph Waldo Emerson,* vol. 16, *1866–1882* (Cambridge, MA: Harvard University Press, 1982), 95, 373, 379.

Julia Sumner Hastings: Andrew Hilen, ed., *The Letters of Henry Wadsworth Longfellow* (Cambridge, MA: Harvard University Press, 1972), 3:409.

85 *"asserted to be originals"* and subsequent quote: TAWJ, 50–51; compare J. B. Thayer to Sophia Thayer, San Francisco, April 30, 1871, folder 3, JBTP.

Pacific Anatomical Museum: J. F. Gibbon, "The Origin and Ending of the Dr. Jordan Museum of Anatomy, Etc., Etc.," *California State Journal of Medicine* 14, no. 1 (January 1916): 27; Barbara Berglund, *Making San Francisco American: Cultural Frontiers in the Urban West, 1846–1906* (Lawrence: University Press of Kansas, 2007), 80–94; John Rollin Ridge, *The Life and Adventures of Joaquín Murieta: The Celebrated California Bandit* (1854; New York: Penguin Books, 2018).

Captain Cragin: J. B. Thayer to Sophia Thayer, San Francisco, April 25, 1871, folder 2, JBTP; compare TAWJ, 50.

"'Joss House'": J. B. Thayer to Sophia Thayer, San Francisco, April 23, 1871, folder 2, JBTP.

Chinatown: A. L. Bancroft, ed., *Bancroft's Tourist's Guide* (San Francisco: A. L. Bancroft, 1871), 197–201; Berglund, *Making San Francisco American,* 95–136.

Chinese theater: Bancroft, *Bancroft's Tourist's Guide,* 123–24; Henry T. Williams, *The Pacific Tourist: William's Illustrated Guide to the Pacific R. R. and California and Pleasure Resorts across the Continent* (New York: Henry T. Williams, 1876), 288–90; Misha Berson, *The San Francisco Stage: From Gold Rush to Golden Spike, 1849–1869,* pt. 1 (San Francisco: San Francisco Performing Arts Library and Museum, 1989), 87–91; Daphne Lei, "The Production and Consumption of Chinese Theatre in Nineteenth-Century California," *Theatre Research International* 28, no. 3 (2003): 294–97.

"the most singular performance" and subsequent quotes: J. B. Thayer to Sophia Thayer, San Francisco, April 25, 1871, folder 2, JBTP; compare TAWJ, 50.

86 *"a sort of Faro game"* and subsequent quote: J. B. Thayer to Sophia Thayer, San Francisco, April 25, 1871, folder 2, JBTP; compare TAWJ, 50. Regarding opium dens, see Williams, *Pacific Tourist,* 278–91.

habitual user: John McAleer, *Ralph Waldo Emerson: Days of Encounter* (Boston: Little, Brown, 1984), 212–13.

"Dreams and drunkenness": ECW, 2:254.

87 *"one may see"* and subsequent quotes: J. B. Thayer to Sophia Thayer, San Francisco, April 25, 1871, folder 2, JBTP.

"heaps" of rice and subsequent quotes: J. B. Thayer to Sophia Thayer, San Francisco, April 25, 1871, folder 2, JBTP.

88 *"If I could tell":* Sarah Forbes Hughes, ed., *Reminiscences of John Murray Forbes,* 3 vols. (Boston: George H. Ellis, 1902), 3:281.

"seemed interested in it all" and subsequent quotes: J. B. Thayer to Sophia Thayer, San Francisco, April 25, 1871, folder 2, JBTP; compare TAWJ, 50.

"little China boys" and subsequent quote: J. B. Thayer to Sophia Thayer, San Francisco, May 19, 1871, folder 3, JBTP.

Elizabeth Barber: J. B. Thayer to Sophia Thayer, San Francisco, April 25, 1871, folder 2, JBTP. For the history of the Barber Family, see sananselmohistory.org/articles /barber-tract/barber-family/, accessed May 28, 2021.

89   *"all shone"* and subsequent quote: Ralph L. Rusk, ed., *The Letters of Ralph Waldo Emerson*, 10 vols. (New York: Columbia University Press, 1939), 6:153–54.

Mission Woolen Mills: Bancroft, *Bancroft's Tourist's Guide*, 160.

mint [. . .] post office: Bancroft, *Bancroft's Tourist's Guide*, 148–50.

"After the American list": J. B. Thayer to Sophia Thayer, San Francisco, May 19, 1871, folder 3, JBTP.

champagne cellar: Brian McGinty, *Strong Wine: The Life and Legend of Agoston Haraszthy* (Stanford, CA: Stanford University Press, 1998), 468–69.

"Wine is not adulterated": Edward Waldo Emerson and Waldo Emerson Forbes, eds., *Journals of Ralph Waldo Emerson, with Annotations*, 10 vols. (Boston: Houghton Mifflin, 1914), 10:352.

Mercantile Library: Rusk, *The Letters of Ralph Waldo Emerson*, 6:152; Glen E. Humphreys, *A Temple of Books: The Mercantile Library in the 1860s* (San Francisco: California Historical Society, 1987), 9–19.

"a capital one" and subsequent quotes: J. B. Thayer to Sophia Thayer, Calistoga, April 27, 1871, folder 2, JBTP.

90   *"peculiar pleasure":* TAWJ, 24.

"the most profound" and subsequent quote: *San Francisco Bulletin*, April 24, 1871. See also *San Francisco Examiner*, April 24, 1871.

committee of Unitarian laymen: *San Francisco Daily Evening Herald*, April 24, 1871. See also *San Francisco Chronicle*, April 25, 1871; *Daily Alta California*, April 25, 1871.

"New Englanders rejoice": *San Francisco Bulletin*, April 26, 1871.

"the most approachable of men" and subsequent quotes: Charles A. Murdock, *A Backward Glance at Eighty: Recollections and Comment* (San Francisco: Paul Elder, 1921), 224–28. See also Charles A. Murdock, *Horatio Stebbins: His Ministry and Personality* (Boston: Houghton, Mifflin, 1921), 65–66, and William Hawley Davis, "Emerson the Lecturer in California," *California Historical Society Quarterly* 20, no. 1 (March 1941): 4–6. Horace Davis would eventually marry Thomas Starr King's daughter Edith in 1875: see Henry C. Meserve, "The First Unitarian Society of San Francisco, 1850–1950," *Proceedings of the Unitarian Historical Society* 9 (1951): 33.

91   *articles duly appeared:* *San Francisco Bulletin*, April 26, 1871; *San Francisco Examiner*, April 26, 1871.

"the over-persistent": Murdock, *Horatio Stebbins*, 65–66; compare Murdock, *Backward Glance*, 226–27.

paraphrasing a line: Ronald A. Bosco and Joel Myerson, eds., *The Later Lectures of Ralph Waldo Emerson, 1843–1871*, 2 vols. (Athens: University of Georgia Press, 2010), 2:357.

"bosses the teachers": J. B. Thayer to Sophia Thayer, May 18, 1871, folder 3, JBTP.

92   *"Society in America":* Bosco and Johnson, *Journals and Miscellaneous Notebooks*, 409.

"stolen in upon us": *San Francisco Chronicle*, April 27, 1871.

"His peculiar manner" and subsequent quotes: Murdock, *Backward Glance*, 226; see also Davis, "Emerson the Lecturer," 4–6.

Based on news reports: Daily Alta California, April 27, 1871; *San Francisco Bulletin*, April 27, 1871; *San Francisco Chronicle*, April 27, 1871.

93 *"American to be proud of"* and subsequent quotes: ECW, 8:85–86, 88. John Murray Forbes was revealed by name as "the American to be proud of" in Emerson and Forbes, *Journals of Ralph Waldo Emerson*, 10:72.

"his figure is slight" and subsequent quotes: *San Francisco Chronicle*, April 27, 1871.

94 *"The lecture was a masterpiece"*: *Daily Alta California*, April 27, 1871.

"The lecturer relied" and subsequent quote: *San Francisco Bulletin*, April 27, 1871.

"his encouraging friendliness" and subsequent quotes: Murdock, *Backward Glance*, 226–28.

95 *Calistoga:* J. B. Thayer to Sophia Thayer, San Francisco, April 25, 1871, and J. B. Thayer to Sophia Thayer, Calistoga, April 27, 1871, folder 2, JBTP; compare TAWJ, 52. See also *Handbook of Calistoga Springs; or, Little Geysers* (San Francisco: Alta California Book and Job Printing House, 1871), and Laura De Force Gordon, *The Great Geysers of California and How to Reach Them* (San Francisco: Bacon, 1877), 8–14.

Occidental Cottage and subsequent quotes: J. B. Thayer to Sophia Thayer, Calistoga, April 27, 1871, folder 2, JBTP. For the Petrified Forest, see *Handbook of Calistoga Springs*, 12; and Gordon, *Great Geysers*, 14–18.

"We live today & every day" and subsequent quotes: Rusk, *Letters of Ralph Waldo Emerson*, 6:151–54.

96 *New England would have remained unpopulated:* Bosco and Myerson, *Later Lectures*, 2:55.

"well & wise & brilliant" and subsequent quotes: Rusk, *Letters of Ralph Waldo Emerson*, 6:152–53.

breakfast about seven o'clock: J. B. Thayer to Sophia Thayer, Calistoga, April 27, 1871, folder 2, JBTP.

Clark T. Foss: Gordon, *Great Geysers*, 14–22; Hannah Clayborn, "Clark Foss: The Most Famous Stagecoach Driver in the World," www.sonic.net/janosko/ourhealds burg.com/history/foss.htm, accessed May 28, 2021.

"intelligent and cheerful": J. B. Thayer to Sophia Thayer, San Francisco, April 30, 1871, folder 3, JBTP.

"fine grassy ranches" and subsequent quotes: J. B. Thayer to Sophia Thayer, San Francisco, April 30, 1871, folder 3, JBTP.

98 *"an easier jaunt"*: J. B. Thayer to Sophia Thayer, Calistoga, April 27, 1871, folder 2, JBTP.

The "Foss Road": Gaye LeBaron, "Artifacts Unearth Story of Early Tourism on Old Foss Road," *Press Democrat* (Santa Rosa), July 8, 2012.

"plumped down right out of the mountains": J. B. Thayer to Sophia Thayer, San Francisco, April 30, 1871, folder 3, JBTP.

"six-in-hand": Gordon, *Great Geysers*, 18.

"a snowy peak" and subsequent quotes: J. B. Thayer to Sophia Thayer, San Francisco, April 30, 1871, folder 3, JBTP; Oliver Wendell Holmes Sr., *Ralph Waldo Emerson* (Boston: Houghton Mifflin, 1884), 263. Alas, Foss eventually came to grief because of his driving: in 1874, he crashed his stage into a ravine between Pine Flat and Fossville, injuring several passengers and killing one young woman; chastened, he moderated his speed from then on, eventually retiring in 1881 (see Clayborn, "Clark Foss").

Geysers Hotel: Gordon, *Great Geysers*, 22–25.

99 *hired a guide:* J. B. Thayer to Sophia Thayer, San Francisco, April 30, 1871, folder 3, JBTP.

"fumarole": Earl Pomeroy, *In Search of the Golden West: The Tourist in Western America* (Lincoln: University Nebraska Press, 2010), 50.

"beautiful green" and subsequent quote: Gordon, *Great Geysers,* 25–26.

"Ascent into Tartarus" and subsequent quotes: Gordon, *Great Geysers,* 29–38.

"We could not but sympathize": J. B. Thayer to Sophia Thayer, San Francisco, April 30, 1871, folder 3, JBTP.

100 *"a rocky promontory":* Gordon, *Great Geysers,* 38.

Arnold Henry Guyot: J. B. Thayer to Sophia Thayer, San Francisco, April 30, 1871, folder 3, JBTP.

influenced both Emerson and Thoreau: Richard J. Schneider, "'Climate Does Thus React on Man': Wildness and Geographic Determinism in Thoreau's 'Walking,'" in *Thoreau's Sense of Place,* ed. Richard J. Schneider (Iowa City: University of Iowa Press, 2000), 45.

"royal mountain fare" and subsequent quote: Gordon, *Great Geysers,* 25.

arrived back from Sonoma the day before: Eleanor M. Tilton, ed., *The Letters of Ralph Waldo Emerson,* 10 vols. (New York: Columbia University Press, 1995), 10:46.

"seized and carried off all letters": J. B. Thayer to Sophia Thayer, San Francisco, April 29, 1871, folder 3, JBTP.

"Resources": San Francisco Bulletin, April 27 and 29, May 1, 1871; Bosco and Johnson, *Journals and Miscellaneous Notebooks,* 409; Davis, "Emerson the Lecturer," 6–7. Since Emerson's lecture was synopsized on the front page of the *San Francisco Bulletin* the next Monday (May 1, 1871)—albeit in a rather jumbled form, or perhaps it was Emerson's reading of it that was jumbled—we can be fairly certain of Emerson's text that night, for although the version of "Resources" published in *Letters and Social Aims* is very different, an earlier draft exists in manuscript that corresponds to the talk he gave in San Francisco (Bosco and Myerson, *Later Lectures,* 2:336–59).

101 *"in communities so exceptional"* and subsequent quotes: *San Francisco Bulletin,* May 1, 1871; compare Bosco and Myerson, *Later Lectures,* 2:340–41, 344, 348.

"He fingers them over" and subsequent quotes: *San Francisco Bulletin,* May 1, 1871.

102 *Monday, May 1:* J. B. Thayer to Sophia Thayer, Yosemite, May 6, 1871, folder 3, JBTP; Bosco and Johnson, *Journals and Miscellaneous Notebooks,* 409.

"Character": a version of the talk was eventually published as "Greatness" in *Letters and Social Aims* (ECW, 8:243–60).

"completeness" and subsequent quotes: ECW, 8:245, 246, 249–51, 255, 257–59.

103 *encomium: San Francisco Bulletin,* May 2, 1871.

"largely attended" and subsequent quotes: *Daily Alta California,* May 2, 1871.

"Mr. Emerson delivered a lecture" and subsequent quote: *San Francisco Bulletin,* May 2, 1871.

"Ralph Waldo Emerson lectured": San Francisco Chronicle, May 2, 1871.

"the people would tire": Murdock, *Backward Glance,* 227; Murdock, *Horatio Stebbins,* 65–66.

104 *"kind and wise and funny"* and subsequent quote: J. B. Thayer to Sophia Thayer, San Francisco, April 30, 1871, folder 3, JBTP.

CHAPTER 5: YOSEMITE

105 *At 7:45 a.m.:* Edith Emerson Forbes line-a-day diary, May 2, 1871, EEFP; TAWJ, 53; Ronald A. Bosco and Glen M. Johnson, eds., *The Journals and Miscellaneous Notebooks of Ralph Waldo Emerson,* vol. 16, *1866–1882* (Cambridge, MA: Harvard University Press, 1982), 409.

"Mr. Coulter": J. B. Thayer to Sophia Thayer, San Francisco, April 30, 1871, folder 3, JBTP.

ferry, railroad, stagecoach, wagon: George A. Crofutt, *Great Trans-Continental Tourist's Guide* (New York, 1871), 193–94.

"My bag had to sweat": J. B. Thayer to Sophia Thayer, Yosemite, May 6, 1871 (5¼ o'c), folder 3, JBTP.

five months pregnant: Edith Emerson Forbes to William H. Forbes, San Rafael, May 7, 1871, EEFP; Ralph L. Rusk, ed., *The Letters of Ralph Waldo Emerson,* 10 vols. (New York: Columbia University Press, 1939), 6:172.

San Rafael to stay with the Barbers: Edith Emerson Forbes line-a-day diary, May 2–14, 1871, EEFP; Edith Emerson Forbes to William H. Forbes, San Rafael, May 3 and 7, 1871, EEFP.

"on the piazza": Edith Emerson Forbes line-a-day diary, May 3, 1871, EEFP; Joseph Mailliard, "Autobiography of Joseph Mailliard," *Condor* 26 (January 1924): 10.

106 *answering letters to Ellen Emerson:* Edith Emerson Forbes line-a-day diary, May 2–14, 1871, EEFP.

bratty antics: Ellen Emerson to Edith Emerson, April 13, 1871, ETEL.

"At the Calaveras Grove Hotel": Charles Nordhoff, *California: For Health, Pleasure and Residence* (New York: Harper & Brothers, 1872), 72.

"frighten Father" and subsequent quote: Edith Emerson Forbes to William H. Forbes, San Rafael, May 3, 1871, EEFP.

The ferry from San Francisco: William H. Forbes to Edith Emerson Forbes, Roberts Ferry, May 3, 1871, EEFP; J. B. Thayer to Sophia Thayer, Coulterville, May 3, 1871, and J. B. Thayer to Sophia Thayer, Yosemite, May 6, 1871 (5¼ o'c.), folder 3, JBTP; TAWJ, 53–56; Bosco and Johnson, *Journals and Miscellaneous Notebooks,* 409.

Drought was on the land: William H. Forbes to Edith Emerson Forbes, Roberts Ferry, May 3, 1871, EEFP; J. B. Thayer to Sophia Thayer, Coulterville, May 3, 1871, folder 3, JBTP.

"jackass rabbits": J. B. Thayer to Sophia Thayer, Yosemite, May 6, 1871 (5¼ o'c.), folder 3, JBTP.

"sat gravely" and subsequent quotes: TAWJ, 54, 56; compare J. B. Thayer to Sophia Thayer, Yosemite, May 6, 1871 (5¼ o'c.), folder 3, JBTP.

107 *"Staging":* J. B. Thayer to Sophia Thayer, Coulterville, May 3, 1871, folder 3, JBTP.

"with the thermometer at 100°": Oliver Wendell Holmes Sr., *Ralph Waldo Emerson* (Boston: Houghton Mifflin, 1884), 264.

"great gifts" and subsequent quote: J. B. Thayer to Sophia Thayer, Coulterville, May 3, 1871, folder 3, JBTP.

108 *"It feels that it is in communication"* and subsequent quotes: J. B. Thayer to Sophia Thayer, Yosemite, May 6, 1871 (5¼ o'c.), folder 3, JBTP.

"To me, the eternal existence": ECW, 8:277; compare J. B. Thayer to Sophia Thayer, Yosemite, May 6, 1871 (5¼ o'c.), folder 3, JBTP; TAWJ, 58.

Roberts Ferry: William H. Forbes to Edith Emerson Forbes, Roberts Ferry, May 3, 1871, EEFP; Bosco and Johnson, *Journals and Miscellaneous Notebooks*, 409.

"chests of tea": TAWJ, 56.

"like a scene in Chaucer": J. B. Thayer to Sophia Thayer, Yosemite, May 6, 1871 (5¼ o'c.), folder 3, JBTP; compare TAWJ, 59.

rushed down to inspect the Tuolumne River: J. B. Thayer to Sophia Thayer, Yosemite, May 6, 1871 (5¼ o'c.), folder 3, JBTP.

"The miners keep Sunday": TAWJ, 57.

109 *"splendid bath"*: William H. Forbes to Edith Emerson Forbes, Roberts Ferry, May 3, 1871, EEFP.

"Boston boy": J. B. Thayer to Sophia Thayer, Yosemite, May 6, 1871 (5¼ o'c.), folder 3, JBTP; William H. Forbes to Edith Emerson Forbes, Roberts Ferry, May 3, 1871, EEFP.

"His wife" . . . "was a Western woman" and subsequent quotes: J. B. Thayer to Sophia Thayer, Yosemite, May 6, 1871 (5¼ o'c.), folder 3, JBTP.

"To me, this is delightful": TAWJ, 57.

Some slept well: J. B. Thayer to Sophia Thayer, Yosemite, May 6, 1871 (5¼ o'c.), folder 3, JBTP.

110 *"swellings of a piecrust"* and subsequent quote: J. B. Thayer to Sophia Thayer, Yosemite, May 6, 1871 (5¼ o'c.), folder 3, JBTP.

"only rocks remained": J. B. Thayer to Sophia Thayer, Coulterville, May 3, 1871, folder 3, JBTP; compare TAWJ, 59–60.

"Water for Horses": J. B. Thayer to Sophia Thayer, Yosemite, May 6, 1871 (5¼ o'c.), folder 3, JBTP; compare TAWJ, 59–60.

Coulterville: William H. Forbes to Edith Emerson Forbes, Leidig's Hotel, Yosemite Valley, May 6, 1871, EEFP; A. L. Bancroft, ed., *Bancroft's Tourist's Guide* (San Francisco: A. L. Bancroft, 1871), 15–16; Bosco and Johnson, *Journals and Miscellaneous Notebooks*, 409. After meeting with Emerson, Clark was reported to have said, "If a god ever did come down from Olympus and talk with a Greek, I know how the fellow felt" (Catherine Coffin Phillips, *Coulterville Chronicle* [San Francisco: The Grabhorn Press, 1942], 184).

"something of the look of decay" and subsequent quote: J. B. Thayer to Sophia Thayer, Coulterville, May 3, 1871, folder 3, JBTP.

"he looked happy" and subsequent quotes: J. B. Thayer to Sophia Thayer, Yosemite, May 6, 1871 (5¼ o'c.), folder 3, JBTP; compare TAWJ, 60–61.

111 *"agreeable" . . . "one who is smoking"* and subsequent quote: TAWJ, 60–61.

"One's respect for him grows constantly": J. B. Thayer to Sophia Thayer, Coulterville, May 3, 1871, folder 3, JBTP.

Hazel Green: TAWJ, 62; Bosco and Johnson, *Journals and Miscellaneous Notebooks*, 409.

"sorry looking horses": William H. Forbes to Edith Emerson Forbes, Leidig's Hotel, Yosemite Valley, May 6, 1871, EEFP.

"four feet": TAWJ, 63.

"alligator skin" and subsequent quote: J. B. Thayer to Sophia Thayer, Yosemite, May 8, 1871, folder 3, JBTP.

"you gentlemen pines" and subsequent quote: TAWJ, 64.

112   *Mr. Dexter:* TAWJ, 64–65.
Bower Cave: William H. Forbes to Edith Emerson Forbes, Leidig's Hotel, Yosemite Valley, May 6, 1871, EEFP; Bosco and Johnson, *Journals and Miscellaneous Notebooks,* 409.
"a picturesque and unique locality": Bancroft, *Bancroft's Tourist's Guide,* 72.
"Open Sesame": J. B. Thayer to Sophia Thayer, Yosemite, May 8, 1871, folder 3, JBTP.
"a small but singularly beautiful lake" and subsequent quotes: Bancroft, *Bancroft's Tourist's Guide,* 74–75.
"a cave and grotto on the stage" and subsequent quotes: J. B. Thayer to Sophia Thayer, Yosemite, May 8, 1871, folder 3, JBTP.
Crane Flat: J. B. Thayer to Sophia Thayer, Yosemite, May 6, 1871, folder 3, JBTP; William H. Forbes to Edith Emerson Forbes, Leidig's Hotel, Yosemite Valley, May 6, 1871, EEFP; Bosco and Johnson, *Journals and Miscellaneous Notebooks,* 409.
"A 'Flat,'" Thayer helpfully explained: J. B. Thayer to Sophia Thayer, Yosemite, May 8, 1871, folder 3, JBTP; compare TAWJ, 62–63.
113   *"a really sumptuous dinner"* and subsequent quote: J. B. Thayer to Sophia Thayer, Yosemite, May 9, 1871, folder 3, JBTP; compare TAWJ, 65.
"These are the only philosophers!": TAWJ, 66; compare J. B. Thayer to Sophia Thayer, Yosemite, May 9, 1871, folder 3, JBTP.
"The uses of travel are occasional and short": ECW, 6:211.
The evening weather: J. B. Thayer to Sophia Thayer, Yosemite, May 9, 1871, folder 3, JBTP; compare TAWJ, 65–67.
"luxurious couch of boughs" and subsequent quote: William H. Forbes to Edith Emerson Forbes, Leidig's Hotel, Yosemite Valley, May 6, 1871, EEFP.
"solid gray rain": William H. Forbes to Edith Emerson Forbes, Leidig's Hotel, Yosemite Valley, May 6, 1871, EEFP.
114   *"monster talent for being tall":* J. B. Thayer to Sophia Thayer, Yosemite, May 9, 1871, folder 3, JBTP; compare TAWJ, 67.
"Yosemite Valley": Bancroft, *Bancroft's Tourist's Guide,* 25–28; compare TAWJ, 72.
the Miwok: Galen Clark, *Indians of the Yosemite* (Yosemite Valley, CA: Galen Clark, 1907); Eugene L. Conrotto, *Miwok Means People: The Life and Fate of the Native Inhabitants of the California Gold Rush Country* (Fresno, CA: Valley Publishers, 2015), 95–103.
"for public use": Jen A. Huntley, *The Making of Yosemite: James Mason Hutchings and the Origin of America's Most Popular Park* (Lawrence: University Press of Kansas, 2014), 107. See also John F. Sears, *Sacred Places: American Tourist Attractions in the Nineteenth Century* (Oxford: Oxford University Press, 1989), 122–55.
115   *"the climb"* and subsequent quotes: J. B. Thayer to Sophia Thayer, Yosemite, May 9, 1871, folder 3, JBTP; compare TAWJ, 67.
"the valley has a wild untamed look": J. B. Thayer to Sophia Thayer, Yosemite, May 6, 1871, folder 3, JBTP.
"barring some want of tinsel and splendor" and subsequent quote: J. B. Thayer to Sophia Thayer, Yosemite, May 6, 1871, folder 3, JBTP; compare TAWJ, 67–70.
"the two elder ladies" and subsequent quotes: Sarah Forbes Hughes, ed., *Reminiscences of John Murray Forbes,* 3 vols. (Boston: George H. Ellis, 1902), 3:279.

"a silly name for a beautiful thing": J. B. Thayer to Sophia Thayer, Yosemite, May 6, 1871, folder 3, JBTP.

"magnificent huge buttress": J. B. Thayer to Sophia Thayer, Yosemite, May 9, 1871, folder 3, JBTP.

toll bridge: J. B. Thayer to Sophia Thayer, Yosemite, May 9, 1871, folder 3, JBTP; compare TAWJ, 70, 85.

three hotels in the valley: J. B. Thayer to Sophia Thayer, Yosemite, May 6, 1871, folder 3, JBTP; Bancroft, *Bancroft's Tourist's Guide*, 21; TAWJ, 71. See also Carl P. Russell, *One Hundred Years in Yosemite* (Berkeley: University of California Press, 1947), 92–99, 101–3.

"piazza" and subsequent quote: J. B. Thayer to Sophia Thayer, Yosemite, May 9, 1871, folder 3, JBTP.

117 *"our sturdy little landlady"*: J. B. Thayer to Sophia Thayer, Yosemite, May 9, 1871, folder 3, JBTP.

some fishing before dinner: J. B. Thayer to Sophia Thayer, Yosemite, May 6, 1871, folder 3, JBTP.

"After traveling a few months in California": quoted in Russell, *One Hundred Years in Yosemite*, 102.

bright Venus: J. B. Thayer to Sophia Thayer, Yosemite, May 9, 1871, folder 3, JBTP; compare TAWJ, 74.

"stands right under 'Sentinel Rock'" and subsequent quotes: J. B. Thayer to Sophia Thayer, Yosemite, May 6, 1871, folder 3, JBTP; compare TAWJ, 71–72.

118 *"spend at least two weeks"* and subsequent quotes: Bancroft, *Bancroft's Tourist's Guide*, 10–11, 51.

119 *Thomas Starr King, on the other hand:* Thomas Starr King, *A Vacation among the Sierra: Yosemite in 1860*, ed. John Adam Hussey (San Francisco: Book Club of California, 1962), ix–xxxiv; Glena Matthews, *The Golden State in the Civil War: Thomas Starr King, the Republican Party, and the Birth of Modern California* (Cambridge: Cambridge University Press, 2012), 135–44; Tyler Green, *Carleton Watkins: Making the West American* (Berkeley: University of California Press, 2018), 68–73.

"grandest piece of rock-and-water scenery": Matthews, *Golden State in the Civil War*, 142.

Whitney's Yosemite Guide-Book: J. D. Whitney, *The Yosemite Guide-Book* (Cambridge, MA: Welch, Bigelow, 1869); Edwin Tenney Brewster, *The Life and Letters of Josiah Dwight Whitney* (Boston: Houghton Mifflin, 1909); Clark A. Elliott, "Whitney, Josiah White," in *American National Biography*, ed. John A. Garraty and Mark C. Carnes (Oxford: Oxford University Press, 1999), 307–8.

he clearly found the book indispensable: J. B. Thayer to Sophia Thayer, San Francisco, April 30, 1871, and J. B. Thayer to Sophia Thayer, San Francisco, May 16, 1871, folder 3, JBTP; TAWJ, 14–15, 63–64, 68–73, 76–77, 84–85, 101–2, 104–5.

Mirror Lake: Bosco and Johnson, *Journals and Miscellaneous Notebooks*, 409.

120 *"broad grassy meadow"* and subsequent quotes: J. B. Thayer to Sophia Thayer, Yosemite, May 7, 1871, folder 3, JBTP; compare TAWJ, 74–76.

"This valley is the only place": Apparently Emerson's comment that Yosemite lived up to the brag became a stock observation that he would repeat to many, including newspaper reporters and Thomas Starr King's widow back in San

Francisco. See the *Chicago Tribune*, Wednesday, June 7, 1871; *Leavenworth Daily Commercial*, June 30, 1871; and Moncure Conway to James Bradley Thayer, December 23, 1884, folder 5, JBTP.

"prostrate Sugar Pine": Bosco and Johnson, *Journals and Miscellaneous Notebooks*, 409.

"not the 'Big Trees'" and subsequent quotes: J. B. Thayer to Sophia Thayer, Yosemite, May 10, 1871, folder 3, JBTP; compare TAWJ, 74–75; see also John Muir, *Our National Parks* (Boston: Houghton Mifflin, 1901), 235–36.

their afternoon smoke: J. B. Thayer to Sophia Thayer, Yosemite, May 7, 1871, folder 3, JBTP.

"I wish the chiefs": J. B. Thayer to Sophia Thayer, Yosemite, May 7, 1871, folder 3, JBTP.

121   *"there is one topic"*: ECW, 6:155.

That day's excursion: TAWJ, 77–78; William H. Forbes to Edith Emerson Forbes, Yosemite Valley, May 7, 1871, EEFP; Bosco and Johnson, *Journals and Miscellaneous Notebooks*, 409.

Mr. Forbes's horse slipped: Hughes, *Reminiscences of John Murray Forbes*, 3:279.

Vernal Fall: Bancroft, *Bancroft's Tourist's Guide*, 35–38.

"pouring straight over" and subsequent quotes: J. B. Thayer to Sophia Thayer, Yosemite, May 7, 1871, folder 3, JBTP; compare TAWJ, 78–79. For "Wreck of the Hesperus," see Henry Wadsworth Longfellow, *Ballads and Other Poems* (Cambridge, MA: John Owen, 1842), 42–47.

Nevada Fall: Bancroft, *Bancroft's Tourist's Guide*, 38–40; Bosco and Johnson, *Journals and Miscellaneous Notebooks*, 409.

"a zig zag trail": William H. Forbes to Edith Emerson Forbes, Yosemite Valley, May 7, 1871, EEFP.

La Casa Nevada: Hank Johnston, "Yosemite's Casa Nevada (The Snow House)," *Yosemite* 66, no. 1 (Winter 2004): 3–5.

"a real kind, genuine Yankee": J. B. Thayer to Sophia Thayer, Yosemite, May 7, 1871, folder 3, JBTP; compare TAWJ, 79–80.

122   *"like rockets"* and subsequent quote: J. B. Thayer to Sophia Thayer, Yosemite, May 7, 1871, folder 3, JBTP.

"'Yes, oh yes, Dante'" and subsequent quote: TAWJ, 80–81, 83.

"maxim of a literary man" and subsequent quote: J. B. Thayer to Sophia Thayer, Yosemite, May 10, 1871, folder 3, JBTP; compare TAWJ, 83.

"fleecy sheets and folds" and subsequent quote: William H. Forbes to Edith Emerson Forbes, Yosemite Valley, May 7, 1871, EEFP.

"the wholeness we admire": ECW, 1:163.

Liberty Cap: Bancroft, *Bancroft's Tourist's Guide*, 40; William H. Forbes to Edith Emerson Forbes, Yosemite Valley, May 7, 1871, EEFP; James Mason Hutchings, *In the Heart of the Sierras* (Oakland, CA: Pacific Press, 1886), 445.

123   *"Why will those madcap boys do that?"*: J. B. Thayer to Sophia Thayer, Yosemite, May 10, 1871, folder 3, JBTP; compare TAWJ, 81–82.

"had some stiff work getting up" and subsequent quotes: William H. Forbes to Edith Emerson Forbes, Yosemite Valley, May 7, 1871, EEFP.

"with quiet happiness": TAWJ, 82; compare J. B. Thayer to Sophia Thayer, Yosemite, May 7, 1871, folder 3, JBTP.

"a day of wonders": Bosco and Johnson, *Journals and Miscellaneous Notebooks*, 409.

"Think on Living": J. B. Thayer to Sophia Thayer, Yosemite, May 10, 1871, folder 3, JBTP; compare TAWJ, 83.

Thoroughly tired by their expedition: J. B. Thayer to Sophia Thayer, Yosemite, May 10, 1871, folder 3, JBTP; Bosco and Johnson, *Journals and Miscellaneous Notebooks*, 409.

singing of robins: J. B. Thayer to Sophia Thayer, Yosemite, May 10, 1871, folder 3, JBTP.

124   "Emerson's mode of living": Holmes, *Ralph Waldo Emerson*, 362.

"But Mr. Forbes!": TAWJ, 95; compare J. B. Thayer to Sophia Thayer, San Francisco, May 20, 1871, folder 3, JBTP.

"One thinks here of the Arab proverb": TAWJ, 83; compare J. B. Thayer to Sophia Thayer, Yosemite, May 10, 1871, folder 3, JBTP. "Allah does not count the days spent in the chase" was one of Emerson's favorite proverbs, appearing in *English Traits* (ECW, 5:57) and *Letters and Social Aims* (ECW, 8:227).

"still we saw fine effects" and subsequent quotes: J. B. Thayer to Sophia Thayer, Yosemite, May 10, 1871, folder 3, JBTP; compare TAWJ, 82–83.

buy some "views": J. B. Thayer to Sophia Thayer, Yosemite, May 10, 1871, folder 3, JBTP.

Thomas C. Roche: Paul Hickman and Peter Palmquist, "J. J. Reilly—Part III: Views of American Scenery," *Stereo World* 12, no. 3 (July/August 1985): 8–10; Louis S. Smaus, "Yosemite in Stereo." *Yosemite* 51, no. 3 (Summer 1989): 8.

125   *Yosemite Falls:* TAWJ, 84; Bosco and Johnson, *Journals and Miscellaneous Notebooks*, 409.

"not even the photogram": Bancroft, *Bancroft's Tourist's Guide*, 45.

"foam and vapor": J. B. Thayer to Sophia Thayer, Yosemite, May 10, 1871, folder 3, JBTP.

"When a man is overwhelmed": Bancroft, *Bancroft's Tourist's Guide*, 45.

James Mason Hutchings: J. B. Thayer to Sophia Thayer, Yosemite, May 10, 1871, folder 3, JBTP; compare TAWJ, 84; see also Bosco and Johnson, *Journals and Miscellaneous Notebooks*, 409–10; Huntley, *The Making of Yosemite*; Kevin Starr, *Americans and the California Dream, 1850–1915* (New York: Oxford University Press, 1973), 181.

"no nonsense": For example, Jack Gyer, ed., *Yosemite, Saga of a Century, 1864–1964* (Oakhurst, CA: Sierra Star Press, 1964), 34.

"owns the landscape": ECW, 1:16.

126   *Hutchings' remained a gregarious and genial host:* J. B. Thayer to Sophia Thayer, Yosemite, May 10, 1871, folder 3, JBTP; Bosco and Johnson, *Journals and Miscellaneous Notebooks*, 409–10.

"dried grubs": TAWJ, 84–85.

guest at Hutchings' House: Huntley, *The Making of Yosemite*, 134–35.

"several of us sat on the shady side" and subsequent quotes: J. B. Thayer to Sophia Thayer, Yosemite, May 10, 1871, folder 3, JBTP.

"Spinoza must now be pretty old": Bosco and Johnson, *Journals and Miscellaneous Notebooks*, 172.

"a mere block": J. B. Thayer to Sophia Thayer, Yosemite, May 10, 1871, folder 3, JBTP.

127 *"he thought that as a man grows"*: TAWJ, 86.
"'What a range'": J. B. Thayer to Sophia Thayer, Yosemite, May 10, 1871, folder 3, JBTP.
"That evening (Monday)": TAWJ, 88–89; compare J. B. Thayer to Sophia Thayer, Yosemite, May 10, 1871, folder 3, JBTP.

CHAPTER 6: THE MARIPOSA BIG TREES

128 *"M" was John Muir*: J. B. Thayer to Sophia Thayer, Yosemite, May 10, 1871, folder 3, JBTP. See also Linnie Marsh Wolfe, *Son of the Wilderness: The Life of John Muir* (Madison: University of Wisconsin Press, 2003), 118–36; Donald Worster, *A Passion for Nature: The Life of John Muir* (Oxford: Oxford University Press, 2008), 149–80; and Jen A. Huntley, *The Making of Yosemite: James Mason Hutchings and the Origin of America's Most Popular Park* (Lawrence: University Press of Kansas, 2014), 134.
"I was then living": William Frederic Badè, *The Life and Letters of John Muir*, 2 vols. (Boston: Houghton Mifflin, 1924), 1:253.
Born in Dunbar: Wolfe, *Son of the Wilderness*, 3–117; Worster, *A Passion for Nature*, 13–157.

130 *"luminous wall of the mountains"* and subsequent quotes: John Muir, *The Mountains of California* (New York: Century, 1894), 2–3. In his essay "Domestic Life" (1870), Emerson wrote, "It is the iron band of poverty, of necessity, of austerity, which, excluding them from the sensual enjoyments which make other boys too early old, has directed their activity in safe and right channels, and made them, despite themselves, reverers of the grand, the beautiful and the good"; if Emerson had known Muir's backstory, he probably would have hailed him as proof of this maxim (ECW, 7:117).
Jeanne Carr: Edmund A. Schofield, "John Muir's Yankee Friends and Mentors: The New England Connection," *Pacific Historian* 29, nos. 2–3 (Summer--Fall 1985): 65–89; Bonnie Johanna Gisel, ed., *Kindred and Related Spirits: The Letters of John Muir and Jeanne C. Carr* (Salt Lake City: University of Utah Press, 2001), 1–11.
"I am feeling as glad": Gisel, *Kindred and Related Spirits*, 138.
"heard the hotel people say" and subsequent quotes: Badè, *Letters of John Muir*, 1:253–54.

131 *"I received today"*: Gisel, *Kindred and Related Spirits*, 139. See also Ralph L. Rusk, ed., *The Letters of Ralph Waldo Emerson*, 10 vols. (New York: Columbia University Press, 1939), 6:154–55.

132 *"Why did you not make yourself known"*: Badè, *Letters of John Muir*, 1:254.
"He is a simple unaffected young fellow": J. B. Thayer to Sophia Thayer, Yosemite, May 10, 1871, folder 3, JBTP.
"urged Mr. Emerson": TAWJ, 90.
"forgetting his age": John Muir, *Our National Parks* (Boston: Houghton Mifflin, 1901), 132.
"was a little rookery": J. B. Thayer to Sophia Thayer, Yosemite, May 10, 1871, folder 3, JBTP; compare TAWJ, 90.
"not easy of access" and subsequent quotes: Badè, *Letters of John Muir*, 1:247–48, 25; sketch of "hang nest" found on 248.

133 *"cat-like love of garrets"*: ECW, 2:182.

"hundreds of capital pencil sketches": J. B. Thayer to Sophia Thayer, Yosemite, May 10, 1871, folder 3, JBTP.

"All these treasures he poured out": TAWJ, 90–91; compare Badè, *Letters of John Muir*, 1:354.

Emerson brought John Murray Forbes: TAWJ, 91; Badè, *Letters of John Muir*, 1:254.

"We all like him exceedingly": J. B. Thayer to Sophia Thayer, Yosemite, May 10, 1871, folder 3, JBTP.

Thérèse Yelverton: Badè, *Letters of John Muir*, 1:228, 278–84, 362–63; Michael P. Branch, "Telling Nature's Story: John Muir and the Decentering of the Romantic Self," in *John Muir in Historical Perspective*, ed. Sally M. Miller (Bern: Peter Lang, 1993), 109–11; Wolfe, *Son of the Wilderness*, 136–42; Worster, *A Passion for Nature*, 175–77.

134 *"miss that noble cliff"*: TAWJ, 91–94.

"sea-green" and subsequent quotes: J. B. Thayer to Sophia Thayer, Yosemite, May 10, 1871, folder 3, JBTP.

"We looked up through the length" and subsequent quote: TAWJ, 93–94.

135 *time for the party to depart*: J. B. Thayer to Sophia Thayer, Yosemite, May 9, 1871, folder 3, JBTP; William H. Forbes to Edith Emerson Forbes, Yosemite Valley, May 7 and 8, 1871, EEFP; TAWJ, 95.

Mariposa Route: A. L. Bancroft, ed., *Bancroft's Tourist's Guide* (San Francisco: A. L. Bancroft, 1871), 16–17.

"I'll go, Mr. Emerson" and subsequent quote: Badè, *Letters of John Muir*, 1:354–55; compare J. B. Thayer to Sophia Thayer, Yosemite, May 10, 1871, folder 3, JBTP; TAWJ, 91; Muir, *Our National Parks*, 132–33.

"The trail was quite as hard" and subsequent quotes: J. B. Thayer to Sophia Thayer, Stockton, May 14, 1871, folder 3, JBTP; compare TAWJ, 96, 98.

"We rode through the magnificent forests": Muir, *Our National Parks*, 133.

136 *"once, when riding down"*: Oliver Wendell Holmes Sr., *Ralph Waldo Emerson* (Boston: Houghton Mifflin, 1884), 264.

Around noon, the party stopped to picnic: J. B. Thayer to Sophia Thayer, Stockton, May 14, 1871, folder 3, JBTP; Badè, *Letters of John Muir*, 1:255.

"How can Mr. Emerson" and subsequent quotes: TAWJ, 96–97.

the party arrived at Clark's Station: J. B. Thayer to Sophia Thayer, May 14, 1871, folder 3, JBTP.

"Where darkness found him": ECW, 9:57.

"was surprised to see the party dismount" and subsequent quotes: Muir, *Our National Parks*, 133–34. Although Emerson was no stranger to camping (see, for example, his sojourn in the Adirondacks in 1857 [John McAleer, *Ralph Waldo Emerson: Days of Encounter* (Boston: Little, Brown, 1984], 552–55), recreational camping in the West did not take off until the 1880s and 1890s. See Earl Pomeroy, *In Search of the Golden West: The Tourist in Western America* (Lincoln: University Nebraska Press, 2010), 141, 145.

137 *"plain country tavern"*: TAWJ, 100.

A photo from the time: Shirley Sargent, *Galen Clark: Yosemite Guardian* (San Francisco: Sierra Club, 1964), 55.

"great stone fireplaces": J. B. Thayer to Sophia Thayer, May 14, 1871, folder 3, JBTP.

138 *"hardly spoke a word"*: Muir, *Our National Parks*, 134.

Galen Clark: J. B. Thayer to Sophia Thayer, May 14, 1871, folder 3, JBTP; TAWJ, 100; Galen Clark, *Indians of the Yosemite* (Yosemite Valley, CA; Galen Clark, 1907), ix–xviii; Sargent, *Galen Clark*, 15–72.

Mariposa Big Trees: Bancroft, *Bancroft's Tourist's Guide*, 57–71.

"Grizzly Giant": Elizabeth Hutchinson, "They Might Be Giants: Carleton Watkins, Galen Clark, and the Big Tree," *October* 109 (Summer 2004), 47.

"guardian": Sargent, *Galen Clark*, 73–80.

two of Clark's brothers were Unitarian ministers: Tyler Green, personal communication, September 18, 2020.

139 *George Nidiver:* ECW, 7:261–63. Elizabeth Hoar was the author of the poem; see Dolores Bird Carpenter, ed., *The Selected Letters of Lidian Jackson Emerson* (Columbia: University of Missouri Press, 1987), 257.

"honoris causa": TAWJ, 100.

Alonzo: Sargent, *Galen Clark*, 95–104.

Charles Warren Stoddard: Gisel, *Kindred and Related Spirits*, 169.

"talked of the trees": TAWJ, 101; compare J. B. Thayer to Sophia Thayer, San Francisco, May 18, 1871, folder 3, JBTP.

"'vegetable Titans'": Charles William Wendte, *Thomas Starr King, Patriot and Preacher* (Boston: Beacon Press, 1921), 134.

"They were 'big trees,'": TAWJ, 102.

through the upper grove: J. B. Thayer to Sophia Thayer, San Francisco, May 18, 1871, folder 3, JBTP; compare TAWJ, 102–6; Ronald A. Bosco and Glen M. Johnson, eds., *The Journals and Miscellaneous Notebooks of Ralph Waldo Emerson*, vol. 16, *1866–1882* (Cambridge, MA: Harvard University Press, 1982), 410.

140 *"hollow tube"* and subsequent quotes: J. B. Thayer to Sophia Thayer, San Francisco, May 18, 1871, folder 3, JBTP.

"That is good!": TAWJ, 106–7.

"mostly in ordinary tourist fashion" and subsequent quote: Muir, *Our National Parks*, 134.

"a chance to sit": J. B. Thayer to Sophia Thayer, San Francisco, May 18, 1871, folder 3, JBTP; compare TAWJ, 107–8.

"in vain to get Mr. Emerson's leave" and subsequent quote: Sarah Forbes Hughes, ed., *Reminiscences of John Murray Forbes*, 3 vols. (Boston: George H. Ellis, 1902), 3:279.

141 *"gave Mr. Clark directions"*: Edward Waldo Emerson and Waldo Emerson Forbes, eds., *Journals of Ralph Waldo Emerson, with Annotations*, 10 vols. (Boston: Houghton Mifflin, 1914), 10:354–55; compare Muir, *Our National Parks*, 134. See also John H. Woodward, "Emerson's Giant Sequoia," *Emerson Society Quarterly* 22, no. 1 (1961): 44–45.

"The greatest wonder": J. B. Thayer to Sophia Thayer, San Francisco, May 18, 1871, folder 3, JBTP; compare TAWJ, 108.

"the poor bit of measured time": Muir, *Our National Parks*, 35.

"It is as if a photographer" and subsequent quote: J. B. Thayer to Sophia Thayer, San Francisco, May 18, 1871, folder 3, JBTP.

"You are yourself a sequoia" and subsequent quotes: Muir, *Our National Parks*, 135.

"he really enjoyed being with us": J. B. Thayer to Sophia Thayer, San Francisco, May 18, 1871, folder 3, JBTP; compare TAWJ, 108–9.

142 *"gazing awhile on the spot"* **and subsequent quotes:** Muir, *Our National Parks*, 135–36. Perhaps tongue in cheek, Emerson later recorded in his journal that Muir "said he slept in a wrinkle of the bark of a Sequoia on the night after we left him"; see Emerson and Forbes, *Journals of Ralph Waldo Emerson*, 10:385.

White and Hatch's: J. B. Thayer to Sophia Thayer, Stockton, May 14, 1871, and J. B. Thayer to Sophia Thayer, San Francisco, May 18, 1871, folder 3, JBTP; TAWJ, 110; Bosco and Johnson, *Journals and Miscellaneous Notebooks*, 410.

Dexter White: "Inn History," meadowcreekranchinn.com/our-inn/inn-history, accessed May 28, 2021.

"to an obscure, low, rather large room": TAWJ, 110–11; compare J. B. Thayer to Sophia Thayer, San Francisco, May 19, 1871, folder 3, JBTP.

143 *"frank sudden way about him"* **and subsequent quotes:** J. B. Thayer to Sophia Thayer, San Francisco, May 19, 1871, folder 3, JBTP. For Caroline Sturgis, see McAleer, *Ralph Waldo Emerson*, 329–30.

"sleep al fresco" **and subsequent quotes:** J. B. Thayer to Sophia Thayer, Stockton, May 14, 1871, folder 3, JBTP; compare TAWJ, 111–13.

"between my helplessness as a traveler": Ralph Waldo Emerson to Georgiana B. Kirby, San Francisco, April 28, 1871, quoted in *The Private Library of Herbert L. Rothchild of San Francisco, California (April 30 and May 1 and 2, 1924)* (New York: American Art Association, 1924), item 491. Kirby had invited the Emerson party to visit her in Santa Cruz (Rusk, *Letters of Ralph Waldo Emerson*, 6:153), but Edith said no ("I fear I shall not win from them any concession to visit Santa Cruz. My daughter Edith is one of those tyrants," Emerson wrote in the above letter to Kirby).

"missed the great mountains" **and subsequent quotes:** TAWJ, 113–14.

144 *Hornitos:* J. B. Thayer to Sophia Thayer, Stockton, May 14, 1871, and J. B. Thayer to Sophia Thayer, San Francisco, May 19, 1871, folder 3, JBTP; Bosco and Johnson, *Journals and Miscellaneous Notebooks*, 410.

"stout Scotch landlady": J. B. Thayer to Sophia Thayer, San Francisco, May 20, 1871, folder 3, JBTP.

Roberts Ferry: TAWJ, 116–17; Bosco and Johnson, *Journals and Miscellaneous Notebooks*, 410.

"in unexpectedly good condition": J. B. Thayer to Sophia Thayer, San Francisco, May 19, 1871, folder 3, JBTP.

"a hopeless subject for Christian education": J. B. Thayer to Sophia Thayer, San Francisco, May 20, 1871, folder 3, JBTP.

"Roberts's, considered as a tavern": TAWJ, 117; compare J. B. Thayer to Sophia Thayer, Stockton, May 14, 1871, folder 3, JBTP.

"handsome, drooping oaks": J. B. Thayer to Sophia Thayer, San Francisco, May 20, 1871, folder 3, JBTP.

"How would it be possible": TAWJ, 118–19.

145 *"a party of nine"* **and subsequent quote:** *Stockton Daily Independent*, May 15, 1871.

Stockton: Bancroft, *Bancroft's Tourist's Guide*, 243–45; Rusk, *Letters of Ralph Waldo Emerson*, 6:159; Bosco and Johnson, *Journals and Miscellaneous Notebooks*, 410.

"like butterflies": TAWJ, 119–20.

Oakland depot: TAWJ, 120.

Thick fog: Badè, *Letters of John Muir,* 1:258.

"a hard day's work" and subsequent quotes: Gisel, *Kindred and Related Spirits,* 140.

146 *"I have laid up in my heart":* Gisel, 140.

ferry back to San Francisco: Bosco and Johnson, *Journals and Miscellaneous Notebooks,* 410.

CHAPTER 7: LAST DAYS IN CALIFORNIA

147 *"theatre of the roughs":* TAWJ, 120; compare J. B. Thayer to Sophia Thayer, San Francisco, April 30, 1871, folder 3, JBTP.

"rude boys": John McAleer, *Ralph Waldo Emerson: Days of Encounter* (Boston: Little, Brown, 1984), 37–38.

"We hardly anticipate" and subsequent quote: A. L. Bancroft, ed., *Bancroft's Tourist's Guide* (San Francisco: A. L. Bancroft, 1871), 124–25.

148 *Barbary Coast:* Doris Muscatine, *Old San Francisco: The Biography of a City from Early Days to the Earthquake* (New York: G. P. Putnam's Sons, 1975), 147–48, 150–51, 203; Barbara Berglund, *Making San Francisco American: Cultural Frontiers in the Urban West, 1846–1906* (Lawrence: University Press of Kansas, 2007), 60–70.

"dodgers" and subsequent quotes: Misha Berson, *The San Francisco Stage: From Gold Rush to Golden Spike, 1849–1869,* pt. 1 (San Francisco: San Francisco Performing Arts Library and Museum, 1989), 59–61; Misha Berson, *The San Francisco Stage: From Golden Spike to Great Earthquake, 1869–1906,* pt. 2 (San Francisco: San Francisco Performing Arts Library and Museum, 1992), 71–77.

149 *"All through the early hours"* and subsequent quote: TAWJ, 120.

the peninsula: Bancroft, *Bancroft's Tourist's Guide,* 223–25; Tyler Green, *Carleton Watkins: Making the West American* (Berkeley: University of California Press, 2018), 253–56.

"whose country seat": Bancroft, *Bancroft's Tourist's Guide,* 224.

150 *Faxon Dean Atherton:* Gertrude Atherton, *Adventures of a Novelist* (New York: Liveright, 1932), 57–61.

"quiet, perfectly unaffected": J. B. Thayer to Sophia Thayer, San Francisco, May 16, 1871, folder 3, JBTP.

"Mrs. Atherton" and subsequent quote: Atherton, *Adventures of a Novelist,* 59.

"homelike": J. B. Thayer to Sophia Thayer, San Francisco, May 16, 1871, folder 3, JBTP.

151 *"abundant magnificent roses"* and subsequent quotes: J. B. Thayer to Sophia Thayer, San Francisco, May 16, 1871, folder 3, JBTP; see also Atherton, *Adventures of a Novelist,* 58.

"model breakfast" and subsequent quotes: J. B. Thayer to Sophia Thayer, San Francisco, May 16, 1871, folder 3, JBTP.

George: Atherton, *Adventures of a Novelist,* 45–54, 61, 74–82, 105–26. After marrying Gertrude Horn in 1876, George Atherton died at sea in 1886 of a hemorrhage caused by a kidney stone. For his body to be returned to his family, it was pickled in a barrel of rum and brought back to the family crypt in Colma, California. Strangely, however, his heart was removed and wound up sealed in a jar of alcohol and deposited in the Edwards Bank of Valparaiso, Chile, where it apparently remains to this day. See Emily Wortis Leider, *California's Daughter: Gertrude Atherton and Her Times* (Stanford, CA: Stanford University Press, 1991), 65.

152 *pick strawberries:* J. B. Thayer to Sophia Thayer, San Francisco, May 18, 1871, folder 3, JBTP.
"a sort of English wagon" and subsequent quote: J. B. Thayer to Sophia Thayer, San Francisco, May 16, 1871, folder 3, JBTP.
Belmont: Philip W. Alexander and Charles P. Hamm, *History of San Mateo County* (Burlingame, CA: Burlingame, 1916), 49; David Lavender, *Nothing Seemed Impossible: William G. Ralston and Early San Francisco* (Palo Alto, CA: American West, 1975), 251–56; Green, *Carleton Watkins*, 253–56.
"extraordinary establishment" and subsequent quotes: J. B. Thayer to Sophia Thayer, San Francisco, May 16, 1871, folder 3, JBTP.
Bank of California assets: J. B. Thayer to Sophia Thayer, San Francisco, May 18, 1871, folder 3, JBTP. In 1875, the bank would indeed collapse, and Ralston would die under circumstances that some suggested was by suicide (Lavender, *Nothing Seemed Impossible*, 362–85).
"gaping about": J. B. Thayer to Sophia Thayer, San Francisco, May 16, 1871, folder 3, JBTP.

153 *"flooded with callers and bores"* and subsequent quote: Edith Forbes to Ellen Emerson, Lake Tahoe, May 20, 1871, EEFP.
"be allowed to enjoy himself": San Francisco Examiner, April 25 1871.
"woman-suffrage committee": Edith Forbes to Ellen Emerson, Lake Tahoe, May 20, 1871, EEFP; compare J. B. Thayer to Sophia Thayer, San Francisco, May 18, 1871, folder 3, JBTP. For articles on the female suffrage convention and bazaar, see *San Francisco Bulletin*, May 18, 1871, and *San Francisco Chronicle*, May 18, 1871.
William Shew's: Wendy Cunkle Calmeson, "'Likeness Taken in the Most Approved Style': William Shew, Pioneer Daguerrotypist," *California Historical Quarterly* 56, no. 1 (Spring 1977): 2–19.
"the shadow for the substance": San Francisco Examiner, May 19, 1871.
"Lack of Preparation": Detroit Free Press, June 1, 1871. News of Emerson's donation of his photograph was also carried by East Coast papers, for example, the *New York Times*, May 27, 1871.
"gentleman came and summoned" and subsequent quote: Edith Forbes to Ellen Emerson, Lake Tahoe, May 20, 1871, EEFP.
Sarah Clarke: J. B. Thayer to Sophia Thayer, San Francisco, May 19, 1871, folder 3, JBTP; compare TAWJ, 121–22.

154 *at the urging of Edith:* Edith Forbes to Ellen Emerson, Lake Tahoe, May 20, 1871, EEFP.
Carleton Watkins: Green, *Carleton Watkins*, 92–93, 107–15, 279–81; Glena Matthews, *The Golden State in the Civil War: Thomas Starr King, the Republican Party, and the Birth of Modern California* (Cambridge: Cambridge University Press, 2012), 146–49.

155 *"The artist, my friend Watkins":* T. S. King to R. W. Emerson, September 9, 1862, MS Am 1280, box 16, Houghton Library, Harvard University, Cambridge, MA.
"two wonderful photographs": Emerson, quoted in Matthews, *Golden State in the Civil War*, 148. Tyler Green suspects that the set of Watkins stereographs

of Yosemite now in possession of the Concord Free Public Library were originally sent to Emerson by Thomas Starr King in the wake of Edward's 1861 trip
(personal communication, September 18, 2020); it is interesting to note that,
perhaps inspired by the photos, Emerson used the Mariposa Big Trees as a
symbol of the amazing fecundity of nature in his 1870 essay "Farming" (ECW,
7:142–43).

156 *"Mr. Emerson, Mr. Watkins told me"* **and subsequent quote:** Edith Forbes to Ellen
Emerson, Lake Tahoe, May 20, 1871, EEFP.

two Watkins photographs: Green, *Carleton Watkins*, 113, 281, Mrs. Russell apparently made a gift of one her Watkins photographs, a picture of Mount Shasta, to
Emerson (Green, 281).

"two gorgeous specimens": Edith Forbes to Ellen Emerson, Lake Tahoe, May 20,
1871, EEFP.

"RALPH WALDO EMERSON—LAST LECTURE!": *San Francisco Bulletin*, May
16 and 17, 1871; Ronald A. Bosco and Glen M. Johnson, eds., *The Journals and
Miscellaneous Notebooks of Ralph Waldo Emerson*, vol. 16, *1866–1882* (Cambridge,
MA: Harvard University Press, 1982), 410.

"An opportunity to hear so eminent a thinker": *Daily Alta California*, May 15, 1871.
Stebbins worked hard: William Hawley Davis, "Emerson the Lecturer in California," *California Historical Society Quarterly* 20, no. 1 (March 1941): 8–9.
Julia King: Moncure Conway to James Bradley Thayer, December 23, 1884, folder
5, JBTP.

157 *Edith was pleased with it:* Edith Forbes to Ellen Emerson, Lake Tahoe, May 20,
1871, EEFP.
"It was disappointing": J. B. Thayer to Sophia Thayer, San Francisco, May 16, 1871,
folder 3, JBTP.
"had extemporized": TAWJ, 120–21.
the précis: *San Francisco Chronicle*, May 18, 1871.
"This had been announced as the last": *San Francisco Examiner*, May 18, 1871.

157–158 *"Ralph Waldo Emerson's lectures":* quoted in Davis, "Emerson the Lecturer," 8.

158 *"Ralph Waldo Emerson addressed":* *San Francisco Bulletin*, May 18, 1871.
"The gentleman's remarks": *San Francisco Chronicle*, May 18, 1871.
Emerson party's final day in the Bay Area: Edith Forbes to Ellen Emerson, Lake
Tahoe, May 20, 1871, EEFP; Bosco and Johnson, *Journals and Miscellaneous Note-
books*, 410.
Henry Augustus Pierce: Ralph L. Rusk, ed., *The Letters of Ralph Waldo Emerson*,
10 vols. (New York: Columbia University Press, 1939), 6:157; *San Francisco Call*,
January 14, 1903.
"along the side of the hills" **and subsequent quotes:** J. B. Thayer to Sophia Thayer,
San Francisco, May 18, 1871, folder 3, JBTP; compare TAWJ, 121.
"delicate viands artistically served": Lois Rather, *R. W. Emerson, Tourist: The Story
of Ralph Waldo Emerson's Visit to California in 1871* (Oakland, CA: Rather Press,
1979), 56–57.
"It was a good illustration" **and subsequent quotes:** J. B. Thayer to Sophia Thayer,
San Francisco, May 18, 1871, folder 3, JBTP.

159 *"Brooklyn":* Rusk, *Letters of Ralph Waldo Emerson*, 6:158; Bosco and Johnson,
Journals and Miscellaneous Notebooks, 410.

"this distinguished metaphysician and philosopher" and subsequent quotes: *Oakland Daily News*, April 27, 1871.

ads for his talk: *Oakland Daily News*, May 18, 1871; *Oakland Daily Transcript*, May 18, 1871.

160 *Meionaon:* Bosco and Johnson, *Journals and Miscellaneous Notebooks*, 122.

"on the beauties of the country home": *San Francisco Bulletin*, May 19, 1871.

"His vivid picture of country life": *Oakland Daily News*, May 19, 1871.

"better mouse-trap": Jean C. S. Wilson and David A. Randall, eds., *Thirteen Author Collections of the Nineteenth Century and Five Centuries of Familiar Quotations* (New York: Charles Scribner's Sons, 1950), 364.

"was well attended": *Oakland Daily Transcript*, May 19, 1871.

161 *"a large and cultivated audience"* and subsequent quotes: *Oakland Daily News*, May 19, 1871.

several calls in Oakland: J. B. Thayer to Sophia Thayer, San Francisco, May 19, 1871, folder 3, JBTP; TAWJ, 121; C. Carroll Hollis, "Whitman and William Swinton: A Co-operative Friendship," *American Literature* 30, no. 4 (1959): 425–49.

"returned at 11": Rusk, *Letters of Ralph Waldo Emerson*, 6:158.

done his packing: Edith Forbes to Ellen Emerson, Lake Tahoe, May 20, 1871, EEFP.

shopping, and the settling up of bills: Edith Forbes to Ellen Emerson, Lake Tahoe, May 20, 1871, EEFP; Bosco and Johnson, *Journals and Miscellaneous Notebooks*, 410.

162 *"silver trout":* Rusk, *Letters of Ralph Waldo Emerson*, 6:158.

announced in the papers: for example, see the *San Francisco Bulletin*, May 18, 1871.

"little bird": J. B. Thayer to Sophia Thayer, San Francisco, May 18, 1871, folder 3, JBTP.

"the corn doctor": J. B. Thayer to Sophia Thayer, San Francisco, May 19, 1871, folder 3, JBTP.

"I would rather have": J. B. Thayer to Sophia Thayer, San Francisco, May 20, 1871, folder 3, JBTP.

a thousand dollars: Apparently, a thousand dollars was actually about par for this trip; see Anne Farrar Hyde, *An American Vision: Far Western Landscape and National Culture, 1820–1920* (New York: New York University Press, 1990), 108.

Woodward's Gardens: J. B. Thayer to Sophia Thayer, San Francisco, May 20, 1871, folder 3, JBTP; Bancroft, *Bancroft's Tourist's Guide*, 130–40; Berglund, *Making San Francisco American*, 70–80.

163 *quiet respite in the Sierra:* Edith Forbes to Ellen Emerson, Lake Tahoe, May 20, 1871, EEFP; TAWJ, 122.

"the forest has lost much of its pretension": Rusk, *Letters of Ralph Waldo Emerson*, 6:157.

Truckee: George A. Crofutt, *Great Trans-Continental Tourist's Guide* (New York, 1871), 155–56; Rusk, *Letters of Ralph Waldo Emerson*, 6:159; Bosco and Johnson, *Journals and Miscellaneous Notebooks*, 410–11.

"excellent soft road" and subsequent quotes: Edith Forbes to Ellen Emerson, Lake Tahoe, May 20, 1871, EEFP; Rusk, *Letters of Ralph Waldo Emerson*, 6:158; Bosco and Johnson, *Journals and Miscellaneous Notebooks*, 411.

164 *"by buying a few acres":* Ronald A. Bosco, "Historical Introduction," in *The Collected Works of Ralph Waldo Emerson*, ed. Ronald A. Bosco, Glen M. Johnson, and

Joel Myerson, vol 8., *Letters and Social Aims* (Cambridge, MA: Harvard University Press, 2010), lxxxvii.

"Prussian-blue thick": Edith Forbes to Ellen Emerson, Lake Tahoe, May 20, 1871, EEFP.

black sand: Edward Waldo Emerson and Waldo Emerson Forbes, eds., *Journals of Ralph Waldo Emerson, with Annotations,* 10 vols. (Boston: Houghton Mifflin, 1914), 10:353.

"a squirrel leaping": ECW, 2:280.

"sunset light" and subsequent quote: Edith Forbes to Ellen Emerson, Lake Tahoe, May 20, 1871, EEFP.

CHAPTER 8: EMERSON AFTER CALIFORNIA

165   *"There was no longer occasion to write":* TAWJ, 122.

Donner Lake: George A. Crofutt, *Great Trans-Continental Tourist's Guide* (New York, 1871), 158–69; Ronald A. Bosco and Glen M. Johnson, eds., *The Journals and Miscellaneous Notebooks of Ralph Waldo Emerson,* vol. 16, *1866–1882* (Cambridge, MA: Harvard University Press, 1982), 411.

Chicago, Milwaukee, and St. Paul Railroad: Jane Maher, *Biography of Broken Fortunes: Wilkie and Bob, Brothers of William, Henry, and Alice James* (Hamden, CT; Archon Books, 1986), 113.

"in Summer Dress" and subsequent quote: Edith Forbes to Ellen Emerson, Lake Tahoe, May 20, 1871, EEFP; compare Edith Emerson Forbes line-a-day diary, May 28 and 29, 1871, EEFP.

166   *"Niagara":* Bosco and Johnson, *Journals and Miscellaneous Notebooks,* 411.

"My long journey to California": Joseph Slater, ed., *The Correspondence of Emerson and Carlyle* (New York: Columbia University Press, 1964), 581. See also Ellen Tucker Emerson, *The Life of Lidian Jackson Emerson,* ed. Dolores Bird Carpenter (Lansing: Michigan State University Press, 1992), 156–57.

Emerson had been warned: Edith E. W. Gregg, ed., *The Letters of Ellen Tucker Emerson,* 2 vols. (Kent: Kent State University Press, 1982), 1:588–89, 592–94.

Old Manse: Gay Wilson Allen, *Waldo Emerson* (New York: Viking Press, 1981), 651–52; Bosco and Johnson, *Journals and Miscellaneous Notebooks,* 410–11.

hid the key: Allen, *Waldo Emerson,* 651–52; Gregg, *Letters of Ellen Tucker Emerson,* 1:594–95.

167   **Parnassus:** Ronald A. Bosco, "Historical Introduction," in *The Collected Works of Ralph Waldo Emerson,* ed. Ronald A. Bosco, Glen M. Johnson, and Joel Myerson, vol 8., *Letters and Social Aims* (Cambridge, MA: Harvard University Press, 2010), cxcii–cxcix.

"Ralph Waldo Emerson, who has arrived": San Francisco Chronicle, June 14, 1871; see also *Sacramento Daily Union,* June 13, 1871, and *San Francisco Chronicle,* June 14, 1871.

"[California's] immense prospective advantages": Ralph L. Rusk, ed., *The Letters of Ralph Waldo Emerson,* 10 vols. (New York: Columbia University Press, 1939), 6:157–58.

"not because of its gold" and subsequent quote: Annie Fields, *Authors and Friends* (Boston: Houghton Mifflin, 1897), 101.

168 *"magnificent adventure"*: Charles Eliot Norton, ed., *The Correspondence of Thomas Carlyle and Ralph Waldo Emerson, 1834–1872*, 2 vols. (Boston: Ticknor, 1886), 2:376.
"I had crowded & closed" and subsequent quote: Norton, *Correspondence*, 2:378–79.
"letter from the Far West" and subsequent quotes: Norton, 2:386–88.

169 *Bret Harte:* Ralph L. Rusk, *The Life of Ralph Waldo Emerson* (New York: Charles Scribner's Sons, 1949), 448–49; Bosco and Johnson, *Journals and Miscellaneous Notebooks*, 247; Ben Tarnoff, *The Bohemians: Mark Twain and the San Francisco Writers Who Reinvented American Literature* (New York: Penguin, 2014), 59, 200.
fascination with frontier and western humor: David S. Reynolds, *Beneath the American Renaissance: The Subversive Imagination in the Age of Emerson and Melville* (New York: Oxford University Press, 2011), 484–97.
"Do you know that" and subsequent quote: Edward Waldo Emerson and Waldo Emerson Forbes, eds., *Journals of Ralph Waldo Emerson, with Annotations*, 10 vols. (Boston: Houghton Mifflin, 1914), 10:362–63.
"Mr Harte," she said pointedly and subsequent quote: Gregg, *Letters of Ellen Tucker Emerson*, 1:618–20.

170 *"My Men"*: Emerson and Forbes, *Journals of Ralph Waldo Emerson*, 10:357.
"I wanted to steal him" and subsequent quote: J. Muir to J. B. McChesney, June 8, 1871, JMP.
"You are in the calm of home" and subsequent quoted letter: John Muir to Ralph Waldo Emerson, July 6, 1871, JMP.

171 *gift of the cones:* John Muir to Ralph Waldo Emerson, January 10, 1872, JMP.

172 *"Here lie your significant cedar flowers"*: William Frederic Badè, *The Life and Letters of John Muir*, 2 vols. (Boston: Houghton Mifflin, 1924), 1:259–60.

173 *"Come to our mountain"*: John Muir to Ralph Waldo Emerson, March 18, 1872, JMP.
earthquake in Yosemite: John Muir to Ralph Waldo Emerson, March 26, 1872, JMP.

174 *"Dear Soul"*: John Muir to Ralph Waldo Emerson, April 3, 1872, JMP.
"I had a letter from Emerson": Badè, *Letters of John Muir*, 1:261; compare Bonnie Johanna Gisel, ed., *Kindred and Related Spirits: The Letters of John Muir and Jeanne C. Carr* (Salt Lake City: University of Utah Press, 2001), 173.
"Runkle": John Daniel Runkle, then President of the Massachusetts Institute of Technology, visited Muir in Yosemite in 1872. See Badè, *Letters of John Muir*, 1:295.
"knew anyone in Cal": John McAleer, *Ralph Waldo Emerson: Days of Encounter* (Boston: Little, Brown, 1984), 607; Stephen R. Fox, *The American Conservation Movement: John Muir and His Legacy* (Madison: University of Wisconsin Press, 1985), 83.

175 *By 1874, Muir was based in Oakland:* Linnie Marsh Wolfe, *Son of the Wilderness: The Life of John Muir* (Madison: University of Wisconsin Press, 2003), 158–287; Donald Worster, *A Passion for Nature: The Life of John Muir* (Oxford: Oxford University Press, 2008), 216–342; John Muir to Ralph Waldo Emerson, May 9, 1874, JMP.
Studies in the Sierra: John Muir, *Studies in the Sierra*, ed. William E. Colby (San Francisco: Sierra Club Books, 1950).

Muir's writing went hand in hand: Wolfe, *Son of the Wilderness*, 238–348; Worster, *A Passion for Nature*, 305–466.

indispensable bridge: John Elder, "John Muir and the Literature of Wildness," *Massachusetts Review* 22, no. 2 (Summer 1981): 376; Steven J. Holmes, "John Muir, Jeanne Carr, and Ralph Waldo Emerson: A Case Study of the Varieties of Transcendentalist Influence," *Journal of Unitarian Universalist History* 25 (1998): 1–25. *"anxiety of influence"*: Russell Powell, "John Muir and the Botanical Oversoul," *Religions* 10, no. 92 (February 2019): 1–13.

176　*never tired of telling the story:* John Muir, *Our National Parks* (Boston: Houghton Mifflin, 1901), 131–36.

"I always grudged": T. Roosevelt to J. Muir, January 27, 1908, JMP.

Muir's later biographers and academic commentators: see, for example, Michael P. Branch, "Telling Nature's Story: John Muir and the Decentering of the Romantic Self," in *John Muir in Historical Perspective*, ed. Sally M. Miller (Bern: Peter Lang, 1993), 99–122; Holmes, "John Muir, Jeanne Carr,"1–25; James Brannon, "Radical Transcendentalism: Emerson, Muir and the Experience of Nature," *John Muir Newsletter* 16, no. 1 (Winter 2006): 1–7; James C. McKusick, *Green Writing: Romanticism and Ecology* (New York: St. Martin's, 2000), 180–85. For the conflict between Transcendentalist monism and Muir's pantheism specifically, see Worster, *A Passion for Nature*, 214–15; for a critique of Transcendental effeteness, see Wolfe, *Son of the Wilderness*, 145–51, esp. 146.

a fact that Muir . . . recognized: e.g., Badè, *Letters of John Muir*, 1:121, 253, 320.

"a grand wide-winged mountain": Badè, *Letters of John Muir*, 1:389.

Emerson's photograph: Elder, "John Muir and the Literature of Wildness," 376; Michael P. Branch, "'Angel Guiding Gently': The Yosemite Meeting of Ralph Waldo Emerson and John Muir, 1871," *Western American Literature* 32, no. 2 (Summer 1997): 106.

"half warm enough until Emerson came": Muir, *Our National Parks*, 131.

"the excursion greatly refreshed": Edward Waldo Emerson, *Emerson in Concord: A Memoir* (Boston: Houghton Mifflin, 1888), 185.

Emerson thus fell back into his old routines: Bosco, "Historical Introduction," cxv–clvi.

177　*"stiff and awkward":* Bosco, "Historical Introduction," cxxvii.

"quite attenuated" and subsequent quote: Bosco, "Historical Introduction," cxx.

increasingly difficult to keep his place: McAleer, *Ralph Waldo Emerson*, 582–84.

disaster struck: Emerson and Forbes, *Journals of Ralph Waldo Emerson*, 10:386–92, 434; Rusk, *The Life of Ralph Waldo Emerson*, 453–56; Allen, *Waldo Emerson*, 655–56; Bosco, "Historical Introduction," clix–clxiii.

"looked pathetically funny": Bosco, "Historical Introduction," clxii.

mild stroke: McAleer, *Ralph Waldo Emerson*, 612; see also Bosco, "Historical Introduction," clxviii.

178　*all calamities had their compensations:* ECW, 2:102–4.

overwhelmed by substantial gifts: Emerson and Forbes, *Journals of Ralph Waldo Emerson*, 10:394–99, 405–19; Allen, *Waldo Emerson*, 657–64; Bosco, "Historical Introduction," clxxi–clxxxi.

Emerson's failing mind: Emerson and Forbes, *Journals of Ralph Waldo Emerson*,

10:419–20; Arthur S. Pier, *Forbes: Telephone Pioneer* (New York: Dodd, Mead, 1953), 77–79.

Hotten volume: By 1873 Hotten had died, due, it was said, to the overconsumption of pork chops—leading one wag to say it was death by cannibalism; however, the obligation for the book was continued under Hotten's company, later known as Chatto and Windus. See Simon Eliot, "Hotten: Rotten: Forgotten? An Apologia for a General Publisher," *Book History* 3 (2000): 61–62.

Letters and Social Aims: Bosco, "Historical Introduction," xxx–xxxvi, clxxxvii, ccii.

"slightly increased love of structure": Bosco, "Historical Introduction," xxvii.

179   *the steady erosion of his memory:* Bosco, "Historical Introduction," cxxxii–cxxxiv, cl–cli, clv–clvi.

"You ought to hear how funny Father is": Gregg, *Letters of Ellen Tucker Emerson,* 1:666.

"that bearded young man in California" and subsequent quote: Carlos Baker, *Emerson among the Eccentrics: A Group Portrait* (New York: Penguin, 1997), 502–3.

"Emerson looks in magnificent health": Robert D. Richardson, *William James in the Maelstrom of American Modernism* (Berkeley: University of California Press, 2006), 353.

"To my father": Albert Bigelow Paine, *Mark Twain: A Biography: The Personal and Literary Life of Samuel Langhorne Clemens* (New York: Gabriel Wells, 1923), 2:603–10.

More modern commentators: Bosco, "Historical Introduction," xxxviii–xlii, cli; David Shenk, *The Forgetting: Alzheimer's: Portrait of an Epidemic* (New York: Doubleday, 2001), 1–3, 16–17, 83–84, 101–10, 216–21; Lynn Casteel Harper, *On Vanishing: Mortality, Dementia, and What It Means to Disappear* (New York: Catapult, 2020), 132–57.

"the senile Emerson": Horace Traubel, *With Walt Whitman in Camden* (New York: D. Appleton, 1908), 1.

180   *"He was . . . beginning to forget":* William Dean Howells, *Harper's Weekly Magazine,* May 16, 1903, 784, quoted in Ronald A. Bosco and Joel Myerson, eds., *Emerson in His Own Time* (Iowa City: University of Iowa Press, 2003), 196.

private correspondence: Bosco, "Historical Introduction," cxxxii, cxlviii, clxvii–clxx, clxxx–clxxxiii, clxxxix–cxcii, cci, cciv–ccxi.

"Old Age": ECW, 7:295–316.

"Memory": ECW, 12:55–71.

"We wonder if he will ever die": Bosco and Myerson, *Emerson in His Own Time,* 34.

181   *"Where are we?"* and subsequent quote: Bosco, "Historical Introduction," ccxii.

take a long walk: Baker, *Emerson among the Eccentrics,* 518.

pneumonia: McAleer, *Ralph Waldo Emerson,* 657–66.

"He did not know how to be sick": Baker, *Emerson among the Eccentrics,* 518.

"fallen down cellar": Bosco, "Historical Introduction," ccxiii.

"I think we may be sure": quoted in Edward Waldo Emerson, "Speech of Edward Waldo Emerson," in *The Centenary of the Birth of Ralph Waldo Emerson* (Boston: Riverside Press, 1903), 126. In "Immortality," Emerson had written: "I think all sound minds rest on a certain preliminary conviction, namely, that if it be best that conscious personal life shall continue, it will continue; if not best, then it will

not: and we, if we saw the whole, should of course see that it was better so" (ECW, 8:268).

culture hero: Robert D. Habich, *Building Their Own Waldos: Emerson's First Biographers and the Politics of Life-Writing in the Gilded Age* (Iowa City: University of Iowa Press, 2011), 127–31. For example, as Habich has observed, in terms of the photographs of Emerson that were extremely popular in his last years, "the formalities of portraiture and the ruin of aphasia made him look dreamy, fragile, and angelic," which "reinforced the expectation of wisdom, piety, and elevation against the engaged and complicated Emerson" of his better days (128).

"Emersonian Cult": The Spectator, August 16, 1884, folder 5, JBTP.

182   *five hundred books and articles:* Bosco, "Historical Introduction," cliii.

"wreccum maris": TAWJ, 5.

thank-you letters: Sarah S. Russell to James Bradley Thayer, June 23, 1884; Ellen Emerson to James Bradley Thayer, June 24, 1884; Horatio Stebbins to James Bradley Thayer, July 28, 1884; James Elliot Cabot to James Bradley Thayer, August 2, 1884; and Edith E. Forbes to James Bradley Thayer, August 15, [1884?], all in folder 5, JBTP. Edith Emerson was miffed that the *Philadelphia Press* reviewer presumed to identify some of the people Thayer had tried so hard to keep anonymous behind initials: it was not Ellen who was the Emerson daughter on the trip, she fumed, nor was Emerson referring to Walt Whitman when he complained that a certain poet wouldn't revise (Edith E. Forbes to James Bradley Thayer, October 10, [1884?], folder 5, JBTP.

"abstract seer": "The Pier Table," *Narragansett Times,* August 1, 1884, folder 5, JBTP.

"generally distributed": "Untitled," *Republic* (Washington, D.C.), July 18, 1884, folder 5, JBTP.

a favorable review: "A Journey with Emerson," *San Francisco Chronicle,* July 13, 1884, folder 5, JBTP.

"a few stones": "Emersoniana," *New York Mail and Express,* June 28, 1884, folder 5, JBTP.

182–183   *smoked cigars and ate pie:* "The Book World," *Philadelphia Press,* July 28 [1884?], folder 5, JBTP.

183   *"gone to higher Sierras"* and subsequent quote: Muir, *Our National Parks,* 136.

Bradford Leavitt: Bradford Leavitt to John Muir, March 9, 1903, JMP.

"every Emersonian blessing": J. Muir to Bradford Leavitt, Martinez, CA, March 1903, JMP (this letter is cataloged as Letter from [John Muir] to [Emily C. Hawley], [1903 Mar ?]).

May 17 event: "Memory of Ralph Waldo Emerson Subject for Glowing Tributes," *San Francisco Call Bulletin,* May 18, 1903; "Honor Name of Poet Emerson," *San Francisco Chronicle,* May 18, 1903; J. Parker Huber, "John Muir and the Emerson Centennial," *Concord Saunterer,* n.s., 11 (2003): 38–49.

184   *On May 18:* "Eulogizes Emerson," *San Francisco Call Bulletin,* May 19, 1903; "Honor Emerson as Poet and Teacher," *San Francisco Chronicle,* May 19, 1903.

185   *May 25, 1903:* "Will Pay High Honor to Emerson's Memory: Congregation of Literary Folks Plans to Dedicate Giant Redwood to Philosopher," *San Francisco Call Bulletin,* May 24, 1903; "Honor Memory of Great Poet with Commemorative Services," *San Francisco Call Bulletin,* May 25, 1903; "Dedicate Tree to Emerson's Memory," *San Francisco Chronicle,* May 26, 1903; Lincoln Fairley, "Literary Associations with Mount Tamalpais," *California History* 61, no. 2 (1982): 88–89, 91–92.

"*Not contented with taking such a heavy load*" **and subsequent quotes:** Sarah Forbes Hughes, ed., *Reminiscences of John Murray Forbes*, 3 vols. (Boston: George H. Ellis, 1902), 3:71. For John Murray Forbes's last trip to California, see Sarah Forbes Hughes, ed., *Letters (Supplementary) of John Murray Forbes* (Boston: George H. Ellis, 1905), 3:231–48.

John Murray Forbes returned to the management: John Lauritz Larson, *Bonds of Enterprise: John Murray Forbes and Western Development in America's Railway Age* (Cambridge, MA: Harvard University Press, 1984), 155–59, 164–69.

Forbes would always retain a lively interest in California: Hughes, *Reminiscences of John Murray Forbes*, 3:286; James L. Coran and Walter A. Nelson-Rees, *If Pictures Could Talk: Stories about California Paintings in Our Collection* (Oakland, CA: WIM, 1989), 66; John Ott, *Manufacturing the Modern Patron in Victorian California: Cultural Philanthropy, Industrial Capital, and Social Authority* (London: Routledge, 2014), 232.

186 "*There is much in Mr. Emerson's writings*": Sarah Hathaway Forbes to John Muir, Boston, April 29, 1872, JMP.

"*He is getting old now*" **and subsequent quote:** Sarah Hathaway Forbes to John Muir, Milton, Winter 1872, JMP.

Of the two daughters, Sarah and Alice: *The New England Historical and Genealogical Register* (Boston: New England Historical and Genealogical Society, 1891), 45:323; Larson, *Bonds of Enterprise*, 200.

187 *Edith and Will Forbes* **and subsequent quotations:** Pier, *Forbes*, 65–69, 92–104, 184–85, 205–12.

Today, Will Forbes is best remembered: Pier, *Forbes*, 111–204, 221–25.

Parnassus: Emerson and Forbes, *Journals of Ralph Waldo Emerson*, 10:437–38; Edith Emerson Forbes, *The Children's Year-Book: Selections for Every Day in the Year* (Boston: Roberts Brothers, 1893); Edith Emerson Forbes, *Favourites of a Nursery of Seventy Years Ago* (Boston: Houghton Mifflin, 1916).

James Bradley Thayer: S. Lothrop Thorndike, "Tribute to James Bradley Thayer," *Proceedings of the Massachusetts Historical Society* 16 (March 1902): 14–19; David J. Langum, "James Bradley Thayer (1831–1902)," in *American National Biography*, ed. John A. Garraty and Mark C. Carnes (Oxford: Oxford University Press, 1999), 490–91.

188 "*He was infinitely patient*": James Parker Hall, "James Bradley Thayer," in *Great American Lawyers*, ed. William Draper Lewis (Philadelphia: James C. Winston, 1907), 8:371.

Chauncey Wright: Hall, "James Bradley Thayer," 8:348, 350, 375. See also Joseph L. Blau, "Chauncey Wright: Radical Empiricist," *New England Quarterly* 19, no. 4 (December 1946): 495–517, and Edward H. Madden, *Chauncey Wright and the Foundations of Pragmatism* (Seattle: University of Washington Press, 1963).

"*Emerson and Religion*": James Bradley Thayer, "Emerson and Religion," *Christian Register* 32, no. 79 (August 9, 1900): 879–81.

"*I don't know the what or the how*": quoted in Thorndike, "Tribute to James Bradley Thayer," 19.

189 *Wilkie moved permanently to Milwaukee:* Maher, *Biography of Broken Fortunes*, 114, 116–17, 135–36, 139, 151–52, 163–64, 168, 199.

"He possessed rare conversational powers" and subsequent quote: Maher, 164, 168.

190 *"I've just come from being married"* and subsequent quote: Thomas M. Davis, "Lines West!—The Story of George W. Holdrege (Part 1),"*Nebraska History* 31 (1950): 46–47.

 Frances Rogers Kimball: Thomas M. Davis, "Lines West!—The Story of George W. Holdrege (Part 2)," *Nebraska History* 31 (1950): 109.

 "the finest private car" and subsequent quote: Thomas M. Davis, "Lines West!—The Story of George W. Holdrege (Part 3)," *Nebraska History* 31 (1950): 208, 224.

191 *Julia Ward Howe:* "Women and the Ballot Box," *Boston Herald*, January 31, 1889.

 Mrs. Russell's cousin, Annie Anthony: Harriet Hyman Alonso, *Growing Up Abolitionist: The Story of the Garrison Children* (Amherst: University of Massachusetts Press, 2002), 243–46, 307, 331.

192 *snarkiness:* Jeanne Olson, "Writing the Wild West: Travel Narratives of the Late Nineteenth Century Tourist" PhD diss., Arizona State University, 1996), 1–32.

 Emerson had startled his son: Emerson, *Emerson in Concord*, 183.

 "Terminus" and following lines: ECW, 9:251–52.

INDEX